Cities, Poverty and Food

Praise for this book...

'The wise use of urban agriculture can significantly contribute to urban poverty reduction, as well as enhancing the resilience of cities in a changing climate. Countries as diverse as Ghana, Peru, Sri Lanka and Yemen are harnessing the potential of urban agriculture. This excellent publication offers a practical methodology to promote sound urban agriculture policies and practices.'

Rafael Tuts, Chief, Urban Environmental Planning Branch, UN-HABITAT, Nairobi

'This is a must-read for researchers and policy makers interested in food security, food policy and urban planning. RUAF has been leading an international network of researchers into exploring the role of urban agriculture in dealing with challenges of urban poverty and economic development, social inclusion of marginalized groups, waste management, food insecurity and malnutrition and potential impacts of climate change in the global South. A very accessible guide with case studies from Asia, Africa and South America, *Cities, Poverty and Food* is a do-it-yourself guide for those who are seeking ways to break away from conventional policy solutions to food insecurity. In a world where most of the people are living in urban areas, *Cities, Poverty and Food* is offering fresh new insights on not only feeding urban populations but, by seeking multi-stakeholder formulations, also democratizing the food system.'

Mustafa Koç, Associate Professor, Department of Sociology and Centre for Studies in Food Security, Ryerson University, Toronto, Canada

Cities, Poverty and Food
Multi-Stakeholder Policy and Planning in Urban Agriculture

Marielle Dubbeling, Henk de Zeeuw and René van Veenhuizen

RUAF Foundation
RESOURCE CENTRES ON URBAN AGRICULTURE & FOOD SECURITY

PRACTICAL ACTION
Publishing

Practical Action Publishing Ltd
Schumacher Centre for Technology & Development
Bourton on Dunsmore, Rugby
Warwickshire, CV23 9QZ, UK
www.practicalactionpublishing.org

ISBN: 978 185339 709 7

Since 1974, Practical Action Publishing (formerly Intermediate Technology Publications and ITDG Publishing) has published and disseminated books and information in support of international development work throughout the world. Practical Action Publishing is a trading name of Practical Action Publishing Ltd (Company Reg. No. 1159018), the wholly owned publishing company of Practical Action. Practical Action Publishing trades only in support of its parent charity objectives and any profits are covenanted back to Practical Action (Charity Reg. No. 247257, Group VAT Registration No. 880 9924 76).

This book was published with support of the International Development Research Centre (IDRC), Ottawa, Canada. www.idrc.ca

Layout, text editing and resources: Femke Hoekstra
Language editing: Ian Tellam

Cover photo: IPES
Cover design by Practical Action Publishing
Typeset by S.J.I. Services
Printed by Replika Press Pvt. Ltd.

CONTENTS

ABOUT THE AUTHORS

Henk **de Zeeuw** is the director of the RUAF Foundation (International network of Resource centres on Urban Agriculture and Food security). He is a senior adviser with ETC Urban Agriculture, the Netherlands with more than 30 years of experience in agricultural development. He coordinated the RUAF Cities Farming for the Future programme (2000–2008).
h.dezeeuw@etcnl.nl

Marielle **Dubbeling** is the global coordinator of the RUAF From Seed to Table Programme (2009–2010) and was the training specialist in the RUAF Cities Farming for the Future Programme. She is a senior adviser at ETC Urban Agriculture, the Netherlands. Before joining ETC and RUAF she worked with IPES (Promoción del Desarrollo Sostenible) and the UN Habitat Urban Management Programme in Latin America, where she supported the development of municipal programmes on urban agriculture in cities in Ecuador, Peru, Argentina, Brazil, and Cuba.
m.dubbeling@etcnl.nl

René **van Veenhuizen** is the knowledge management officer of the RUAF From Seed to Table Programme and earlier in the RUAF Cities Farming for the Future Programme. He is a senior adviser with ETC Urban Agriculture, the Netherlands. He has been working in research, knowledge and information management, training and networking related to sustainable agricultural development, land and water management and poverty alleviation. Since 2000, he is the editor of the Urban Agriculture Magazine and has edited a number of leading publications on urban agriculture.
r.van.veenhuizen@etcnl.nl

Femke **Hoekstra**, assistant editor, is the programme assistant of the RUAF From Seed to Table Programme and earlier in the RUAF Cities Farming for the Future Programme. She is a junior adviser with ETC Urban Agriculture, the Netherlands.
f.hoekstra@etcnl.nl

Authors of Case Studies

Case study	Authors
Accra, Ghana	**Theophilus Otchere-Larbi** RUAF training officer in Anglophone West Africa, and at IWMI, Ghana t.larbi@cgiar.org **Olufunke Cofie** Regional coordinator RUAF for Anglophone West Africa & Senior researcher, IWMI, Ghana o.cofie@cgiar.org
Beijing, China	**Cai Jianming** Regional coordinator RUAF for China, and Professor, Department of Urban and Rural Studies, Institute of Geographic Sciences and Natural Resources Research, Chinese Academy of Sciences, China caijm@igsnrr.ac.cn
Bulawayo, Zimbabwe	**Takawira Mubvami** Regional coordinator RUAF for Eastern and Southern Africa, and Coordinator, Urban Agriculture Programme Municipal Development Partnership (MDP), Zimbabwe tmubvami@mdpafrica.org.zw **Percy Toriro** RUAF training officer in Eastern and Southern Africa, and Urban agriculture and planning specialist at MDP, Zimbabwe ptoriro@mdpafrica.org.zw
Freetown, Sierra Leone	**Olufunke Cofie** Regional coordinator RUAF for Anglophone West Africa, and Senior researcher, IWMI, Ghana o.cofie@cgiar.org **Marco Serena** Country director at COOPI – Cooperazione Internazionale, Sierra Leone m.serena@etcnl.nl **Theophilus Otchere-Larbi** RUAF training officer in Anglophone West Africa and at IWMI, Ghana t.larbi@cgiar.org
Gampaha, Sri Lanka	**Priyanie Amerasinghe** Regional coordinator RUAF for South and South East Asia, and Senior researcher, IWMI, India p.amerasinghe@cgiar.org
Lima, Peru	**Gunther Merzthal** Regional coordinator RUAF for Latin America and the Caribbean, and Coordinator, Urban Agriculture Programme IPES, Peru gunther@ipes.org.pe **Noemi Soto** Advisor urban agriculture projects, IPES, Peru Noemi@ipes.org.pe
Sana'a, Yemen	**Salwa Tohme Tawk** RUAF knowledge management officer, and Environmental and Sustainable Development Unit, Faculty of Agricultural and Food Sciences, American University of Beirut (AUB-ESDU), Lebanon salwatawk@gmail.com **Ziad Moussa** Regional coordinator RUAF for the Middle East and Northern Africa, AUB-ESDU, Lebanon ziadmoussa@yahoo.com **Layal Dandache** RUAF monitoring and evaluation officer, AUB ESDU, Lebanon ld11@aub.edu.lb

FOREWORD

Over the last decade and under the leadership of ETC, the RUAF Foundation (International network of Resource centres on Urban Agriculture and Food security) has developed what can be considered to be today the single most comprehensive international capacity building programme for municipal policy on urban agriculture and food security.

The RUAF network was established in 1999 to respond to the increasing urban poverty and food insecurity due to the problems cities are facing in creating sufficient formal employment opportunities for their growing populations. A growing body of research indicates that urban agriculture is making important contributions to reduction of urban poverty and food insecurity, social inclusion of disadvantaged groups (such as female-headed households with children and HIV/AIDS-affected families), the improvement of the urban environment (urban greening, reuse of wastes, biodiversity management) and reduction of vulnerability to climate change.

With this book the partners in the RUAF Foundation share the experiences they have gained in the Cities Farming for the Future (CFF) programme that they implemented between 2005 and 2008. It tells of the efforts of a large number of organizations – including municipal authorities, NGOs, producer groups, community-based organizations, universities, agricultural extension organizations and others – to jointly develop policies and action programmes on urban agriculture aiming at participatory governance, urban food security, urban poverty alleviation and enhanced urban environmental management.

The CFF programme focused on the development of regional training and planning capacities and facilitating multi-stakeholder policy formulation and action planning in 20 partner cities in 7 regions. The CFF programme sought to develop the capacity of local stakeholders to engage in participatory and multi-stakeholder diagnosis and strategic action planning on urban agriculture and to facilitate the integration of urban agriculture in local policies and institutional budgets and programmes.

The CFF programme was funded by the Environment and Development Department of the *Directorate General for International Co-operation* (DGIS, the Netherlands) and the *International Development Research Centre* (IDRC, Canada) with important contributions from the organizations participating in the RUAF Foundation and from local partners (especially the cooperating municipalities).

Experiences gained in each of the partner cities were periodically shared and systematized in order to learn from doing and adding bit by bit to a growing body of experience regarding the multi-stakeholder planning approach and effective policies and action programmes on urban agriculture.

The RUAF 'Cities Farming for the Future' programme has been evaluated as highly successful both by the stakeholders in the partner cities as well as by external evaluators. The latter judged that:

> CFF has been very successful in changing the attitude of urban actors towards urban agriculture, has put urban agriculture high on the local policy agenda, has strongly contributed to the strengthening of participatory governance at city level, and at the same time the empowerment of urban producers, contributed to changes in sector and territorial policies at national level (e.g. Brazil, Ghana, Senegal and China) as well as to municipal policies and programmes in the RUAF partner cities (e.g. Lima, Bulawayo and Beijing) and has been able to reach diverse poor and very poor groups and to tailor the projects to their specificities (Y. Cabannes and M. Pasquini, Report on the Mid Term Review of the RUAF Cities Farming for the Future Programme, London, 2008).

The RUAF partners share these experiences in the expectation that these will be of value for all persons and organizations interested in contributing to the development of safe and sustainable agriculture in and around our cities that provides fresh and nutritious food at affordable prices, generates income and employment, especially for the urban poor, and makes important contributions to urban environmental management and adaptation to climate change.

Dr Luc Mougeot
Senior Program Specialist, Canadian Partnerships Programme
International Development Research Centre (IDRC)
Ottawa, Canada.

ACRONYMS/ABBREVIATIONS

AGRITEX	National Agricultural Extension Service, Zimbabwe
AMA	Accra Metropolitan Assembly
AWGUPA	Accra Working Group on Urban and Peri-urban Agriculture
CBO	Community Based Organization
CFF	Cities Farming for the Future programme (RUAF Foundation, 2004–2008)
CSA	City Strategic Agenda
DFID	Department for International Development, UK
DGIS	Dutch Ministry of Foreign Affairs
ESDU	Environmental and Sustainable Development Unit of the Agricultural University of Beirut, Lebanon
FAO	United Nations Food and Agriculture Organization
FCC	Freetown City Council
FSTT	From Seed to Table programme (RUAF Foundation, 2009–2010)
FUPAP	Freetown Urban and Peri-Urban Agriculture Platform
GDP	Gross Domestic Product
GFA	Greater Freetown Area
GIS	Geographical Information System
IAGU	Institut Africain de Gestion Urbaine (African Institute for Urban Management)
IASC	Inter Agency Standing Committee
IDRC	International Development Research Centre
IFAD	International Fund for Agricultural Development
IGSNRR	Institute of Geographical Sciences and Natural Resource Research of the Chinese Academy of Sciences
IMF	International Monetary Fund
IPES	IPES Promoción del Desarrollo Sostenible
IWMI	International Water Management Institute
M&E	Monitoring and Evaluation
MAFFS	Ministry of Agriculture, Forestry and Food Security, Freetown
MDP	Municipal Development Partnership
MoFA	Ministry of Food and Agriculture, Ghana
MMDAs	Metropolitan Municipal and District Assemblies, Accra
MPAP	Multi-stakeholder Policy formulation and Action Planning
MSF	Multi-Stakeholder Forum

MSP	Multi-Stakeholder Platform
NAFSL	National Association of Farmers of Sierra Leone
NGO	Non Governmental Organization
PRA	Participatory Rapid Appraisal
PROVE	Programa de Verticalização da Pequena Produção (Programme for market integration of small-scale production)
RUAF	RUAF Foundation, international network of Resource centres on Urban Agriculture and Food security
SPC	Sustainable Production and Consumption
ToT	Training of Trainers
UMP-LAC	Urban Management Programme – Latin America and the Caribbean
UNCHS/UN HABITAT	United Nations Centre for Human Settlements
UNCTAD	United Nations Conference on Trade and Development
UNDP	United Nations Development Programme
UNEP	United Nations Environment Programme
UNESCO	United Nations Educational, Scientific and Cultural Organization
USDA	United States Department of Agriculture
WHO	World Health Organization
YASAD	Yemeni Association for Sustainable Agriculture and Development

Chapter 1
INTRODUCTION

Poverty and food insecurity: a growing urban concern

The year 2008 will go down in history as the year in which the world's urban population outnumbered its rural population for the first time in history. According to the United Nations Population Fund, the world's urban population is expected to double from 3.3 billion in 2007 to 6.4 billion by 2050, and it is predicted that by 2030, 60 per cent of the world's population will live in cities (UNFPA, 2007).

Rapid urbanization in many developing countries, especially those with lower incomes, is taking place at a time when the availability of non-farm jobs is limited. In fact, non-farm productivity in the least developed countries declined 9 per cent from 1980–83 to 2000–03 (UNCTAD, 2006). As a result, the urbanization process is accompanied by a phenomenon referred to as the '*urbanization of poverty*': rural-to-urban migration combined with limited employment opportunities in cities is leading to a shift in the locus of poverty from rural to urban areas. The percentage of the poor living in cities is expected to increase from 30 per cent in 2000 to 50 per cent by 2035 (UNCHS, 2001).

Credit: IPES

More people worldwide now live in urban than rural areas (Lima, Perú)

A recent World Bank and IMF report based on more than 200 surveys conducted in 90 developing countries showed that the growth in urban poverty was 30 per cent higher than that of rural poverty during the 1993–2000 period. This translated into an additional 50 million urban poor in a period of just seven years (IMF, 2007). In most developing countries, more than half of the urban population is below the poverty line. The total number of urban poor (those living on less than US$1 a day) in developing countries is estimated at 1.2 billion (UN, 2008).

Increasing urban poverty goes hand in hand with growing food insecurity and malnutrition in the cities. Urban food insecurity is often overlooked since at aggregate level economic and social conditions in urban areas are much better than those in rural areas. The familiar images of 'famine' situations are often from rural areas and rarely depict urban areas. But such aggregate figures do not account for inequality within the urban population that is generally much greater than within the rural areas (World Bank, 2000). Besides, such data mask the deep food insecurity and hunger issues in urban areas, which remain under-reported problems (FAO, 2004). Unlike in rural areas, problems of food insecurity in urban areas are strongly related to the inadequate purchasing power of the urban poor which limits their access to adequate quantities of nutritious food. Hunger in the cities is chronic but is less visible and attracts much less attention from the media and policy makers. Moreover, the nutritional value of food consumed by the urban poor is often very low (Mutonodzo, 2009).

The urban poor often live in neighbourhoods with poor sanitary conditions, limited access to clean water, high environmental pollution and consequently high and chronic exposure to health hazards. Such *unhealthy living conditions aggravate food insecurity*. Chronic infections compromise the ability of the human body to make effective use of nutrients from consumed food (including malabsorption and part of the nutrients being used to mitigate toxic effects of environmental contaminants) amplifying the impacts of an already poor diet (Yeudall, 2007).

Although already in 1999 the FAO Committee on Agriculture (COAG), during its 15th meeting, urged the member states to give more attention to urban and peri-urban agriculture – production of food within and close to the urban centres – in order to enhance urban food security, in many countries the growing urban food insecurity and malnutrition problem remained largely unattended and did not yet translate into policy action. Poverty and hunger were still viewed by many as a largely rural problem (Shapouri et al., 2009), although many good examples exist of cities and countries that have developed innovative policies and programmes on urban and peri-urban agriculture. We will see various examples of this later in this book.

The recent *food and economic crises* have made city and national governments realize that urban food security is a major issue that requires policy intervention. In over 30 major cities food riots broke out due to the sharp increase in food prices and the deteriorating access to food for the urban poor.

As a consequence of these crises the number of people that were undernourished increased by about 170 million people in just one and a half years and the urban poor are among the hardest hit. The 136th Council meeting of the FAO reported *'World hunger is projected to reach a historic high in 2009, with 1,020 million people going hungry every day (from 850 million in 2007). The urban poor will probably face the most severe problems in coping with the global recession].'* (FAO, 2009).

The urban poor are particularly vulnerable to changes in food prices and variations in income since food makes up a large part of their household expenses (often over 60–70 per cent) and urban consumers are almost exclusively dependent on food purchases. They are the first to lose their jobs. Variations in income or food prices have a significant and direct impact on their diets (lower food intake, turning to cheaper/less nutritious food) and lead further to reduced expenditure in health care and schooling or the sale of productive assets (FAO, 2008). The most vulnerable groups are the underemployed or unemployed citizens, refugees, the disabled, people dislocated by rural violence and conflict and immigrants escaping from poverty and hunger and especially the children and women within these groups (FAO, 2009).

Inevitably, also the *effects of climate change* will disproportionally affect the urban poor, since they are often located in the most vulnerable parts of the cities in slum and squatter settlements on steep hillsides or in low lying and poorly drained areas and have the lowest capacity to adapt to such changes (Commission on Climate Change and Development, 2009).

Recent *natural disasters and human-induced emergencies* (e.g. Iraq, Georgia, Darfur, Democratic Republic of Congo and Afghanistan) have led to large numbers of refugees. Often, a large proportion of these refugees end up living permanently in and around urban areas, even after short periods of displacement, further exacerbating the pressure on urban systems to provide basic services and accelerating processes of massive slum formation, growing urban poverty, rising food insecurity and chronic malnutrition and poor health. Food security is a specific concern to recent refugees in urban areas as they have very limited resources to help them cope (IASC Task Force on Meeting Humanitarian Challenges on Urban Areas, 2009).

Credit: Jorge Castro Henriques

Urban agriculture reduces the distance for transporting food (Lisbon, Portugal)

These are urgent and pressing challenges that need an equally urgent and adequate response from city and national authorities and international support organizations. Urban policies need to incorporate food security considerations and focus more on building cities that are more resilient to crises.

The United Nations High Level Task Force on the Global Food Crisis states (p. 15):

> A paradigm shift in design and urban planning is needed that aims at: ... reducing the distance for transporting food by encouraging local food production, where feasible, within city boundaries and especially in immediate surroundings. Without sacrificing core principles to observe public health standards, this includes removing barriers and providing incentives for urban and peri-urban agriculture, as well as improved management of water resources in urban areas (UN, 2008).

Urban agriculture

Urban agriculture is used throughout this book as the term to describe both intra-urban and peri-urban agriculture. It is defined as the growing of plants and the raising of animals within and around cities and related activities (production of inputs, processing, marketing, provision of services to agricultural producers and agro-enterprises).

A wide variety of different types of urban agriculture and all sorts of classifications can be made based on different classification criteria. According to Mougeot (2000) the most important aspects to characterize urban agriculture are the following: who are the main actors involved; where is the activity taking place (location); what kind of products are produced; which technologies are used and at what scale of production; what are the main motives of the people involved; and to what degree is processing and marketing taking place?

Characteristics of urban agriculture

Types of actors involved. A large proportion of the people involved in urban agriculture are the urban poor. Contrary to general belief they are often not the most recent immigrants from

Credit: IPES

rural areas (since the urban producers need time to get access to urban land, water and other productive resources). In many cities, one will often also find lower and mid-level government officials, school teachers and the like involved in agriculture, as well as richer people who are seeking a good investment for their capital. Women constitute an important section of urban producers, since agriculture and related processing and selling activities can often be more easily combined with their other tasks in the household. It is, however, more difficult to combine household responsibilities with urban jobs that require travelling to the town centre, industrial areas or to the houses of the rich.

Women constitute an important proportion of urban producers (Lima, Perú)

Locations. Urban agriculture may take place in locations inside the cities (intra-urban) or in the peri-urban areas. The activities may take place on the homestead (on-plot) or on land away from the residence (off-plot), on private land (owned, leased) or on public land (parks, conservation areas, along roads, streams and railways), or semi-public land (schoolyards, grounds of schools and hospitals).

Products. Urban agriculture includes food products from different types of crops (grains, root crops, vegetables, mushrooms, fruits) and animals (such as poultry, rabbits, goats, sheep, cattle, pigs, guinea pigs and fish) as well as non-food products (like aromatic and medicinal herbs, ornamental plants and tree products), or combinations of these. Often the more perishable and relatively high-valued vegetables and animal products and by-products are favoured. Production units in urban agriculture tend in general to be more specialized than rural enterprises, and exchanges take place across production units.

Scale of production and technology used. In the city we may encounter individual or family farms, group or cooperative farms and commercial enterprises at various scales ranging from micro- and small farms (the majority) to medium-sized and some large-scale enterprises. The technological level of the majority of urban agriculture enterprises in developing countries is still rather low. However, the tendency is towards more technically advanced and intensive agriculture and various examples of such can be found in all cities.

Types of economic activities involved. Urban agriculture includes agricultural production activities as well as related processing and marketing activities and delivery of inputs and services delivery (e.g. compost production from organic wastes, animal health services) by specialized micro-enterprises or NGOs. In urban agriculture, production and marketing tend to be more closely interrelated in terms of time and space than for rural agriculture, thanks to greater geographic proximity and quicker resource flow.

Credit: Marielle Dubbeling

Rooftop gardening in Dakar

Producing different types of lettuce for the market in Chicago

Credit: René van Veenhuizen

Managing the urban
space in Havana, Cuba

A night wholesale
market in Hanoi

Degree of market orientation. In most cities in developing countries an important part of urban agricultural production is for self-consumption, with surpluses being traded. However, the importance of market-oriented urban agriculture, both in volume and economic value, should not be underestimated (as shown in the following section of this chapter). Products are sold at the farm gate, by cart in the same or other neighbourhoods, in local shops, on local (producers') markets or to intermediaries and supermarkets. Mainly fresh products are sold, but part of the produce is processed for use by farmers themselves, cooked and sold on the streets or processed and packaged for sale to one of the outlets mentioned above.

Policy relevance of urban agriculture

Cities are quickly becoming the principal territories for intervention and planning of innovative strategies that aim to eradicate urban hunger and improve livelihoods. Urban agriculture provides a strategy that contributes to enhanced food security and improved nutrition of the urban poor. Further, it contributes to local economic development, poverty alleviation and social inclusion of the urban poor – and women in particular – as well as to the greening of the city, the productive reuse of urban wastes, and reduced vulnerability to climate change. Research findings related to each of these potential contributions of urban agriculture are reviewed in the following sub-sections.

Food security and nutrition

The contribution of urban agriculture to food security and healthy nutrition is probably its most important asset. Food production in the city is in many cases a response of the urban poor to inadequate, unreliable and irregular access to food, and the lack of purchasing power.

Urban agriculture may improve both food intake and the nutritional quality of the food. Locally produced food is fresher, more nutritious and diverse than food products bought in supermarkets or in fast food chains; it also leads to more regular food intake. This is of crucial importance for young children, the elderly or sick household members (e.g. HIV/AIDS and TB patients) and pregnant and lactating women. Involvement in local food production also leads to better mitigation of diseases (better nutrition, home-grown medicinal plants), more physical exercise, less dependency on gifts and food aid and enhanced self-esteem (Maxwell and Armar-Klemesu, 1998; Yeudall, 2007).

In addition to enhanced food security and nutrition of the urban producers themselves, urban agriculture produces large amounts of food for other categories of the population (Nugent, 2000). It has been estimated that about 15–20 per cent of the world's food is produced in urban and peri-urban areas (Armar-Klemesu, 2000). The volume of crops and animal products produced in urban and peri-urban agriculture often represents a substantial part of the total urban annual food requirements, e.g. in Nakuru (Kenya) 8 per cent (Foeken, 2006), Dakar (Senegal)

Credit: IGSNRR

The importance of market-oriented urban agriculture should not be underestimated (Beijing)

10 per cent (Mbaye and Moustier, 2000), Kampala (Uganda) 40 per cent (International Potato Center, 2007) and Hanoi (Vietnam) 44 per cent (Mubarik et al., 2005). For certain products (especially perishable products like leafy vegetables, poultry, eggs and milk) often 60–90 per cent is produced by urban and peri-urban producers (Table 1.1).

Urban agriculture improves access of the urban poor to fresh and nutritious food not just by making it available at close proximity to cities but also by reducing the costs of food (since

Credit: Hans Peter Reinders

As well as own consumption, urban agriculture also produces food for sale to others (Cuba)

locally-produced food involves fewer intermediaries and less transport, cold storage, processing and packaging). Marketing chains in urban agriculture are normally much shorter and more varied than in rural agriculture, reducing the costs of wholesalers and retailers in the total chain; transport costs are lower, while more products are sold fresh and unpackaged soon after harvest, thus reducing related storage, packaging and cooling costs. Consequently, the price differential between producer and final consumer (which may go up to 1:10 in rural agriculture) is lowered to 1:2 or 1:3 in urban agriculture (Moustier and Danso, 2006).

Intensive horticulture can be practised on small plots, making efficient use of limited water and land resources. Horticultural species, as opposed to other food crops, have a considerable

Table 1.1 Food provided by urban agriculture

City	Percentage of urban demand met by urban agriculture						
	Leafy vegetables	All vegetables	Eggs	Poultry	Milk	Pork	Fruit
Havana, Cuba (Gonzalez Novo and Murphy, 2000)		58					39
La Paz, Bolivia (Kreinecker, 2000)		30					
Dakar, Senegal (Mbaye and Moustier, 2000)		70–80		65–70	60		
Dar Es Salaam, Tanzania (Jacobi et al., 2000)	90				60		
Addis Ababa, Ethiopia (Tegegne et al., 2000)		30			79		
Accra, Ghana (Cofie et al., 2003)		90					
Ibadan, Nigeria (Olajide-Taiwo et al., 2009)	80						
Brazzaville, Congo (Moustier, 1999)	80						
Nouakchott, Mauretania (Laurent, 1999)	90						
Antananarivo, Madagascar (Moustier, 1999)	90						
Jakarta, Indonesia (Purnomohadi, 2000)		10					16
Shanghai, China (Yi-Zhang and Zhangen, 2000)		60	90	50	90–100	50	
Hong Kong, China (Smit et al., 1996)		45		68		15	
Singapore (Smit et al., 1996)		25					
Hanoi, Vietnam (GTZ, 2000; Phuong Anh et al., 2004)	80	0–75 seasonal variation	40	50		50	
Vientiane, Laos (Kethongsa et al., 2004)	100	20–100 seasonal variation					

Source: Compiled by RUAF Foundation

yield potential and can provide up to 50 kg of fresh produce per m² per year depending on the technology applied. In addition, due to their short cycle, horticultural crops provide a quick response to emergency needs for food (several species can be harvested 60–90 days after planting).

Urban agriculture complements rural agriculture and increases the efficiency of the national food supply by:

- providing products that rural agriculture cannot easily supply, such as perishables that require rapid delivery upon harvest (e.g. fresh milk and vegetables) especially where road conditions are poor and cold storage facilities scarce;
- complementing rural production in the dry season and/or when rural areas are poorly accessible during the rainy period and thus also acting as a market stabilizer (Moustier and Danso, 2006);
- substituting for food imports intended for urban consumption and thereby saving on foreign exchange.

Poverty alleviation and local economic development

Households involved in urban and peri-urban agriculture are mainly (but not exclusively) the urban poor, each working small pieces of land intensively or keeping small numbers of animals. Smit et al. (1996) estimated that 800 million people worldwide are involved in urban agriculture of which 200 million are full-time farmers. Not only do household farms produce goods through family labour, but numerous other people are employed in the farming, marketing and processing activities. Table 1.2 summarizes data on employment generated in urban agriculture in a number of cities.

Poor households involved in urban and peri-urban agriculture benefit economically from their production activities by:

- saving on food expenditure. Since food is a major part (often 60–70 per cent) of the expenditures of a poor urban household such savings can be substantial and the freed up cash can be used for other livelihood essentials (water, medicines, rent, schooling and clothing). For example, in Windhoek, Namibia, research found that households involved in urban agriculture saved an average of 60 Namibian dollars a month on food expenditure, which is a significant amount (Frayne, 2005);
- sales of surplus crop and livestock production to neighbours and local shopkeepers and to local and city markets, supermarkets, school feeding programmes and hospitals.

In addition, poor urban households may benefit from:

- production and sales of processed products (meals, jams, shampoos and other products) on the street, in local restaurants and shops, and other outlets;

Table 1.2 Contribution of urban agriculture production to urban employment

City	Urban producers
Accra, Ghana (Sonou, 2001; Maxwell and Armar-Klemesu, 1998)	13.6% of all households in 16 city areas are involved in farming, among them 700 market farmers (1997)
Dakar, Senegal (Mbaye and Moustier, 2000)	3,000 family vegetable farms (14,000 jobs) of which 1,250 fully commercial (9,000 jobs); 250 poultry units (1996)
Dar es Salaam, Tanzania (Sawio, 1993)	15–20% of all families in 2 city areas have a home garden; urban agriculture forms at least 60% of the informal sector and was the second largest urban employer (20%) in 1997
Kumasi, Ghana (Drechsel et al., 2000; AQ 2006 in Ref Poynter and Fielding, 2000)	1,470 registered farms and 30,000 unregistered farmers; 500 cattle owners; 100 registered poultry farms (+ 200 unregistered)
Kampala, Uganda (International Potato Center, 2007)	35% of households are engaged in urban agriculture
Nairobi, Kenya (Foeken and Mwangi, 2000)	150,000 households (30% of population); agriculture provided (in 1993) the highest self-employment earnings among small-scale enterprises
Cienfuegos, Cuba (Socorro, 2003)	17,000 jobs were generated between 1995 and 2003; 1.17% of city GDP
Governador Valadares, Brazil (Lovo and Pereira Costa, 2006)	45% of population practices some form of urban agriculture
Habana, Cuba (Gonzalez and Murphy, 2000)	117,000 direct and 26,000 indirect jobs in urban agriculture
Lima, Peru (IPC, 2007)	20% of the population of Lurigancho-Chosica District of Lima is involved full-time or part-time in agriculture
Shanghai, China (Yi-Zhang and Zhangen, 2000)	2.7 million farmers (31.8% of all workers) 2% of city GDP
Beijing, China (Liu et al., 2003)	Peri-urban agriculture is absorbing high amounts of migrant labour (between 500,000 and 1 million people)
Manila, Philippines (IPC, 2007)	120,000 low-income households in the Manila region depend economically on local jasmine production (including jasmine farmers, garland makers, garland sellers)

Source: Compiled by RUAF Foundation

Backyard gardening in Cape Town

Credit: Henk de Zeeuw

- production and sales of agricultural inputs (e.g. production of compost or animal feed from collected organic waste; irrigation equipment from recycled materials) and provision of services (e.g. transport, animal health care services).

Although the production levels and turnover of individual urban producers in many cases will be small, the high number of urban producers in each city makes their overall contribution to the urban economy highly significant, generating employment for many poor urban households and providing incomes equivalent to or higher than the official minimum wage (Moustier and Danso, 2006).

Table 1.3 summarizes data from a number of studies regarding net income generated in (mainly peri-urban) irrigated open space vegetable production in a number of African and Asian cities, showing that monthly net farm income figures usually range between US$30 and US$70, but can go up to $200 or more. In the same countries, the minimum monthly wage is in the range $20–40 indicating that urban irrigated vegetable production could indeed be a profitable business compared to other urban jobs and also compared to rural vegetable farming (in Ghana irrigated urban vegetable farmers are earning an average annual income that is two to three times higher than that of rural farmers (Danso et al., 2003).

Danso et al. (2003) provide some data on the profitability of urban livestock in and around Kumasi. Cattle-raising within or close to the city is a highly profitable enterprise but only when the herd size falls within one to five animals. Space requirements, waste disposal and feed availability are major factors to be considered for larger herd sizes. Also, raising animals such as pigs, sheep and goats is profitable. Studies in Nairobi have shown the generation of significant incomes in urban livestock keeping, with pig and poultry farming as profitable ventures that guarantee a quick return on capital (Mireri, 2002).

Most poor families rarely have sufficient space for profitable urban animal husbandry within their homesteads. However, many urban producers keep smaller herds/flocks or only smaller

Table 1.3 Monthly net income from mixed vegetable farming with irrigation

City	Typical net monthly income in US$ per farm	Net income per capita in this country
Accra, Ghana	40–57	27
Bamako, Mali	10–300	24
Bangui, Central African Republic	n.d-320	22
Banjul, Gambia	30-n.d.	26
Bissau, Guinea Bissau	24	12
Brazzaville, Congo	80–270	53
Cotonou, Benin	50–110	36
Dakar, Senegal	40–250	46
Dar es Salaam, Tanzania	60	24
Kumasi, Ghana (Eriksen-Hamel and Danso, 2009)	35–160	27
Lagos, Nigeria (Ezedinma and Chukuezi, 1999)	53–120	27
Lomé, Togo	30–300	26
Nairobi, Kenya	10–163	33
Niamey, Niger	40	17
Ouagadougou, Burkina Faso	15–90	25
Yaoundé, Cameroon	34–67	53
Ho Chi Minh City, Vietnam (Jansen et al., 1996)	40–125	
Jakarta, Indonesia (Purnomohadi, 2000)	30–50	

Source: for data on West and East African countries: Drechsel et al, 2006

animals (e.g. guinea pig, rabbit, guinea fowl and poultry) with low space and input require-ments and still generate a good income. For example, in Addis Ababa (Ethiopia), profits above average are earned with very low capital input by backyard owners of inner city dairy units of even the smallest scale, a large part of which is managed by women (Tegegne et al., 2000).

A sizeable proportion of urban middle- and high-income families do have adequate land for commercial livestock keeping. The high start-up capital requirements of livestock keeping means that the majority of urban livestock producers (especially of cattle and of larger herds/ flocks) maintain their livestock enterprises as secondary to other ventures, for example, trad-ing or salaried employment, from which the capital is derived.

Ornamental plant and/or flower production is another profitable urban agricultural activity that can achieve annual benefits of US$400 up to $4700 (Nigeria) or $5000 (Lomé) if suf-ficient cash is available for labour and the purchase of seeds and seedlings (Kessler, 2002; Ezedinma and Chukuezi, 1999).

Recent work by FAO analysed the importance of urban agriculture for the urban poor from a comparative international perspective, making use of a Rural Income-Generating Activities (RIGA) database, which brought together comparable, nationally-representative household survey data for 15 developing and transition countries (FAO, RIGA website). The results show that the share of income from agriculture by poor urban households is highest in Nigeria with over 50 per cent of the income of the urban poorest quintile derived from agriculture, while this is around 20 per cent or somewhat higher in the other three African countries in the sample. Outside Africa the numbers are much lower (Zezza and Tasciotti, 2008).

Recent studies show that urban horticulture and urban livestock-raising have much higher growth rates than rural agriculture and are even comparable to or higher than in some other urban sectors. According to the World Bank (2007), intensive peri-urban horticultural and livestock rearing are extremely fast growing sectors that employ many workers and produce high value-added products that yield reasonable incomes and returns.

Urban agriculture has a comparative advantage over rural farming due to its proximity to urban consumers and lower transport and cooling costs, which is particularly important for perishable products (green vegetables, milk, eggs, etc.) and in places where roads and other infrastructure facilities such as refrigeration are poor.

Urban agriculture, to a large extent, makes productive use of land that is not fit for construc-tion (flood or earthquake-prone areas, land under power lines and in buffer zones) and adds value to land that might not otherwise have an economic output. It can generate income from temporarily idle land through urban and peri-urban infill, and is compatible with public parks and open space planning. Urban agriculture can also compete with alternative land uses. However, questions are sometimes raised regarding the sustainability of urban agriculture in the context of a dynamic urban market with high competition for land, soaring land prices and largely uncontrolled urban growth, if it is not protected by municipal laws and programmes and combined with other functions like recreation, water management, urban greening, lowering urban temperature and adaptation to climate change (see Chapter 2).

Social inclusion

Alongside the economic and employment aspects, urban agriculture can play a role in the social inclusion of marginalized groups (the aged without a pension, unemployed youth, persons with disabilities, those afflicted by HIV-AIDS, refugees, female-headed households, etc.) by providing them an opportunity to feed their families and raise an income, while enhancing self-management and entrepreneurial capacities.

Several examples exist of municipalities or NGOs that have initiated urban agriculture projects focusing on disadvantaged groups, with the aim to integrate them more strongly into the urban network and to provide them with a decent livelihood. The participants in such projects feel enriched by the possibility of working constructively, building their community, working together and, in addition, producing food and other products for consumption and for sale. Providing marginalized groups with a decent livelihood prevents social problems (Gonzalez Novo and Murphy, 2000).

A majority of the world's urban producers are women (around 65 per cent). Urban agriculture may provide some advantages over other jobs and income-earning opportunities such as the low capital needed to start farming, lower food expenditures, the possibility of combining this activity with caring for children, less travelling (and related costs in money and time) to the city centre or better-off neighbourhoods for an informal job as housekeeper or other low-paid job.

Children visiting an agro-centre in Shanghai

Credit: IGSNRR

In more developed cities, urban agriculture may be undertaken for the physical and/or psychological relaxation it provides, rather than for food production *per se*. Also, urban and peri-urban farms may take on an important role in providing recreational opportunities for citizens (recreational routes, food buying and meals on the farm, visiting facilities) or having educational functions (such as bringing youth in contact with animals and teaching ecology).

Urban waste management

Productive reuse of solid organic wastes. Urban agriculture is part of the urban ecological system and can play an important role in urban environmental management. A growing city will produce increasing organic wastes. For most cities the disposal of wastes has become a serious problem. Urban agriculture can help to solve such problems by turning urban wastes into a productive resource.

In many cities, local or municipal initiatives exist to collect household wastes and organic refuse from vegetable markets and agro-industries in order to produce compost or animal feed. Quality compost is an important input that can fetch a good price, and allows an urban farmer to use less chemical fertilizers (and by so doing also preventing problems related to the contamination of groundwater with residues of agrochemicals). The composted organic solid wastes generated by a city contain large amounts of nutrients (nitrogen, phosphorus, potassium and others) that can be used for soil improvement and fertilization. Drechsel et al., (2007) calculated that the nutrient value of the uncollected solid waste in Kumasi would be sufficient to pay the service costs of solid waste management for the whole city (US$180,000 per month). Moreover, about 80 per cent of this amount is spent on waste collection and transportation to disposal sites, which could be drastically reduced through composting for the additional benefit of the farming community. In addition, compost-making initiatives create employment and provide income for the urban poor. Diverting solid organic waste from landfill sites by composting is also one of the simplest ways to prevent emissions of methane (a greenhouse gas) and to reduce the pollution of groundwater due to leachates from the landfill. Recovering methane from landfills has proven to be only partially successful because up to 60 per cent of the methane generated escapes through leakage. And it is clearly much better to prevent organic waste coming into landfills.

Fresh waste from vegetable markets, restaurants and hotels, as well as food processing industries, is regularly used as a source of feed for urban livestock (Allison et al., 1998). Organic wastes are also used as a source of energy, either by incineration in an electricity-producing plant, by capturing methane from composting sites for biogas or by making briquettes for household use.

Productive reuse of wastewater. As competition for water in densely populated zones intensifies, producers close to cities increasingly make use of wastewater for irrigation in agriculture and

Compost production in Gampaha, Sri Lanka

Credit: IWMI India

aquaculture (either treated wastewater, wastewater diluted in rivers or other water bodies and untreated wastewater). Wastewater provides the poor urban and peri-urban producer with a regular supply of irrigation water as well as nutrients (replacing expensive industrial fertilizers). A study by IWMI of 53 cities in the developing world revealed that in four out of every five cities surveyed wastewater is used in urban and peri-urban agriculture on approximately 0.4 million ha, involving a farmer population of 1.1 million with 4.5 million family dependants. The total number of farmers worldwide irrigating their plots with treated, partially treated or untreated wastewater is estimated at 200 million farming on at least 20 million ha (Raschid-Sally and Jayakody, n.d.).

The World Health Organization (WHO) expects that 'urban agriculture, with urban wastewater as a common resource, will play a more important role in supplying food for the cities'. They indicate that a city of 1 million people can produce enough wastewater to irrigate approximately 1500–3500 ha land in a semi-arid country (WHO, 2006).

It seems obvious to view wastewater as a major source of irrigation water supply in urban and peri-urban horticulture, agro-forestry and aquaculture,while taking into account the WHO guidelines (WHO, 2006) to reduce associated health risks. (See IWMI, 2007 for a clear and practical overview). Benefits of using wastewater include:

- Productive (safe) use of wastewater in urban agriculture will help to reduce the demand for freshwater supply and mitigate the stress on water resources.
- Local reuse of wastewater will reduce the discharge of wastewater into rivers, canals and other surface water sources and thus diminish water pollution.
- Reuse of wastewater will reduce the need for artificial fertilizers and the energy used to produce them, and lower the depletion of certain minerals (e.g. phosphorus) by making productive use of the nutrients in the wastewater. Wastewater, excreta and urban organic waste are an accessible source of plant nutrients, such as phosphorus, nitrogen and potassium. The amount of nutrients in urban wastewater is substantial (but can vary considerably: 16–62 kg total nitrogen, 4–24 kg phosphorus, 2–69 kg potassium, 18–208 kg calcium, 9–110 kg magnesium, and 27–182 kg sodium per 1,000 m^3) and its economic value is sizeable (Manzoor et al, 2007). It should be noted that the world's resources of readily available phosphorus are limited and will run out in 25 years (Rosemarin, 2004).

However, wastewater use is still not clearly incorporated into national or local policy in most countries. The fear of health impacts, increasing focus on water supply instead of managing the demand for water and, occasionally, cultural factors influence the lack of clear policies in support of safe water reuse. The common point of view of researchers, decision-makers, and service providers is that the use of untreated wastewater is unacceptable and that important benefits can be obtained only when the water is appropriately treated. This approach has resulted in a marginalization of poor farmers who use low quality water since the alternative of using 'appropriately treated water' is in many cases an illusion.

Treatment of wastewater in centralized treatment plants is prohibitively expensive for many cities in developing countries. A further disadvantage is that conventional treatment methods remove the nutrients in wastewater, thus reducing the economic benefits to its users. The last two decades have seen a strong move towards alternative decentralized and low-cost treatment of wastewater that allows reuse of wastewater and nutrients or even includes aquaculture or agriculture as part of the wastewater treatment process. Stabilization ponds are used extensively in mid-income countries, especially in the Middle East. Other technologies have and are being developed that allow decentralized and low-cost treatment – and reuse of wastewater and nutrients – close to the source (e.g. cluster approach, constructed wetlands, up-flow anaerobic sludge reactors – see UNEP, 1997 for an overview). However, very low-income countries cannot be expected to provide wastewater treatment facilities of appropriate quality to even a small percentage of the population in the foreseeable future. The adoption of an integrated and productive approach to water development and the use of alternative decentralized wastewater treatment technologies needs to be strongly supported with a view to enhancing coverage while enabling productive reuse.

Further, the use of wastewater does not need to be restricted to fully treated wastewater. Where only partial or no wastewater treatment is available, the health risks of productive reuse of wastewater can be reduced through complementary health risk reduction measures as explained in the new WHO guidelines for safe use of excreta and wastewater (WHO, 2006). The new guidelines assist decision-makers in planning how to achieve the required levels of pathogen reduction by choosing and combining a number of different health risk reduction measures and entry points for action along the 'farm to fork' pathway, depending on what is feasible locally. The new WHO guidelines should be extensively applied as this allows for incremental and adaptive change (in contrast to the earlier strict water quality thresholds). This is a cost-effective and realistic approach for reducing health and environmental risks in low-income countries (see IWMI Policy Water Briefing no. 17 for a good overview of this low cost risk reduction strategy and recommended measures; IWMI, 2007).

Adaptation to climate change

Urban agriculture is receiving increasing recognition as an important strategy for climate change adaptation (taking steps to minimize the predicted impacts of climate change) and (to a lesser extent) mitigation (reduction of greenhouse gas emissions).

The Conference 'Urban challenges and Poverty Reduction in African, Caribbean and Pacific Countries' organized by UN Habitat with EU and ACP countries, 8–10 June 2009 in Nairobi, identified urban agriculture, including agro-forestry, as having a high potential for climate change adaptation (UN Habitat, 2009). The Asian Cities Climate Change Resilience Network (ACCCRN) earmarked urban agriculture as an important strategy to building resilient cities (defined as cities that are able to respond to, resist and recover from changing climatic conditions) (Rumbaitis del Rio, 2009).

Urban agriculture helps cities to adapt to climate change and become more resilient by:

1. Reducing energy use and greenhouse gas emissions by producing fresh food close to the city (less energy used in transport, cooling, storage, processing and packaging thus lowering the ecological footprint), and enabling synergic and cyclical processes between urban domestic and industrial sectors and agriculture (e.g. use of excess heat, cooling water or CO_2 from industry in greenhouses). Urban food production also contributes to reduction of the ecological food(t)print of the city (the energy and water needed to produce and transport the food consumed by a city).

2. Maintaining green open spaces and enhancing vegetation cover in the city with important adaptive (and some mitigation) benefits:
   - reduction of the heat island effect by providing shade and enhanced evapotranspiration (and thus more cooling, less smog);
   - fewer floods and reduced impacts of high rainfall by storage of excess water, increased water interception and infiltration in green open spaces. Urban agriculture also keeps flood zones free from construction and reduces rapid storm water runoff and floods downstream and facilitates more replenishment of groundwater;
   - improvement of water quality by natural cleaning in low lying agricultural areas (e.g. natural or constructed wetlands, aquaculture in maturation ponds etc.);
   - capturing CO_2 and dust (and thus contributing to mitigating the global warming effect of the city) through urban (agro-)forestry;
   - preventing landslides by agro-forestry on steep slopes (and preventing building on such sites).

3. Reducing the vulnerability of the most vulnerable urban groups and strengthening community-based adaptive management by:
   - diversifying urban food sources, enhancing access of the urban poor to nutritious food, reducing the dependency on imported foods and making the city less vulnerable to periods of low food supply from rural areas due to floods, droughts or other natural or man-made disasters;
   - diversifying income opportunities of the urban poor and functioning as a safety net in times of economic crisis;
   - being a source of innovation and learning about new strategies/technologies for high land and water-efficient food production.

Municipal policy making and action planning on urban agriculture

An increasing number of national and city governments have policies and programmes on urban agriculture, or are in the process of formulating these. The growing attention of local and national policy makers and practitioners is also reflected in the growing demand (e.g. to the RUAF

A vision for agriculture in Metro-Vancouver

partners) for inspiring examples of successful policies and programmes on urban agriculture as well as for training and (co-)funding of research and action programmes.

Main policy perspectives on urban agriculture

It is useful to distinguish between three main policy perspectives (social, economic and ecological), which are helpful in designing alternative policy scenarios for the development of sustainable urban agriculture. These perspectives are related to the vision of municipal governments regarding the role they expect urban agriculture to play and the kind of contributions they expect urban agriculture to make to the realization of certain policy goals, namely, to make the city more food-secure and socially inclusive, to reduce poverty and enhance local economic development, or to make the city environmentally more sustainable. Figure 1.1 summarizes the three policy perspectives on urban agriculture (Cabannes, 2006).

The **social perspective** is mainly (but not exclusively) associated with *subsistence-oriented* types of urban agriculture that form part of the livelihood strategies of urban low income households with a focus on producing food and medicinal plants for home consumption. Examples include home gardening, community gardening, institutional gardens at schools and hospitals, and open field farming at the micro scale with low levels of investment. These activities do not generate a major cash surplus but provide for food or medicinal plants, thus reducing the food and health expenses of the family. Since food is such a substantial part of the expenditures of a poor urban household (and can be between 50 and 70 per cent of their budget), such savings can be substantial and the freed cash can be used for other livelihood essentials (such as water, rent, schooling and clothing). This contribution to food security and nutrition is one of the important benefits of

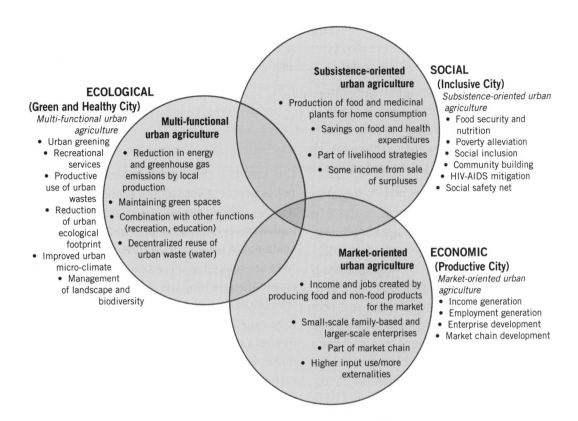

ECOLOGICAL
(Green and Healthy City)
Multi-functional urban agriculture
- Urban greening
- Recreational services
- Productive use of urban wastes
- Reduction of urban ecological footprint
- Improved urban micro-climate
- Management of landscape and biodiversity

Multi-functional urban agriculture
- Reduction in energy and greenhouse gas emissions by local production
- Maintaining green spaces
- Combination with other functions (recreation, education)
- Decentralized reuse of urban waste (water)

Subsistence-oriented urban agriculture
- Production of food and medicinal plants for home consumption
- Savings on food and health expenditures
- Part of livelihood strategies
- Some income from sale of surpluses

SOCIAL
(Inclusive City)
Subsistence-oriented urban agriculture
- Food security and nutrition
- Poverty alleviation
- Social inclusion
- Community building
- HIV-AIDS mitigation
- Social safety net

Market-oriented urban agriculture
- Income and jobs created by producing food and non-food products for the market
- Small-scale family-based and larger-scale enterprises
- Part of market chain
- Higher input use/more externalities

ECONOMIC
(Productive City)
Market-oriented urban agriculture
- Income generation
- Employment generation
- Enterprise development
- Market chain development

Figure 1.1 Main policy perspectives on urban agriculture

these types of urban agriculture, coupled with other important social impacts such as social inclusion, poverty alleviation, community development, and HIV/AIDS mitigation.

The **economic perspective** focuses on income generation and employment creation, and on *market-oriented producers* that not only or mainly produce for self-subsistence but also or primarily for the market. In this case the rationale for urban agriculture is its capacity to generate local economic development through enterprise development in local agricultural production, processing and marketing. Market-oriented urban agriculture may constitute the primary or be a complementary source of income for urban residents. Activities usually involve small-scale family-based enterprises and sometimes, larger scale entrepreneurial farms run by private investors or producer associations. The activities not only include food production (such as irrigated vegetable production and stall-fed dairy production) but also non-food production (such as medicinal and aromatic herbs, flowers and ornamental plants). Commercial urban agriculture also includes enterprises involved in the delivery of inputs (like the collection and composting of urban wastes, seed and fodder supply, production of organic pesticides, fabrication of tools, delivery of water, buying and transport of chemical fertilizers), the provision of services (such as transport, animal health care services), and the processing and marketing of primary or processed products (including marmalades, shampoos and other products) on the street, in local restaurants and shops, or at producers' markets.

Market-oriented types of urban agriculture have a more pronounced economic impact and higher profitability, but their externalities for the city and urban populations, especially those of the intensive larger scale enterprises, tend to be higher especially through risk of water and soil contamination due to intensive use of agrochemicals, health risks from use of contaminated water for irrigation and risks of animal–human disease transfers (zoonosis).

The **ecological perspective** mainly focuses on the role of urban agriculture in urban environmental management. Besides provision of food and generating income, urban agriculture plays a role in environmental management through nutrient recycling via decentralized composting and reuse of organic wastes and wastewater. Urban agriculture can also provide other functions (in addition to food and income) such as: provision of recreational services; reduction of the city temperature; capturing CO_2 and dust; keeping buffer zones and flood plains free from construction; storm water storage and flood prevention; ecological education of youth; and care for people with a handicap. In order to enable such a combination of functions, urban agriculture will have to adopt agro-ecological production methods, link up with eco-sanitation and decentralized sustainable waste management systems and also become an integral part of the planning and management of parks, nature reserves and recreational services.

The three policy perspectives on urban agriculture suggest different scenarios for the development of urban agriculture and will lead to a different set of policy measures. For example, when the focus is mainly on the social perspective the policy will mainly support home-, community- and school-gardening and groups of disadvantaged citizens will be assisted by providing access to municipal land, and will receive basic training in group work skills and in food growing and providing basic materials (such as seeds and equipment) in exchange. However, when the emphasis shifts to the economic perspective, more market-oriented producers will be supported with, for example, technical assistance, credit, strengthening producer groups and small-scale enterprises, infrastructure development and market chain development.

However, it should be stressed that the three perspectives certainly are not mutually exclusive and, in practice, most policies on urban agriculture will be based on a *specific mix* of the three perspectives, giving different emphasis to a certain perspective in certain locations and with certain categories of the population and another perspective in other parts of the city territory and with other actors.

Multi-stakeholder approach to policy development and action planning

Due to the cross-cutting and multifunctional nature of urban agriculture, policy development and action planning on urban agriculture should involve various sectors and disciplines, including: agriculture; urban land use planning; health; waste management; social housing and slum upgrading; and park and nature management.

Moreover, urban producers, and the CBOs and NGOs supporting them, should be involved in the planning process. According to Allen (2001) the most important aspect of strategic urban planning is related to the participation of the urban poor themselves in the analysis of the situation, in the definition of priorities and in action planning and implementation. Such consultative processes will make the outcomes of policy development and action planning not only robust and comprehensive, but also accepted and sustainable. Increasingly, this is being recognized and incorporated in urban planning approaches such as the multi-actor planning methodologies adopted by Local Agenda 21 and the Sustainable Cities Programme.

In Chapters 2 to 4, the partners in the RUAF Foundation present the experiences they gained during the last five years in the 'Cities Farming for the Future' programme regarding multi-stakeholder policy formulation and action planning (MPAP) on urban agriculture in over 20 cities in 17 countries (see also www.ruaf.org).

Chapter 2 focuses on the MPAP approach: the principles and main working procedures of the approach are explained and the main experiences gained regarding each of the phases in the strategic planning process are presented.

In Chapter 3 seven city cases are briefly presented to further illustrate the practical application of the MPAP approach and the results achieved to date.

In Chapter 4 an overview is provided of a range of policy measures and development strategies regarding urban agriculture that have been applied with success in a number of cities as 'food for thought' for policy makers and practitioners in other cities.

Finally, a number of resources on urban agriculture and multi-stakeholder planning are provided.

References

Allen, A. (2001) *Environmental planning and management of the peri-urban interface*, Keynote Paper for the Conference Rural-Urban Encounters: Managing the Environment of the Peri-urban Interface, London, 9–10 November 2001.

Allison, M., Harris, P.J.C., Hofny-Collins, A.H. and Stevens, W. (1998) *A Review of the Use of Urban Waste in Peri-Urban Interface Production Systems*, Henry Doubleday Research Association, Coventry, UK.

Armar-Klemesu, M. (2000) 'Urban agriculture and food security, nutrition and health', in N. Bakker, M. Dubbeling, S. Guendel, U. Sabel-Koschella and H. de Zeeuw (eds), *Growing Cities, Growing Food, Urban Agriculture on the Policy Agenda*, pp. 99–117, DSE, Feldafing.

Cabannes, Y. (2006) 'Financing and investment for urban agriculture', in R. van Veenhuizen (ed.), *Cities Farming for the Future-Urban Agriculture for Green and Productive Cities*, pp. 87–123, RUAF Foundation, IDRC and IIRR, Philippines.

Cofie, O., Van Veenhuizen, R. and Drechsel, P. (2003) *Contribution of urban and peri-urban agriculture to food security in sub-Saharan Africa*. Paper presented at the Africa session of 3rd World Water Forum, Kyoto, 17 March 2003.

Commission on Climate Change and Development (2009) *Closing the gaps: Disaster risk reduction and adaptation to climate change in developing countries*, Ministry of Foreign Affairs, Sweden.

Danso, G., Drechsel, P., Akinbolu, S.S. and Gyiele, L.A. (2003) *Review of studies and literature on the profitability and sustainability of urban and peri-urban agriculture*, Final Report submitted to FAO-Rome, International Water Management Institute, Accra.

Deutsche Gesellschaft für Technische Zusammenarbeit (GTZ) (2000) *Fact sheets on urban agriculture: Ho Chi Minh City, Mexico City and Accra*, GTZ, Eschborn.

Drechsel, P., Graefe, S., Sonou, M. and Cofie, O.O. (2006) *Informal irrigation in urban West Africa: An overview*, IWMI research report 102, IWMI (with RUAF, FAO and Urban Harvest), Colombo.

Drechsel, P., Graefe, S. and Fink, M. (2007) *Rural-urban food, nutrient and virtual water flows in selected West African cities,* IWMI research report 115, Colombo.

Eriksen-Hamel, N.S. and Danso, G. (2009) 'Urban compost: a socio-economic and agronomic evaluation in Kumasi, Ghana', in M. Redwood (ed.), *Agriculture in Urban Planning, Generating Livelihoods and Food Security*, chapter 2, Earthscan, London.

Ezedinma, C. and Chukuezi, C. (1999) 'A comparative land analysis of urban agriculture enterprises in Lagos and Port Harcourt, Nigeria', *Environment and Urbanization* 11(2): 135–144.

Food and Agriculture Organization of the United Nations (FAO) (2004) *The State of Food Security in the World*, FAO, Rome.

FAO (2008) *State of Food Insecurity in the World 2008: High food prices and food security – threats and opportunities,* FAO, Rome.

FAO (2009) *Follow-up to the high-level conference on world food security: FAO contribution to the implementation of the comprehensive framework for action*, Document for FAO Council 136th session, 15–19 June, Rome.

FAO, Rural Income Generating Activities website, available at: http://www.fao.org/es/ESA/riga/english/index_en.htm [last accessed 25 March 2010].

Foeken, D. (2006) *To Subsidise My Income: Urban farming in an East African Town,* Brill, Leiden.

Foeken, D. and Mboganie Mwangi, A. (2000) 'Increasing food security through urban farming in Nairobi', in N. Bakker, M. Dubbeling, S. Guendel, U. Sabel-Koschella and H. de Zeeuw (eds), *Growing Cities, Growing Food, Urban Agriculture on the Policy Agenda*, pp. 303–28, DSE, Feldafing.

Frayne, B. (2005) 'Survival of the poorest: migration and food security in Namibia', in L.J.A. Mougeot (ed.), *AGROPOLIS: The Social, Political and Environmental Dimensions of Urban Agriculture*, pp. 31–50, Earthscan, London.

Gonzalez Novo, M. and Murphy, C. (2000) 'Urban agriculture in the City of Havana: A popular response to a crisis', in N. Bakker, M. Dubbeling, S. Guendel, U. Sabel-Koschella and H. de Zeeuw (eds), *Growing Cities, Growing Food: Urban Agriculture on the Policy Agenda*, pp. 329–47, DSE, Feldafing.

IASC Task Force on Meeting Humanitarian Challenges on Urban Areas (2009) *Meeting Humanitarian Challenges in Urban Areas: Assessment and Strategy*; Draft annotated outline, Geneva.

International Monetary Fund (IMF) (2007) *Finance and Development Report 2007*, IMF, Washington D.C.

International Potato Center (IPC) (2007) *Impacts of urban agriculture: Highlights of Urban Harvest research and development 2003–2006,* Urban Harvest, Lima.

International Water Management Institute (IWMI) (2007) *Recycling realities: Managing health risks to make wastewater an asset*, Water Policy Briefing no. 17, IWMI Global Water Partnership.

Jacobi, P., Amend, J. and Kiango, S. (2000) 'Urban agriculture in Dar es Salaam: Providing for an indispensable part of the diet', in N. Bakker, M. Dubbeling, S. Guendel, U. Sabel-Koschella and H. de Zeeuw (eds), *Growing Cities, Growing Food: Urban Agriculture on the Policy Agenda*, pp. 257–83, DSE, Feldafing.

Jansen, H.G.P., Midmore, D.J., Binh, P.T., Valasayya, S. and Tru, L.C. (1996) 'Profitability and sustainability of peri-urban vegetable production system in Vietnam', *Netherlands Journal of Agricultural Science* 44: 125–43.

Kessler, A. (2002) *Farming systems in Urban agriculture in four West Africa Cities*, IWMI, Accra.

Kethongsa, S., Thadavong, K. and Moustier, P. (2004) *Vegetable marketing in Vientiane*, SUSPER project AVRDC/CIRAD/French MOFA, Hanoi.

Kreinecker, P. (2000) 'La Paz: Urban agriculture in harsh ecological conditions', in N. Bakker, M. Dubbeling, S. Guendel, U. SabelKoschella and H. de Zeeuw (eds), *Growing Cities, Growing Food, Urban Agriculture on the Policy Agenda*, pp. 391–412, DSE, Feldafing.

Laurent cited by Moustier, P. (1999) 'Urban horticulture in Africa and Asia', *ISHS Acta Horticultura* 762.

Liu, S., Cai, J. and Yang, Z. (2003) 'Migrants' access to land in peri-urban Beijing', *Urban Agriculture Magazine* 11: 6–8.

Lovo, I.C. and Pereira Costa, Z.R. (2006) 'Making laws for urban agriculture: The experience of Governador Valadares, Brazil', *Urban Agriculture Magazine* 16: 45–7.

Manzoor, Q. et al. (2007) 'Agricultural use of marginal-quality water: Opportunities and challenges', in D. Molden (ed.), *Water for Food, Water for Life: A Comprehensive Assessment of Water Management in Agriculture*, pp. 425–57, Earthscan, London; IWMI, Colombo.

Maxwell, D. and Armar-Klemesu, M. (1998) *Urban agriculture: Introduction and review of literature*, Noguchi Memorial Institute for Medical Research, Accra

Mbaye, A. and Moustier, P. (2000) 'Market-oriented urban agricultural production in Dakar', in N. Bakker, M. Dubbeling, S. Guendel, U. Sabel-Koschella and H. de Zeeuw (eds), *Growing Cities, Growing Food, Urban Agriculture on the Policy Agenda*, pp. 235–56, DSE, Feldafing.

Mireri, C. (2002) 'Private investment in urban agriculture in Nairobi, Kenya', *Urban Agriculture Magazine* 7: 19–21.

Mougeot, L.J.A. (2000) 'Urban agriculture: Definition, presence, potentials and risks', in N. Bakker, M. Dubbeling, S. Guendel, U. Sabel-Koschella and H. de Zeeuw (eds), *Growing Cities, Growing Food, Urban Agriculture on the Policy Agenda*, pp. 1–42, DSE, Feldafing.

Moustier, P. (1999) 'Complémentarité entre agriculture urbaine et agriculture rurale', in B. Olanrewaju Smith (ed.), *Agriculture Urbaine en Afrique de l'Ouest: Une Contribution à la Securité Alimentaire et à L'assainissement des Villes*, pp. 41–55, TCA and IDRC, Wageningen/Ottawa.

Moustier, P. and Danso, G. (2006) 'Local economic development and marketing of urban produced food', in R. van Veenhuizen (ed.), *Cities Farming for the Future: Urban Agriculture for Green and Productive Cities*, pp. 172–208, RUAF Foundation/IDRC/IIRR, Leusden.

Mubarik, A., De Bon, H. and Moustier, P. (2005) 'Promoting the multifunctionality of urban and periurban agriculture in Hanoi', *Urban Agriculture Magazine* 15: 11–13.

Mutonodzo, C. (2009) 'The social and economic implications of urban agriculture on food security in Harare, Zimbabwe', in M. Redwood (ed.), *Agriculture in Urban Planning – Generating Livelihoods and Food Security*, chapter 4, Earthscan/IDRC, London.

Nugent, R. (2000) 'The impact of urban agriculture on the household and local economies', in N. Bakker, M. Dubbeling, S. Guendel, U. Sabel-Koschellaand H. de Zeeuw (eds), *Growing Cities, Growing Food: Urban Agriculture on the Policy Agenda*, pp. 67–97, DSE, Feldafing.

Olajide-Taiwo, L., Cofie, O.O., Odeleye, O.M.O., Olajide-Taiwo, F.B., Olufunmi, Y., Adebayo, O.S. and Alabi, O.O. (2009) *Effect of capacity building on production of safe and profitable leafy vegetables among farmers in Ibadan city of Nigeria*. Paper presented to the All Africa Horticulture Congress, Nairobi, August 2009.

Phuong Anh, M.T., Ali, M., Lan Anh, H. and Thi Thu Ha, T. (2004) *Urban and peri-urban agriculture in Hanoi: Opportunities and constraints for safe and sustainable food production*, Technical bulletin No. 32, AVRDC, CIRAD, SUSPER, Tainan.

Poynter, G. and Fielding, D. (2000) 'Urban livestock in Kumasi: Survey findings', *Urban Agriculture Magazine* 2: 28–9

Purnomohadi, N. (2000) 'Jakarta: Urban agriculture as an alternative strategy to face the economic crisis', in N. Bakker, M. Dubbeling, S. Guendel, U. Sabel-Koschella and H. de Zeeuw (eds), *Growing Cities, Growing Food: Urban Agriculture on the Policy Agenda*, pp. 453–66, DSE, Feldafing.

Raschid-Sally, L. and Jayakody, P. (no date) *Drivers and characteristics of wastewater agriculture in developing countries – results from a global assessment*, IWMI research report.

Rosemarin, A. (2004) 'In a fix: The precarious geopolitics of phosphorous', *Down to Earth,* June 2004, pp. 27–31.

Rumbaitis del Rio, C. (2009) *Cities Climate Change Resilience and Urban Agriculture*, Powerpoint presentation at Strategic Partnership meeting on Urban Agriculture, IDRC, Marseille, July 2, 2009.

Sawio, C. (1993) *Feeding the urban masses? Towards an understanding of the dynamics of urban agriculture and land use change in Dar es Salaam, Tanzania*, PhD. Thesis, Graduate School of Geography, Clark University, Worcester, MA, USA.

Shapouri, S., Rosen, S., Meade, B. and Gale, F. (2009) *Food Security Assessment 2008–2009*, United States Department of Agriculture (USDA), Washington D.C..

Smit, J., Ratta, A. and Nasr, J. (1996) *Urban agriculture: Food, jobs and sustainable cities.* UNDP, New York.

Socorro, A. (2003) 'From empty lots to productive spaces in Cienfuegos', *Urban Agriculture Magazine* 11: 26–7.

Sonou, M. (2001) 'Peri-urban irrigated agriculture and health risks in Ghana', *Urban Agriculture Magazine* 3: 33–4.

Tegegne, A., Tadesse, M., Yami, A. and Mekasha, Y. (2000) 'Market-oriented urban and peri-urban dairy systems', *Urban Agriculture Magazine* 2: 23–4.

United Nations (UN) (2008) *Comprehensive Framework for Action, High level Task Force on the global Food Crisis*, July 2008, New York.

United Nations Centre for Human Settlements (UNCHS) (2001) *State of the World's Cities Report*, UNCHS, Nairobi.

United Nations Conference on Trade and Development (UNCTAD) (2006) *The Least Developed Countries Report: Developing Productive Capacity*, UNCTAD, Geneva.

United Nations Environment Programme (UNEP) (1997) *Source book of alternative technologies for freshwater augmentation in Latin America and the Caribbean*, UNEP Environmental Technology Centre, Osaka.

United Nations Population Fund (UNFPA) (2007) *State of the World Population; Unleashing the potential of urban growth*, UNFPA, New York.

UN Habitat (2009) *International tripartite Conference on Urban challenges and Poverty Reduction in African, Caribbean and Pacific Countries*, 8–10 June 2009, Nairobi.

World Bank (2000) *World Development Report 2000/2001: Attacking Poverty*, World Bank, Washington D.C.

World Bank (2007) *Agricultural Investment Source book* (First update), World Bank, Washington D.C.

World Health Organization (WHO) (2006) *Guidelines for the safe use of wastewater, excreta and grey water*, WHO, Geneva.

Yeudall, F. (2007) 'Nutritional perspectives in urban and peri-urban agriculture', in A. Boischio, A. Clegg and D. Mwagore (eds), *Health Risks and Benefits of Urban and Peri-Urban Agriculture and Livestock in Sub-Saharan Africa*, pp. 25–34, Urban Poverty and Environment Series Report No. 1, IDRC, Ottawa.

Yi-Zhang, C. and Zhangen, Z. (2000) 'Shanghai: Trends towards specialised and capital-intensive urban agriculture', in N. Bakker, M. Dubbeling, S. Guendel, U. Sabel-Koschella and H. de Zeeuw (eds), (2000) *Growing Cities, Growing Food, Urban Agriculture on the Policy Agenda*, pp. 467–76, DSE, Feldafing.

Zezza, A. and Tasciotti, L. (2008) *Does Urban Agriculture Enhance Dietary Diversity?* Empirical Evidence from a Sample of Developing Countries, FAO, Rome.

Chapter 2
MULTI-STAKEHOLDER POLICY FORMULATION AND ACTION PLANNING ON URBAN AGRICULTURE

Introduction

Multi-stakeholder processes are increasingly considered to be an important element of policy design, action planning and implementation. By involving multiple stakeholders in decision-making, it is much more likely that policies and programmes will be developed that are more inclusive and more successful in their implementation. This chapter seeks to describe the characteristics, benefits and challenges involved in setting up and managing multi-stakeholder processes and will illustrate the approach taken and lessons learned by RUAF partners in 20 cities who have been involved in such processes in the past five years (2004–2008).

Credit: IWMI

Involving multiple stakeholders in decision-making in Gampaha, Sri Lanka

Characteristics of multi-stakeholder policy formulation and action planning

When a government collaborates – preferably from an early stage – with other stakeholders such as citizens, farmers, civil organizations, private sector companies and other governmental entities in the preparation, implementation and evaluation of policies and related action plans, we speak of participatory and multi-stakeholder policy and action planning (MPAP).

Our municipal administration assumed from the start the challenge to fight against poverty and create new policies and programmes based on consultative, participatory and democratic processes of policy formulation. The policies and programmes that have been developed respond to the needs expressed by the population to combat hunger, environmental degradation, analphabetism and urban violence. One of the programmes created is the Zero Hunger programme. Also, a municipal sub-department of urban agriculture was created to promote urban agriculture in the municipality. I would like to reaffirm our commitment to keep working together with our citizens, community-based organizations, and public and private institutes towards the further development and modernisation of urban agriculture to improve our municipality and, most importantly, the quality of life and well-being of its population (Dr. Washington Ipenza Pacheco, Mayor of the Municipality of Villa Maria del Triunfo, Lima, Peru, 2006).

The multi-stakeholder policy formulation and action planning approach was developed in the 1990s in the context of the UNEP Local Agenda 21 programmes and the UN Habitat city consultation strategies (UN Habitat and UNEP, 1999).

The concept of *stakeholders* has emerged in recent decades as crucial for understanding decision-making and policy formulation on a wide range of issues. It supplements (and to a certain extent supplants) the related concept of *actors*. 'Stakeholders' refers to all individuals, groups and organizations that play a role in a policy process and have an interest in the policies or plans that are to be developed, either as individuals or as members of a group or organization. This includes people who influence a decision, or can influence it, as well as those affected by it.

If a participatory and multi-stakeholder approach is chosen, action plans and policies are formulated in collaboration with and interaction between a local (or national) government and other relevant stakeholders, including citizen groups, community-based organizations (CBOs), non-governmental organizations (NGOs), municipal departments, regional or national governmental organizations, credit institutions, private enterprises, etc. This collaboration must surpass 'window-dressing' and mere informative or consultative forms of participation. Instead, the goal is to establish 'partnerships where degrees of decision-making are increased, trade-offs are made and responsibilities shared; decision-making capacities are transferred to non-governmental groups; and where community groups share control of all stages of planning, policy-making and management, including funds' (Arnstein, 1969).

In this perspective, multi-stakeholder policy and planning processes are characterized by the following:

- participation of both governmental and a variety of non-governmental actors in joint policy-making and action planning;
- a variety of non-governmental actors are given an equal chance to contribute to the preparation, implementation and evaluation of a policy and related action plans;
- an open and transparent process;
- final decisions honour – to the greatest extent possible – the contributions from the various actors involved.

For sustainable urban agriculture development, such multi-stakeholder participation is particularly important, since urban agriculture involves a large diversity of direct actors (e.g. input providers, vegetable producers, fish or livestock farmers, micro-entrepreneurs, traders and retailers) and touches on a large number of urban management areas (e.g. land use planning, environmental and waste management, economic development, public health, social and community development, housing programmes and management of parks and green structures). Urban agriculture can thus be understood as a cross-cutting issue involving a wide range of often disconnected actors or stakeholders. To be effective, any urban agriculture policy or programme should address the needs and specific conditions of the different stakeholders as well as the specific socio-economic and political-institutional context in which it will have to operate.

The multi-stakeholder planning process is normally built around the following phases (UN Habitat and UNEP, 1999):

- diagnosis, assessment and stakeholder inventory;
- consultation to confirm political support and consolidate stakeholder participation;
- joint strategy development and action planning;
- implementation;
- follow-up and consolidation;
- integrated monitoring and evaluation.

Benefits of the application of a participatory and multi-stakeholder approach include the following (Hemmati, 2002; Partners and Propper, 2004). A multi-stakeholder approach contributes to more participatory governance, encourages public–private partnerships, and helps overcome distrust and bridge the gap between citizen groups and the government. The approach improves the quality of the diagnosis of the actual situation and the decision-making on the courses of action needed. This comes about through a better understanding of priority issues and the needs of different stakeholders involved and a better linking of different sources of knowledge, information and expertise. Moreover, there is a greater likelihood of success and sustainability of implementation through enhanced acceptance and ownership

Participatory diagnosis, assessment and stakeholder inventory (Freetown, Sierra Leone).

Credit: René van Veenhuizen

of the policy, improved mechanisms and processes for coordination of the implementation and by mobilizing and pooling scarce human, technical and financial resources. Finally, the approach strengthens the problem-solving and political lobbying capacities of the participating institutions and contributes to the empowerment of citizens' groups (in this case especially resource-poor urban producers).

A major aim of the application of the multi-stakeholder approach is to contribute to building participatory and democratic governance in cities. Multi-stakeholder policy and planning processes are based on principles of participation, ownership and commitment, mutual trust and collaboration (in planning, decision-making and control). They are thus, in fact, political processes through which power relations are redefined and (if well organized) lead to a more participatory governance and increased participation of civil society in decision-making. But even in cases when the multi-stakeholder process does not lead to a stronger role of civil society in decision-making, it may well prove to have very positive impacts. For example, in China, evaluation of the MPAP process on urban agriculture in three cities showed that although the direct involvement of the urban producers in the planning process was minimal, it was positively evaluated by all concerned since it was particularly instrumental in enhancing a higher participation of civil servants and a better coordination within the government sphere: among the various government sectors that play a role in urban agriculture (urban planning, agriculture, land and water management, recreation and parks, etc.) and between the various tiers of government (local, regional, central).

Participatory and multi-stakeholder processes of policy formulation and action planning also present some challenges, which should not be underestimated. Such processes require skilled facilitators and sufficient financial means; they also may require more time than conventional approaches, not least to allow for changes that may be required in institutional cultures. They may also lead to an undue increase in the influence of some stakeholders, for example, those that have a higher capacity to actively participate in the process and to convince other stakeholders. It may prove difficult to build true participation among stakeholders who may never have worked together, have had conflicts in the past, hold strongly differing views on the key issues at stake or are not interested in new forms of collaboration and management.

Moreover, the experiences gained to date point out that the results of multi-stakeholder policy and planning processes can be disappointing if the MPAP process is not properly managed. Causes of a low degree of success of a multi-stakeholder process that are often mentioned are the following:

- insufficient preparation and planning of the process;
- insufficient embedding of the process in participating institutions; and
- lack of transparency and communication throughout the process.

That is to say, municipal authorities planning to engage in an MPAP process will require well-designed methods and tools and trained staff to successfully implement a multi-stakeholder policy and action planning process.

Important elements of a successful MPAP process

Analysis of the experiences gained in UNEP Local Agenda 21 programmes and the UN Habitat city consultation strategies (UN Habitat and UNEP, 1999) demonstrate that successful multi-stakeholder policy and planning processes should integrate the following elements:

Enhancing awareness in participating organizations; before starting a multi-stakeholder policy and action planning process, one should first reflect on the following questions.

Is there sufficient room for new ideas and for a style of working that is different from the current style of operation within the local government and the other organizations that will be involved in such a process? In other words, is there really room to develop plans and policies in a participatory way together? Are the stakeholders prepared to engage in dialogue and to change their current ideas and plans based on inputs provided by other actors? Are they committed to implement the outcomes of the joint planning process? Is there sufficient trust among the different stakeholders? Is the government involved willing to cede part of its 'power' and allow for public participation in policy making?

If such questions cannot be answered positively, one should first undertake activities to build up mutual trust and to create more 'room for manoeuvre' and commitment for the multi-stakeholder process as described below (or abstain from the plan to engage in such a process).

Capacity building among stakeholders for the development of participatory processes of diagnosis, problem identification and the implementation of solutions according to previously established priorities, conflict mediation and negotiation, policy design and joint implementation of actions, systematization, monitoring and control of municipal policy changes.

Continuous building of trust and cooperation among the main actors during the process (building commitment). Permanent and transparent information flows among the different stakeholders is crucial in this respect, as is communication on the implementation and results of agreements that are made. Commitments among different actors can be formalized by means of an inter-actor agreement or any other formal arrangement for promoting transparency and institutionalization of the process.

Policy making as well as joint action planning and implementation; efforts to establish policies before initiating action planning/implementation often result in policies that do not work due to lack of political will, lack of resources or severe distortions during translation into actions later on in the process. On the other hand, actions that are not translated into

Credit: IAGU

Coordinator of the local
team of the pilot project
in Bobo Dioulasso

adequate guiding/facilitating policies tend to stay rather localized with few or less sustained impacts on the livelihoods of larger segments of the population.

Shared budgeting and resource mobilization through incorporation of priority actions into the operational plans and budgets of the various participating organizations and institutions. For example, the inclusion of urban agriculture in the municipal budget was an essential component in the promotion of urban agricultural activities in Rosario (Argentina), where the City Council guaranteed resources for promotion, training, and marketing activities (Cabannes et al., 2003). Dependence on external (project) funding will severely limit, delay or even inhibit the possibility of implementing the developed action plans, leading in turn to conflict, distrust, de-motivation and finally a break-up of the entire process.

Early implementation of initial actions (such as pilot projects, new techniques) at local level: actions that produce tangible results help to reinforce the commitment and participation of those involved and inform public policy-making. It is useful to develop, from the outset of the process, pilot projects or actions that produce outputs or have an impact in the short term, in order to create a positive environment for more complex and long-term processes.

Multi-stakeholder policy formulation and action planning on urban agriculture

Based on a systematic review of the earlier experiences developed by UNEP and UN Habitat, RUAF partners have over the past years developed their own methodology for multi-stakeholder policy formulation and action planning for urban agriculture. Urban agriculture MPAPs have been undertaken in 20 cities in 17 countries. The process they followed has been built around the following phases (see also Figure 2.1):

1. preparatory activities;
2. situation analysis;
3. broadening commitment and participation;
4. establishment of a multi-stakeholder forum on urban agriculture;
5. development of a City Strategic Agenda on urban agriculture;

6. operationalization;
7. implementation and monitoring; adaptation/innovation.

Preparatory activities. Within the RUAF partner cities (mainly capital cities or other large cities) a municipality (or district) was identified that was interested to undertake a multi-stakeholder planning process on urban agriculture. The territory of that municipality would be selected as the focus area for the MPAP. A basic agreement was established between a restricted number of organizations committed to jointly implement the MPAP process in this municipality regarding the main principles of the MPAP, working procedures, communication strategies and staffing and financial aspects. A facilitating team (or MPAP core team) was established and the participating staff were trained in the MPAP process and tools and a work plan was made for the team.

Situation analysis. The facilitating team (sometimes with the support of contracted university staff or consultants) reviewed available secondary data, made an inventory of the main stakeholders in urban agriculture and analysed their main interests in and views on urban agriculture as well as their actual and planned activities in this field. Existing agricultural land use was mapped and available open spaces in the city were identified and classified. After identification of the main urban farming systems in the city, participatory rapid analysis techniques were applied to identify main problems and potentials of each of these farming systems. Also, the existing policies, norms and regulations regarding urban agriculture were critically reviewed. To some extent also the local and regional economic, political and funding environment was analysed. On the basis of the situation analysis the key issues to be addressed in policies and programmes on urban agriculture could be identified as well as potential courses of action.

Broadening commitment and participation. In this phase the findings of the situation analysis were shared with a wider group of stakeholders and actions were undertaken to involve them in the MPAP process and/or strengthen their commitment.

Establishment of a multi-stakeholder forum on urban agriculture. A multi-stakeholder forum on urban agriculture was established in each partner city. The forum provides a mechanism to bridge the communication gap between the direct stakeholders in urban agriculture and the institutional actors. In the platform the dialogue on the actual situation of urban agriculture and the policies and programmes needed were taking place and the platform coordinated the next steps in the process of policy development and action planning and implementation, with the support of the core team. The platform was also instrumental in mobilizing resources for the realization of the concerted plans, the integration of these plans within the programmes of the participating institutions and the coordination and monitoring of the implementation of the concerted city agenda on urban agriculture. The relation between this forum and the municipal authorities was different in each city.

Development of a City Strategic Agenda on urban agriculture. The multi-stakeholder forum partners, supported by the core team, developed a City Strategic Agenda on urban and peri-urban agriculture. The Agenda outlines policy objectives and key issues in urban agriculture on which the city wants to focus. It also describes proposed policies and intervention strategies needed for further development of safe and sustainable urban agriculture. The City Strategic Agenda forms the basis for the elaboration of new laws and regulations on urban agriculture and detailed action plans at a later stage. The level of detail and operationalization of the City Strategic Agenda varied greatly.

Operationalization. In this phase the forum members (in various sub groups) further developed the project profiles included in the City Strategic Agenda operational project plans, including the budget. The required changes in the actual policies, by-laws and norms and regulations on urban agriculture were prepared in detail. Also, the sustainability and consolidation of these projects and policies was sought through their inclusion into institutional programmes, and their integration into existing plans (e.g. city strategic development and zoning plans) and budgets. Such 'institutionalization' of urban agriculture often also included the establishment of specific urban agriculture programmes or unit within the municipality and other institutions and the development of new mechanisms for the allocation of resources (e.g. inclusion of urban agriculture in the 'participatory budgeting' scheme of the municipality or creation of specific tax regulations for urban agricultural producers). These activities were coordinated in periodic multi-stakeholder forum meetings (or with the core team).

Implementation and monitoring; adaptation/innovation. The various stakeholders, each according to their mandate and resources, took responsibility for implementation of the various planned activities and the monitoring of their results.

During periodic meetings of the multi-stakeholder forum or its core team, progress regarding the implementation of the City Strategic Agenda is reviewed and monitoring results are shared. Where needed, the strategies of the City Strategic Agenda are adapted or new elements are added. The degree of implementation of the City Strategic Agenda varies from city to city.

The duration of the MPAP process varies widely and is influenced by the degree of commitment of the forum members, the complexity of the issues and other factors. Sometimes tangible results become visible within a relatively short time period, whereas in other cases it may take some time before things start falling into place. In Accra, Ghana, for example (see the 'Gradual institutionalization of urban agriculture in Accra, Ghana' case study in Chapter 3), it took two years to create a sufficient basis for policy change and the development of the Strategic Agenda. It was only in the third year that bye-laws on urban agriculture were actually revised and changes were made in land use plans, integrating urban agriculture within the zoning plan as a legitimate urban land use.

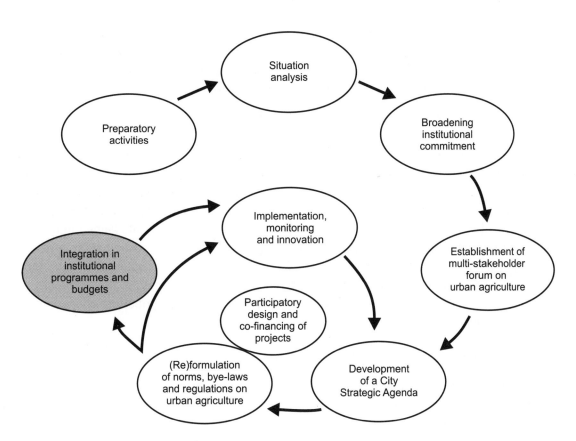

Figure 2.1
Steps in the MPAP

Each of the seven MPAP phases are described in further detail below and experiences are provided from the RUAF partner cities.

Phase 1: Preparatory activities

City and MPAP focus area selection

Selection of a partner city and MPAP focus area was carried out by preparing a short 'City Dossier' on potential partner cities. Basic selection criteria include: 1) The current presence of urban agriculture and the availability of vacant land for urban agriculture; 2) The potential for urban agriculture to contribute to food security, poverty alleviation, local economic development and improved environmental management and adaptation to climate change; 3) The presence of good local MPAP partners (with organizational expertise in urban agriculture, in participatory action-research, in policy design and project formulation etc.); 4) Initial local government interest and commitment to participate in and contribute to an MPAP on urban agriculture; and 5) A period of at least two years before the next governmental elections (so that at least a City Strategic Agenda can be formulated and approved and a multi-stakeholder forum put in place that will be strong enough to continue working and to lobby for new political support after possible changes in government take place following the elections).

Especially when working in a larger city or metropolis, which often consists of various municipalities, or when working in a larger municipality consisting of different municipal departments or administrative zones, it proved important to select one focus area (preferably independent, with its own decision-making structure and budget) for the MPAP. It proved difficult to implement an MPAP directly at the level of the metropolis (like in Hyderabad, India or Lima, Peru) and far easier to start working at a lower and smaller level of administration, and undertake upscaling activities at a later stage, backed by the experiences and results gained in the selected focus area (see, for example, the 'Enhancing urban producers' participation in policy making in Lima, Peru' case study in Chaper 3). In view of future upscaling it is important that, in the selection of the focus area, its degree of representativeness of the whole city is taken into account in terms of its population density, types of urban agriculture encountered, and socio-economic status of its population, etc.

Establishment of a local MPAP facilitating team

To start the MPAP in the selected city or focus area, a local MPAP core or facilitating team was formed. This team is responsible for coordinating, planning, organizing and implementing the MPAP process and facilitating and strengthening dialogue with the larger group of stakeholders who will become involved in further communication, analysis, action planning and policy design. Most local MPAP teams integrated community members/urban producers, NGO or University staff and (local) government representatives from the start. Representatives of urban producers provided insights into their experiences, views and needs, and facilitated the identification of the urban agriculture systems in the city. NGO and University staff brought in action-oriented research tools and methods and often facilitated the dialogue between producers and government representatives. Local government representatives helped with access to certain information (for example, statistics on food production, land use maps, laws and regulations related to urban agriculture) and provided support in describing and analysing the legal and institutional context in which urban agriculture is taking place or will take place in the near future (depending on strategic city development plans, for example). Choosing a small and manageable team composed of one or two representatives of each one of the main categories of actors has proven the most appropriate. The team members liaised with other staff in their organization.

In some cities, such as Cape Town, South Africa, a separate management committee has been set up – next to the MPAP team – made up of directors/coordinators of the institutional partners and governmental administration involved. This committee acted as an overall supervising body and ensured institutional commitment and institutional backing for the staff in the core team.

The MPAP teams agreed on meeting schedules to regularly discuss implemented activities, progress, problems encountered, lessons learned and recommendations. Minutes were made on decisions taken and actions planned in each MPAP team meeting and were shared among all team members and with their organizations. This facilitates monitoring of team performance and stimulates implementation of the agreed activities by team members.

Awareness raising and formalizing commitments

Awareness raising might be needed regarding the multi-stakeholder approach itself (process, costs and benefits) as well as urban agriculture (its presence, potential and constraints, and the need for policy intervention). Awareness raising will especially be directed to councillors and other political leaders, heads of municipal departments and senior staff of support organizations and opinion leaders (university, press). RUAF partners paid a lot of attention to such awareness raising on urban agriculture by providing adequate data and information on the role of urban agriculture in sustainable city development, its potential positive and negative impacts (fact sheets) and its contributions to existing policy goals (policy briefs), as well

Seeking commitment with members of the community garden in Lima

Credit: IPES

as by providing examples of policies and programmes of urban agriculture implemented by other cities. Policy awareness seminars to brief local councillors, heads of departments and other key stakeholders turned out to be a very effective instrument. Additionally, taking such persons to the field to meet with urban farmers, organizing city to city exchanges or study visits on urban agriculture and publishing on urban agriculture in the local media (newspaper article, video on TV, radio programme) are other effective strategies that have been used.

In some cities, the heads of the organizations participating in the local MPAP team and/or a main decision-maker (e.g. the Mayor) made a formal statement laying out their policy intentions regarding urban and peri-urban agriculture and their support to the formulation of an urban agriculture policy and action programme on urban agriculture through a participatory and multi-stakeholder process (see, for example, the declaration formulated by the programme committee in Serilingampally, Hyderabad, India (Box 2.1)).

Box 2.1 Declaration on promotion of urban and peri-urban agriculture in Serilingampally, Hyderabad, India

Our vision is to contribute to the reduction of urban poverty and food insecurity through sustainable urban- and peri-urban agriculture (UPA) and to stimulate participatory and gender-inclusive governance for the municipality of Serilingampally, Hyderabad.

We acknowledge that:

- UPA is a widely practised activity in and around towns and cities within the region on parcels of land with alternative competing uses;

- UPA has generally been practised informally without appropriate policy, legislative and institutional frameworks;

- UPA will continue to play a significant role in addressing food security, employment creation and income generation, health and nutrition and improving the economies of urban areas; some governments in the region have made significant progress in incorporating UPA in their urban development plans, and others are now beginning to rise to the challenge.

Recognizing the existence and increasing practice of UPA and also noting the many challenges that it faces, including:

- the absence of, inadequacy of and / or inconsistency between the policies, legislation and institutional arrangements for regulating UPA;

- the limited availability of and access to resources;

- the lack of sufficient research, documentation and information-sharing, both nationally and regionally;

- the need for environmental sustainability.

Accepting,

that the foregoing challenges require immediate and prudent reform of policies, legislative and institutional arrangements in order to effectively integrate UPA into planning activities in the municipality of Serilingampally, Hyderabad.

We therefore,

call for the promotion of a shared vision of UPA that takes into account the specific needs and conditions in the municipality of Serilingampally, Hyderabad, and accordingly commit ourselves to developing policies and appropriate instruments that will create a gender-sensitive enabling environment for integrating UPA into our urban planning processes.

Signed by:
Mr. S.A. Kadhar Saheb, Municipal Reform Officer (SWM) Hyderabad;
Mrs. Gayatri Ramachandran, DG EPTRI;
Ms. Anna Matthew, Principal Ruda Mistry College;
J. Venkatesh, HOD, Centre for Spatial Information and Technology JNTU

Source: International Water Management Institute, 2006

Training and work planning

Once the local MPAP teams had been put in place, team members as well as representatives of the different key stakeholders who were to take part in the MPAP process were trained in principles, process and methods of the MPAP process.

RUAF applied a two-tier approach to MPAP training. First, regional Training of Trainers (ToT) workshops were organized to train se-lected regional and local trainers in the various subjects. The ToT also served to harmonize un-derstanding of the various definitions, concepts and frameworks used, as well as to strengthen capacities of the trainers on adult-learning methods. The trainers who were trained were made responsible for organizing the MPAP training/planning workshops for the core teams in each of the RUAF partner cities. They also translated the various training modules and adapted these to the local conditions.

Credit: René van Veenhuizen

Training in principles, process and methods in Beijing

The MPAP training and planning workshops for the core teams were split into blocks. In most cases, the first block dealt with a general introduction to urban agriculture and to the MPAP process and methods, with emphasis on situation analysis and stakeholder motivation. During the following training and planning workshops the other phases of the MPAP process, such as the setting up of a multi-stakeholder forum, development of a City Strategic Agenda on urban agriculture, operationalization (project planning, revision of norms and regulations) and implementation/monitoring were dealt with in detail. In each workshop the training on a specific phase was directly linked to the planning of the work to be done by the core team to prepare and implement each phase of the MPAP process, identifying the activities to be implemented, roles and responsibilities, time-schedules, budgets, monitoring and commu-nication procedures.

Lessons learned regarding the preparatory phase

Need for clarity on expected results and decision-making procedures. From the very start of an MPAP, there should be clarity regarding the results expected from the process and what will be done with these results. What will the MPAP, in a specific time-period, realistically achieve in a given local situation? To what extent will it be possible to advance in the formulation and adoption of revised or new bye-laws or regulations, or in the setting up of a new urban agriculture programme or unit? How will the City Strategic Agenda be implemented and with what sources of funding?

It will also be important to clarify how and by whom formal decisions regarding adoption and implementation of proposed policies and action plans will be taken. In Bulawayo (Zimbabwe), for example, it was agreed that the City Strategic Agenda would be developed by the multi-stakeholder forum on urban agriculture. The Agenda was then presented to one of the Municipal Council Committees that reviewed the proposals and made certain adaptations and subsequently presented the plan to the full Municipal Council for its approval and formalization. The council approved the plan and made a budget available for its implementation (see the 'Joint action planning on urban agriculture in Bulawayo, Zimbabwe' case study in Chaper 3).

Importance of organization, building trust and mutual respect. The MPAP process should be well organized from the start with a clear time-schedule, division of labour and agreements on funding. The MPAP core team should ensure that sufficient financial and human resources are made available for the realization of the MPAP process (including local coordination, situation analysis, team meetings, forum meetings, monitoring). Preferably, some funds should also be made available for the implementation of some 'early implementation' activities during the planning process in order to enhance credibility and participation of the urban producers and show concrete results early on in the process.

It is important to work with a committed and capable core team with good skills in facilitation, conflict resolution and inter-institutional coordination.

Institutional commitments and contributions to the process should be clarified and – whenever possible – formalized. Minutes on discussions held, agreements made and results obtained should be shared among all stakeholders to continuously build trust, cooperation and commitment. Mutual understanding and respect should be seen as a basis for dialogue and negotiation.

Specific attention has to be paid to facilitating the participation of the urban producers. Urban farmers are often not at all or only loosely organized and rarely participate in representative bodies. Hence, special efforts are needed in order to involve urban farmers, especially poorer and female farmers, in the multi-stakeholder policy formulation and action planning process. Informal farmer groups and leaders have to be identified and existing farmer groups have to be brought into contact with each other, to present their proposals to the policy formulation process. Moreover, leadership training is required.

In Villa Maria del Triunfo, Lima, Peru, a key factor for the success of the MPAP was the establishment of the Villa Maria urban producers' network, as further described in the 'Enhancing urban producers' participation in policy making in Lima, Peru' case study in Chapter 3. That organization proved to be a crucial partner in lobbying for continued local government support for urban agriculture, after a new Mayor had been elected. Unless urban producers groups are organized and obtain some form of formal recognition, it will be very hard for them to make claims on public resources or participate in policy decisions which impact on them.

Phase 2: Situation analysis

Before being able to plan for the development of urban agriculture in a given city, it will be important to better understand the present state, potentials and constraints of urban agriculture in that city. In RUAF partner cities qualitative and quantitative information on urban agriculture was collected to better understand:

- the local socio-economic, institutional and legal context in which urban agriculture takes place;
- the variation in urban agriculture farming types, their functions and impacts (positive or negative); and,
- the locations where urban agriculture already takes place or can take place and its characteristics.

Different tools and techniques were applied to collect the necessary data and information, including:

- analysis of existing literature and research reports and review of available statistics;
- analysis of city maps and available Geographic Information System (GIS) materials, including visits to various parts of the city and its surroundings;
- identification and mapping (e.g. with GIS and local observations) of agricultural activities in the city and of available open spaces that could be used for urban agriculture, and classification of the suitability of those areas according to various criteria;
- interviews with key informants and meetings with representatives of the various stakeholders and farmers;
- Participatory Rapid Appraisal (PRA) exercises (e.g. focus group interviews with different types of urban producers) in selected areas.

In most cases, the initial situation analysis was followed by more focused in-depth studies of specific problems and potential solutions in later stages of the planning process.

The information collected served as a basis for the identification of the *main key issues* (needs, problems, potentials and opportunities) to be addressed for the development of safe and sustainable urban agriculture in the city, as well as the identification of *possible strategies and interventions* (information campaigns, training, research, projects, changes in norms and regulations, etc.) to respond to those problems and opportunities and to enhance the contributions of urban agriculture to urban poverty alleviation, urban food security, local economic development, and creation of a better living environment.

The joint situation analysis also contributes to *building up the mutual understanding, dialogue and collaboration between different stakeholders in urban and peri-urban agriculture* (various types of urban farmers, food vendors, community organizations, NGOs, municipal authorities, urban planners, health authorities, water and waste management authorities, etc.) and to enhancing their commitment to participate in concerted actions regarding urban agriculture.

The situation analysis included four main components, each of which will be further described below:

1. stakeholder inventory and analysis;
2. land use mapping;
3. participatory farming system analysis; and
4. critical policy review.

Stakeholder inventory and analysis

The identification of the stakeholders to be involved in the MPAP is crucial. To be effective, as far as possible all institutions, organizations and groups that have a stake in urban agriculture should be identified, including categories of the population involved in urban agriculture and organizations with a regulatory mandate or with relevant technical knowledge. The type of stakeholders involved in urban agriculture and their level of participation in the process will vary depending on local circumstances. It is important to identify (by means of literature and web searches, questionnaires and interviews) organizations that can contribute to solving problems encountered by urban farmers and to realizing the development potentials in urban agriculture (see Box 2.2).

In RUAF, the stakeholder inventory is mainly focused on the *indirect* stakeholders in urban agriculture: institutions, organizations and networks that have expertise and/or resources that can be mobilized for the development of urban agriculture in the city. The analysis of the *direct* stakeholders (the urban producers) was undertaken in the context of the participatory appraisal of selected urban and peri-urban farming types.

Key questions to identify and analyse the indirect stakeholders in urban agriculture included:

*   Which institutions/organizations do play and can/should play a role in the development of urban and peri-urban agriculture? What is their mandate? Where do they work and with whom?
*   What are their views on urban and peri-urban agriculture?
*   What type of services do they provide (or could they provide) to urban producers?
*   What contributions (human and/or financial) can they provide to the MPAP and the future implementation of the City Strategic Agenda?

Box 2.2 Stakeholders in urban agriculture

Local, provincial and national governments play a key role in urban agriculture and are engaged in many areas of service provision and regulation, such as urban planning, land use zoning, water treatment, waste collection and management of green spaces, which have direct interactions with urban agriculture. Therefore, it is essential to involve government representatives in the discussions throughout the MPAP process, in order to acknowledge their opinion and suggestions, overcome possible resistance and gain support for policy review and formulation. An MPAP process that does not involve those who influence decision-making (Mayor, council members, heads of departments, policy advisers) may achieve little in the long term.

Special attention has to be paid here to the different levels of responsibility and decision-making.

The main focus should be on the municipal level. However, the involvement of key actors from other levels may be crucial. For example, the Government of Senegal regulates and controls land use in the cities and its lack of participation in the local MPAP process in Pikine, Dakar, proved to be an obstacle. On the other hand, participation of representatives of the Provincial Government has facilitated the local MPAP process in Gampaha, Sri Lanka and, in addition, allowed for quick upscaling of initial project activities from the municipal to the provincial and even national level.

Interaction between different levels of government is especially important where urban agriculture 'crosses political boundaries'. Often the peri-urban interface is a highly contested political arena with a wide range of interests vying for influence and resources. At the same time this zone has confusing administrative competences and responsibilities which can easily be exploited. For example, in the case of Lima, there is overlap and ambiguity in the responsibilities of Lima Metropolitan Municipality and of the local district municipalities with regard to land use planning. In this situation it was important that the poverty alleviation and environmental benefits of urban agriculture were constantly communicated to local and metropolitan decision-makers alike (Gonzales et al., 2007).

On the other hand, overdependence on government support should also be avoided. In Gampaha the MPAP has so far been driven mainly by local and provincial government actors, and there the challenge remains to strengthen civil society participation in the MPAP process and encourage stronger participation of the urban producers in the multi-stakeholder forum.

NGOs, community-based organizations and universities

Urban producers may lack expertise regarding specific aspects of urban agriculture (i.e. specific production or processing techniques). Universities and research centres can support the development of appropriate technologies for urban food production and processing and provide methodological and technical support in the situation analysis, planning, and monitoring activities. NGOs and community-based organizations can play a crucial role in organizing the urban producers, linking them with governmental authorities or research institutes, and supporting them during the MPAP process. Such organizations often also play an important role in the design and implementation of specific action projects with the producers. For example, in

Universities and research centres can support the development of appropriate technologies, Beijing

Credit: IGSNRR

Bulawayo, Zimbabwe, various NGOs are active members of the forum and are implementing urban agriculture projects, mainly using their own resources (see the 'Joint action planning on urban agriculture in Bulawayo, Zimbabwe' case study in Chapter 33).

Private sector and support organizations
The private sector and support organizations can play a role in facilitating access to inputs and services (e.g. marketing). In Villa Maria (Lima, Peru), for example, an agreement was signed with the National Electricity Company, whereby the company took responsibility to lease institutional land (lying under power lines) to vegetable farmers free of charge. Also, the participation of financing institutions (including micro-finance institutions and credit-cooperatives) should be considered.

Commercial and subsistence farmers and gardeners and their organizations
It should be borne in mind that urban producers do not form a homogeneous group. Livestock farmers have different interests from horticulture or aquaculture farmers. Commercial farmers differ in their interests from subsistence or hobby farmers. Promotion of different urban agriculture production systems therefore requires different policies and interventions (see the ' participatory farming system analysis' sub-section below). Taking into account the expertise, local knowledge and views of different producers and producer groups is important in this regard. As direct stakeholders, urban farmers should also play a key role in project management and coordination, and in the evaluation and control of the activities carried out.

The stakeholder analysis helps to decide which organizations should be involved in the MPAP and to develop a strategy to motivate these organizations to participate in the planning process. It also helps to identify their potential roles in and contributions to the planning process and the future implementation of the City Strategic Agenda on Urban Agriculture.

Land use mapping

Land use mapping in RUAF partner cities was undertaken with a view to answering the following questions:

- What types of urban agriculture are currently undertaken in and around the city (or the MPAP focus area)?
- Where are these various types of urban agriculture practised? Under which tenure systems?
- Are there any vacant open spaces where urban agriculture could possibly take place? What is their accessibility and suitability for urban agriculture?
- What changes in land use are expected or being planned that may affect agriculture in and around the city?

By analysing existing maps and GIS materials the location of the land that is currently in agricultural use (both formal and informal land use) was identified. Then an identification was made of the location and characteristics of available open spaces in and around the city that might be used for urban agriculture (permanent or temporary).

Land is of course a basic requirement for urban food production. Improved access to land for production and more secure land tenure is therefore a primary requirement for urban producers. The first reaction of many local government officials is that there is no land for urban agriculture available in the city due to high competition from other uses. But analysis of the vacant open spaces in a city normally clearly shows that there is far more land available then is recognized by the city officials. Land that can be used for urban agriculture is not limited to communal or private farms and gardens. For example, riverbanks and roadsides, parks, land under high-voltage electrical towers, flood plains and other areas that are not fit for construction, public and semi-public land around schools and hospitals, empty lots due to speculation and abandoned industrial sites may all be used for urban agriculture (eventually under certain restrictions).

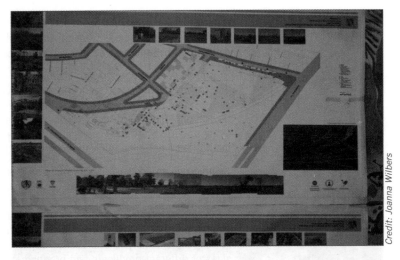

Credit: Joanna Wilbers

Identification, mapping and analysis of both productive and vacant land (Rosario, Argentina)

Identification, mapping and analysis of both productive as well as vacant land areas will provide important data such as the area of land already under cultivation, the presence of certain types of urban agriculture, the area of vacant land that potentially can be used for urban agriculture, and its characteristics. The mapping will visualize the presence of urban agriculture, which is important for awareness raising, and will facilitate discussion on the problems and potentials of urban agriculture in various locations. It also provides a basis for enhancing access to land for the urban poor that want to engage in food production and for the integration of urban agriculture into municipal physical planning policies.

Box 2.3 Mapping urban agriculture land use in Bogota, Colombia

In Bogota, Colombia, the mapping included identification of:

1) non-built up areas where different types of urban agriculture already take place (crop production, tree production, livestock, aquaculture);

2) open or vacant land areas and water bodies that can potentially be used for urban agriculture.

For each of the identified areas of land, information was collected on its property and tenure status, such as: private land; institutional land (belonging to schools, hospitals etc); and public land.

Urban agriculture in Bogota was found to take place in and around the house (in backyards and patios), on institutional land (for example, school-gardens), on open areas of land in the city and on larger areas of land surrounding the city.

But it was also found that urban agriculture is also very much present on Bogota's rooftops in the more densely populated low-income areas. It was therefore decided to also map available rooftop areas and analyse their potential for food production. This formed the basis for a pilot project regarding the design and running of rooftop gardens in a later stage of the MPAP process.

Through field visits the information obtained from topographical and GIS maps was checked on the ground through field visits and 'community mapping': the drawing of maps indicating agricultural land use in a certain area by some residents of that area.

Participatory farming systems analysis

In order to better understand the problems encountered by different types of urban producers and their development potentials and to more strongly involve the direct stakeholders in the MPAP process, a participatory rapid appraisal was implemented in selected areas where urban agriculture is practised.

Credit: René van Veenhuizen

Firstly, on the basis of the information collected from secondary sources and the mapping exercise, the main types of urban agriculture present in this city, as well as their main locations, were identified.

Although the RUAF partners often started from the global classification of farming types, in each city or focus area this is further specified according to the local insights. When making the classification it is important to bear in mind that the identified urban farming types should be meaningful for planning purposes and preferably should be rather homogeneous internally but differ strongly from other types in their main production characteristics, the

Transect walk as part of the situation analysis in Accra

types of actors involved and their motivations, main problems and development potentials (see Box 2.4).

Secondly, for each main type of urban agriculture a representative area was selected in which a participatory situation analysis was undertaken with the urban producers, applying focus group interviews, transect walks and other participatory techniques. Special attention was given to gender differences in interests and needs of men and women (including the gender division of labour and differences in position of men and women in the given society). For further information on the use of gender sensitive PRA techniques and gender mainstreaming in urban agriculture, see the Resources section following Chapter 4.

The PRA in the selected areas of the main urban farming types provided valuable insight in the characteristics of the urban producers, the problems and potentials of the main urban farming systems, and the viewpoints of the urban producers on required policy measures and support strategies. The participatory analysis also gave insights into the social, economic, health/nutrition and ecological benefits and risks of each type of urban and peri-urban

> ### Box 2.4 Global classification of urban farming types
>
> 1. **Micro-farming in and around the house:** growing of food and herbs or keeping small animals (poultry, rabbits, grass-cutter) in front- and back-yard, patio, on rooftops, in cellar or barn, especially in marginal urban settlements, mainly for subsistence and some barter.
>
> 2. **Community gardening:** growing of food, fruits and herbs for subsistence and generation of some income through sale of surpluses, sometimes also provision of food for the needy in the community (soup kitchens).
>
> 3. **Institutional gardens (at schools, hospitals, prisons):** growing of nutritious food for the clients of these institutions (vegetables, poultry or pigs); school gardens have an educational function; hospital and prison gardens in addition have a function in recycling of food wastes and therapy.
>
> 4. **Small-scale (semi-) commercial horticulturalists:** mainly fresh vegetables production (but also other food crops, medicinal herbs, berries/fruits, plant seedlings) mainly for the market plus family self-consumption.
>
> 5. **Small-scale (semi-) commercial livestock keeping and fish-farming:** Zero grazing dairy units, poultry and pig raising units; fish farming in cages in open water bodies or in tanks/ponds.
>
> 6. **Small-scale specialist producers:** Small-scale production of mushrooms, pot plants, flowers (also for oil extraction), tree seedlings, earthworms, piglets and chicks and compost.
>
> 7. **Larger scale agro-enterprises:** intensive larger scale livestock keeping, large nurseries or other intensive form of agriculture (e.g. irrigated and climate protected horticulture), often urban investors hire a manager and labour to work the farm.

agriculture in the city. It also helped to identify the main constraints and potentials for the development of each farming type.

Leading questions for the participatory analysis of each type of urban farming are the following:

- What is the pattern of production of this type of urban agriculture: crops grown, animals raised, inputs used (including recycling of organic wastes and wastewater); level of technologies applied and capital invested; what is the output produced and its use (autoconsumption, barter, market)?
- Who is involved in this type of urban agriculture: number of households and persons involved (male/female); their characteristics and socio-economic profile (level of income, origin, other jobs); their objectives for urban farming; land ownership and tenure situation; gender aspects; local leadership and factions; social networks of farming groups and coping mechanisms; and access to inputs, credit, extension services and business support services?
- What is the contribution of this type of urban agriculture to:
  – Income generation?

Box 2.5 Participatory farming system analysis in Sana'a, Yemen

Participatory farming system analysis in Sana'a, Yemen, helped to identify the presence of various types of urban agriculture in the city, including vegetable production (leeks, coriander, radishes, onions and tomatoes), fruits (grapes, berries, nuts, peaches and apricots); forage production (alfalfa, maize, and barley); and livestock-keeping (dairy, sheep and goats, camels and donkeys, poultry and bees).

These agricultural activities constitute an essential part of the urban livelihoods and supply food for consumption and income. Access to reliable sources of water, technical training and secure access to and tenure of land were identified by the urban producers as key issues for the further development of urban agriculture. As a result, strategies for increasing water availability (amongst others by recycling of wastewater) and more efficient use of irrigation water and more agriculture extension services for urban producers were developed and steps were taken to reformulate some laws and land use regulations in order to preserve the agricultural areas and to enhance access to municipal land, specifically for grazing (see also 'The integration of food production in Sana'a urban planning, Yemen' case study in Chapter 3).

- Nutrition and food security (especially of low income groups and HIV-Aids affected families)?
- Recycling of urban organic wastes and wastewater and improvement of the urban climate (greening, capturing dust/CO_2, shade)?
- Community development and social inclusion (urban agriculture as a catalyser in run-down communities, creating access to productive inputs and new development chances to disadvantaged groups such as single women with children, youth without jobs, people with a handicap, etc.)?
- What are the health and environmental risks associated with this type of urban agriculture (e.g. evidence of incidence of diseases or environmental pollution due to urban agriculture)?

Critical policy review

For the multi-stakeholder planning process it is also important to develop a good understanding of the current legal and planning framework in which urban agriculture takes places:

- What are the city's current main policy goals and priorities? How could urban agriculture contribute to them?
- Which are the actual policies, norms and regulations and urban development and zoning plans that effect urban agriculture? How successful and effective are these policies and instruments to date (do they have the intended effects; and if not: why not?)

- Are there any inconsistencies between the various sectors regarding their views on and treatment of urban agriculture (e.g. between economic and social development policies, public health or environmental management policies) or between policies at different levels (e.g. local versus national)?
- Do outdated or unnecessary restrictive norms and regulations regarding urban agriculture exist (in municipal bye-laws, ordinances, zoning regulations, etc.) that should be removed or adapted?
- Which needs and possibilities to improve the effectiveness of existing policies and plans on urban agriculture and/or their relevance for certain categories of the population (e.g. women, the poor) do you encounter?
- What opportunities exist to integrate urban agriculture better into the various sector policies and/or to harmonise better their treatment of urban agriculture?
- What are current decision-making structures of relevance for urban agriculture in the city? What are current forms and level of public participation in these structures? What is the most effective way to relate the multi-stakeholder forum on urban agriculture to these structures?

To be able to answer these questions, a critical policy review (through desk studies and interviews with key informants) of existing policies, plans, norms and regulations – of relevance to urban agriculture – was implemented. This analysis includes policies and plans that deal specifically with urban agriculture (a bye-law regulating livestock keeping in the city) as well as policies and plans that have a strong influence on urban agriculture (e.g. city and land use plans and zoning norms, health regulations). Although the focus of the policy review is mainly on the municipal level, influential national policies and regulations are also taken into account.

Box 2.6 Critical policy review in Accra, Ghana

A situation analysis on urban agriculture in the Accra metropolis was conducted from June to September 2005 also including a critical policy review. At that time no specific policies for urban agriculture existed in Accra, but several bye-laws and regulations of the Accra Metropolitan Area were found to be too restrictive regarding livestock production (due to health and environmental concerns). As part of the Strategic City Agenda, a reformulation of the existing livestock bye-laws and regulations were undertaken involving livestock and health specialists who removed ungrounded limitations and assisted in the development of new policies that promote the adoption of safe space, confined, and non-traditional livestock production systems (grass-cutters, rabbits, mushrooms and snails) and their integration within land use planning.

Integration of results and reporting

An example of a Policy Narrative document

Finally, all information collected in the situation analysis was analysed to identify the *local factors that facilitate or constrain the development of safe and sustainable urban agriculture* in the city. These findings were then summarized and presented in the form of a short and concise 'policy narrative': a document that presents essential information on urban agriculture in the city, its presence, types, benefits and risks, development potentials and constraints, and possible course of action. The document will be used to share the results of the situation analysis with all stakeholders identified and to create a good starting point for the reflection, discussions, joint visioning and strategic planning in the multi-stakeholder forum (see further Phase 3 below).

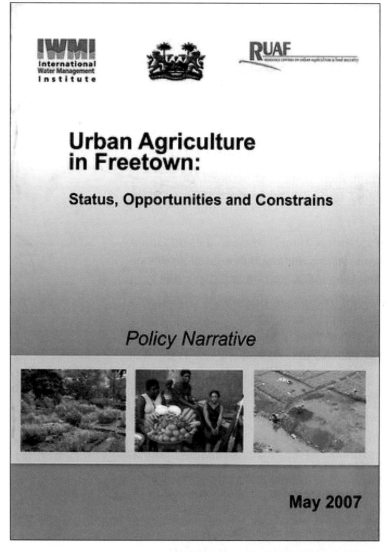

The document contains the following information:

- presentation of key data regarding the presence and main characteristics of different types of urban agriculture. For each type of urban agriculture a brief analysis is presented of:
  - the main benefits and risks associated with this type of urban agriculture in the actual situation;
  - the main problems encountered by this type of urban producers (gender differentiated); and
  - the main potentials for the safe and sustainable development of this type of urban agriculture.
- the identification of current and potential relevance of urban agriculture for the various policy domains (health/nutrition, local economic development and poverty alleviation, urban environmental management, etc.);
- the identification of key issues for the development of safe and sustainable urban agriculture;
- presentation of possible strategies to reduce certain risks associated with urban agriculture, to overcome existing problems and to realize identified potentials;

- presentation of the results of the stakeholder analysis: institutional actors, their views on urban agriculture and their role in and possible contributions to the development of safe and sustainable urban agriculture and their activities;
- the identification of some specific 'early implementation' actions that might be undertaken already while developing the City Strategic Agenda on urban agriculture.

Lessons learned regarding implementation of the situation analysis

Develop the situation analysis in sub-teams instead of contracting it out to one organization. As it will be unlikely that one local partner organization has the required capacity and means to implement all components of the situation analysis, conformation of sub-teams of the local MPAP core team (each one with their own coordinator and each implementing one component of the situation analysis) has proven to be more successful. This also helps creating further interest in and commitment to the process. The local coordinator (or coordinating organization) will remain responsible for supervising the overall implementation of the situation analysis. Contracted consultants may play a role in data gathering but should act always in direct coordination with members of the core team.

Make optimum use of the limited financial means available. Generally, only limited (financial) means are available to conduct a situation analysis. Hence it is very important:

- to always keep in mind the main focus of the situation analysis: to collect information needed for preparing the City Strategic Agenda on urban agriculture. Avoid collecting information just because someone finds it 'interesting'; and aim for information that enhances understanding of the main issues, trends and factors in urban agriculture;
- to apply a step wise approach: first the review of existing information and the land mapping. This will enable an identification of the main types of urban agriculture and its locations. This makes it possible to select smaller areas where a more detailed analysis of a certain type of urban agriculture can be implemented;
- to pay attention to the level of detail. Make maximum use of existing available information. If collecting additional data, use PRA (mainly qualitative) methods to deepen insight related to the main problems and potentials of the various types of urban agriculture in the city and keep the collection of quantitative data that are statistically representative for the whole city to a minimum (e.g. only for the number of farmers per type of urban agriculture and size of land holdings);
- to triangulate data: seeking verification of certain data by combining different sources of information (such as literature reviews, interviews with key stakeholders, use of maps and participatory farming system analysis);
- to motivate members of the MPAP core team to implement their part of the situation analysis as much as possible using their own resources, reserving available project funds for those costs that cannot easily be covered by the partner organizations.

Do not strive for a one-dimensional picture. Different viewpoints may exist of the same reality. It is therefore always important to make note of who provided specific information (person/organization), with what objectives and in what perspective, especially when it comes to the interpretation of certain 'facts' and the conclusions and recommendations that are derived from the information. For example, a health department will look differently at the reuse of urban wastes and wastewater in agriculture than an environmental officer or the officer in charge of poverty alleviation, let alone the poor urban farmers involved in these practices. It is important not to highlight only one opinion or viewpoint but to identify and show such different views on the existing reality, identified problems or potentials and desired developments.

Phase 3: Broadening commitment and participation

Once findings of the situation analysis have been synthesized in the form of a policy narrative, the results are shared more widely and activities are undertaken to involve new stakeholders, strengthen the commitment of existing partners and to establish a multi-stakeholder platform that will guide and coordinate policy design and action planning.

Before really starting the planning process, it is necessary to inform and motivate the stakeholders that have been identified during the situation analysis and to enhance their willingness to participate in the development of the City Strategic Agenda on urban agriculture.

RUAF partners have applied the following strategies for informing and motivating stakeholder participation:

Sharing of the '*policy narrative*' (the synthesis document on the situation analysis) with all identified stakeholders to inform them of the present situation (presence, types, problems and potentials) of urban agriculture in the city and to provide a basis for the coming discussions in the stakeholder forum.

Organizing *individual visits to important stakeholders* in order to discuss in-depth the most important problems/issues identified in the situation analysis and to explore alternative solutions and intervention strategies. In these visits their possible role in – and available human and financial resources for – development of urban agriculture would also be discussed as well as the desired organizational set-up for the multi-stakeholder platform on urban agriculture.

Organization of *policy awareness seminars* to raise awareness among policy makers and high ranking officials of the benefits and risks of urban agriculture and the potential contribution of urban agriculture to the city's policy goals and priorities. These seminars also help to raise motivation and commitment of the institutions to collaborate together in policy formulation and action planning on urban agriculture. Conclusions and agreements reached during the discussions can be summarized in an official declaration, agreement or memorandum of understanding. Such documents will provide a firm basis for follow-up (and may be used to help partners to remember their commitments where necessary).

Organization of *study visits* to more advanced cities. Such study visits can be very instrumental in raising the motivation of senior officers and officials to participate in the MPAP, enhance their understanding of the multi-stakeholder approach, and to broaden their knowledge on (certain types of) urban agriculture, and their potential for the realization of the City's development objectives (e.g. policy alleviation, social inclusion, gender equity, local economic development, and waste recycling). The basic idea behind these study visits is that a policy maker or senior officer is more easily convinced by another policy maker or fellow senior officer than by other actors or sources of information. These visits can even result in long-standing relationships between cities and mutual co-operation programmes. Study visits may also involve other types of stakeholders (producers, researchers, entrepreneurs).

Taking high officials to field sites to expose them to urban producers, their interests and potentials and to make them reflect about the ways in which their institution might contribute to the development of safe and sustainable urban agriculture. Such a visit, if properly prepared, can be a very effective way of communicating a need and raising motivation to participate in the MPAP. It may show a policy maker that certain things are actually present (of which he or she may not have been aware), it will provide the agricultural producers (forming part of the policy makers' constituency!) the opportunity to voice their concerns and proposals and will provide the policy maker with insight

Credit: René van Veenhuizen

A field visit to urban producers provides opportunities to reflect on safe and sustainable urban agriculture

into what he or she may actually do to support these people. Such field visits are also a good opportunity to 'boost' public opinion on the policy makers' involvement. However, the visit should be well prepared, with sufficient anticipation. The expectations of the persons in the locations to be visited should be clarified and they should be instructed on how to avoid potential conflicts with policy makers.

Developing policy briefings and other written and visual communication materials: briefing papers and other communication materials can be used as a general strategy to target a wider audience then the ones that can be reached through personal dialogue. These materials are less likely to be misquoted than oral presentations, and provide a readily available record that can be used whenever a staff member or policy maker needs to address the issue. But these materials offer fewer opportunities for interaction and dialogue, although they can also be used as the basis for a personal meeting or as background reading material. Such communication materials are generally short, illustrative, user-friendly and concise and aim to raise awareness and mobilize political support. The policy briefs present the key issues and

Credit: IPES

Organization of special events, like the 'Lima week of urban agriculture', broadens commitment

policy relevance of urban agriculture in a concise way and provide suggestions on how local governments may support the development of safe and sustainable urban agriculture. RUAF partners have also produced various short videos showing different types of urban agriculture and examples of successful governmental and civil society programmes and projects supporting the development of urban agriculture.

Involvement of press/media: RUAF partners have continuously informed the media (press, radio and television) and influential opinion leaders through personal contacts, sharing of videos, briefing papers and reports and the publication of a newsletter, which has led to good coverage of the subject in the media and a rapidly growing public interest in urban agriculture. This has also counterbalanced some historic misconceptions about urban agriculture. For example, in Zimbabwe it was assumed for a long time by city officials that urban maize-growing increased malaria risks. Dissemination of international research data proving that this is not the case helped to overcome this bottleneck.

Lessons learned regarding stakeholder motivation and participation

In order to actively participate in an MPAP process an organization needs:

- to be *aware* of urban and peri-urban agriculture, its potentials and problems;
- to be *willing* to participate in its development (which mainly depends on the contribution that urban agriculture can make to the main interests of the actor involved);
- to be *able* to contribute (which mainly depends on the organization's mandate and available human and financial resources).

All three conditions have to be fulfilled to a certain degree.

In this perspective, the main obstacles for active involvement at an organizational and personal level often relate to:

Sharing and making available information, at the Information Centre in Freetown

- a *lack of awareness/information*: information is not available/not accessible, or only at one level in the organization (technical level or decision-making level); or the available information is not relevant to the user, is not what he/she needs to get interested and take a decision; or the available information is not presented in a way that is attractive to the user (in terms of communication channels used, the way the information is packaged, the moment the information is presented, by whom and to whom this is done);

- a *lack of interest*: the person/organization is not well informed on the potentials of urban agriculture for pursuing his/her interests; they have other priorities;

- a *lack of mandate or lack of resources*: the person/organization does not have the mandate to work with poor urban farmers; they lack required expertise/skills, equipment and/or economic means; or the person/organization does not have the right relations/power.

An organization will thus be more committed to actively contribute to an MPAP if the following conditions are fulfilled:

A strong link with the institutional policy / interests
The institution will be more motivated to participate:

- when decision-makers are well informed on urban agriculture and its relevance for their main institutional goals and priorities;
- when urban agriculture fits relatively well within their mandate and actual programmes and budget headings;
- when the organization might be blamed later when problems arise regarding urban agriculture due to a lack of attention by this organization (the cost of doing nothing);
- when the organization leans towards innovation and learning and has a less dominant 'disciplinary' and 'sectoral' orientation;
- when the organization is less hierarchical, has more democratic attitudes and has gained (positive) experiences with participatory or multi-stakeholder processes;
- when funding flows for urban agriculture are increasing and accessible for the organization;

- when the core partners in the MPAP process are seen as 'trustworthy' and with sufficient 'leverage power';
- when no shorter / cheaper routes to arrive at the same results are available;
- when there is less corruption / more transparency in the organization and thus less resistance to sharing of information and outsiders knowing about planned activities and their participation in the monitoring of results.

A strong link with individual interests of staff in those organizations
Staff will be more motivated to participate:

- when there are more staff in the organization that have a positive opinion on and experience with urban agriculture;
- when some high ranking officer acts as internal advocate for urban agriculture; the higher rank the better;
- when a person's involvement in the MPAP matches with his/her personal interests;
- when the participation in the MPAP process is rewarding (intrinsic values, development of relevant knowledge/skills, better chances for access to scholarship, certificate, economic incentives, etc.);
- when their participation in the MPAP is formalized and included in the routine work planning and does not come as an extra activity on top of the 'normal' duties.

Outside pressures call for attention to urban agriculture:

- from persons that can influence the institution directly (their agenda, resource allocation, etc.) like local and national policy makers, donor organizations, etc.;
- from clients;
- from the media.

Phase 4: Establishment of a multi-stakeholder forum and development of a city strategic agenda

Establishment of a multi-stakeholder forum (MSF)

The organizations that had shown interest and commitment were invited to be part of a multi-stakeholder forum on urban agriculture. Such a forum should include all key stakeholder groups (municipal departments, farmer groups, NGOs and CBOs, universities and research institutes, relevant governmental and private sector organizations and, if possible and desired, international organizations) required to design and to implement, in a participatory manner, adequate solutions to the problems or potentials identified in the situation analysis (and summarized in the policy narrative).

The objectives and tasks of such a forum include:

- bridging the communication gap between the various stakeholders involved in urban and peri-urban agriculture and functioning as a platform for information exchange and dialogue;
- building effective and sustainable partnerships for coordination, planning, implementation and monitoring of a concerted City Strategic Agenda on urban agriculture;
- stimulating the creation of a facilitating policy and institutional environment for urban agriculture and the integration of urban agriculture in institutional policies, programmes and budgets.

In the RUAF partner cities the activities of the MSF included the development of a City Strategic Agenda on urban agriculture (definition of objectives, selection of key issues and strategies, definition of coordination and monitoring mechanisms and operational framework), the operationalization of the Agenda into concrete projects and revised or new bye-laws, norms and regulations on urban agriculture, and the 'institutionalization' of urban agriculture.

The multi-stakeholder forum is established by defining its role and mandate and the signing of an inter-actor agreement indicating the common goals and strategies that are to be pursued jointly and the commitments of the organizations participating in the forum (see, for example, Box 2.7).

The MSF is coordinated by a coordinating committee (or similar name) consisting of the members of the former MPAP core team plus some other key stakeholders in the MSF. The MSF and committee are chaired by a forum member known for his/her proven capacities in coordination, conflict resolution and negotiation and participatory action planning.

Experience indicates that the forum has to be independent from the political structure though preferably formally recognized and supported by the municipality (and other stakeholders) as the main advisory platform for dialogue, planning and coordination regarding urban agriculture in the city. The forum preferably should be linked to the most relevant Council committee in order to have a channel to the Council to formalize proposals put forward by the MSF.

Important factors for the successful functioning of a multi-stakeholder forum include:

- Clear and formalized initial commitments of the participating institutions and organizations. Continuous trust and commitment building.
- Clarity about the importance of local ownership and member contributions to the functioning of the multi-stakeholder forum and the implementation of activities is needed. A central justification for building such multi-stakeholder partnerships has – after all – to do with making the best use of available local financial and human resources. In addition, external resources may be mobilized by involving donor agencies in the MSF and presenting project proposals to national and international sources of funding, although this should never become the driving factor.

Box 2.7 Collaboration agreement signed by members of the MSF in Freetown, Sierra Leone

1. Concept
The multi-stakeholder forum on urban and peri-urban agriculture in Freetown will serve as a platform where problems, potentials and strategies for the development of intra- and peri-urban agriculture in Freetown are discussed. It integrates stakeholders from civil society, research organizations, private enterprises, farmer groups, local and national governments and international organizations. The forum counts with recognition from the local/national government and the commitment of all its member organizations to actively participate in the forum.

2. Principles
The forum is:
- Characterized by the participation of different stakeholders (multi-stakeholder), from both civil society as well as local/national government;
- Open to all stakeholders that commit to its principles, roles and responsibilities of its members;
- A space where democratic decisions are taken in a consensual approach.

3. Role of the forum
The forum has as its role the identification, planning and formulation, prioritization, implementation, articulation and monitoring/evaluation of strategies and policies that promote the development of urban and peri-urban agriculture in Freetown/Western Area. It will effectively coordinate and implement programmes and projects on urban agriculture, building on activities and efforts implemented by its member organizations and on their human and financial resources, without replacing or competing with these activities.

4. Membership and structure
Membership of the forum is open to all organizations, institutions, (government) departments and programmes working on intra- and peri-urban agriculture or related activities (such as waste management, community development, employment creation). Membership is institutional, each institution officially assigning one or two representatives to participate in the Forum (meetings). Institutional representatives have the obligation to communicate the results of the Forum meetings and activities to their organizations, to follow up on institutional commitments and to bring in institutional viewpoints and contributions to the Forum meetings.

The Forum is made up of an MSF Coordinating team and MSF Platform. The MSF Coordinating team is made up of a smaller group of active MSF-members taking the lead in formalizing the City Strategic Agenda on urban agriculture and coordinating its implementation. The MSF Platform involves all members of the forum. Specific *Working Groups* can be formed for implementing specific activities.

5. Participants
The following organizations participate in the MSF:
[A list of member organizations is included]

6. Roles and responsibilities
Each member organization commits:
- to avail our representative on the multi-stakeholder platform for all planning and implementation of activities as agreed upon by the forum;
- to endorse the legitimacy of the multi-stakeholder platform and mandate our representative to make contributions to decision-making within the platform;

- to collaborate and strengthen dialogue among the various member organizations of the forum, and to discuss and prioritize broad strategies to address key issues for the development of urban agriculture;
- to jointly develop Actions Plans (e.g. projects) and formulate policies to address the key issues and provide human, financial and logistical support for the implementation thereof;
- to formally adopt the City Strategic Agenda on urban agriculture as developed by the forum and to incorporate relevant decisions taken by the multi-stakeholder forum and strategies proposed in their institutional and development programmes; and
- to coordinate all the efforts needed to implement – in a participatory and multi-stakeholder way – the aforementioned objectives and to ensure the foreseen results.

7. Endorsement

We, the following listed institutions with representatives on the multi-stakeholder platform agree to sign this document as an indication of our cooperation and commitment to the cause of the multi-stakeholder vision and City Strategic Agenda for urban agriculture in Freetown and the terms defined in this document:

Signatories:

The Director
(name organization)
Date:

The Director
(name organization)
Date:

The Director
(name organization)
Date:

- A stimulating coordinating committee that keeps all members well informed, helps to structure and organize the tasks of the MSF and monitors the realization of agreed activities and other commitments. Good and effective communication is central to achieve openness and transparency.
- Clear rules on how and when decision-making will take place, and how progress and results will be monitored.
- MSF meetings that are well prepared and that are led by a skilled facilitator capable of creating an open atmosphere, building mutual respect and conflict management and constructive use of diverging views. Ground rules for effective facilitation include involving partners in agenda setting, using participatory methods of decision-making and encouraging an atmosphere of sharing and learning. The MSF meetings require a clear agenda and time-schedule and a good division of labour.

MSF meeting in Villa Maria del Triunfo, Lima

Credit: IPES

Box 2.8 Factors for success: the multi-stakeholder forum in Belo Horizonte, Brazil

In Belo Horizonte a city forum on urban agriculture was formed in 2006. The forum is made up of various organizations and institutions (including universities, NGOs, CBOs and urban producer groups, national governmental institutions, international organizations and private enterprises).

Several factors can be identified relating to the successful functioning of this forum.

Regular, well-organized meetings facilitated good information exchange among members. The date and time of the meetings are set by the forum members and meetings are well-planned and moderated.

The agenda of the MSF meetings always included the presentation of audiovisual material on urban agriculture experiences in other Latin America cities. The forum also realized exchange visits. The presentations and exchange visits serve as important incentives for participation and the creation of personal commitment, which is strengthened by taking sufficient time to allow for joint learning and exchange among partners.

Several new and very motivated stakeholders entered the forum, as a result of previous awareness raising and sensitization activities developed by the local MPAP facilitating team and included urban agriculture as part of their own activities. For example, a programme working on urban planning and design developed an interest to integrate urban agriculture into the (re)design of low-income neighbourhoods. Participation of such new stakeholders provides new dynamism to the work of the forum.

The participating institutions included the time and resources needed for the elaboration and operationalization of the City Strategic Agenda into their institutional plans and set aside institutional funding for this purpose based on clear agreements on the division of tasks and responsibilities and related resources. This may take the form of financial contributions, but may also be in the form of materials, transport, meeting rooms, meals and printing and ICT services.

Progress and results of activities implemented are regularly shared. Further, the discussions and agreements made at the meetings are documented and sent to all members after each meeting, including those who were not present.

- At a personal level, the participation in the MSF should not be seen as a route to acquiring 'easy money' (e.g. DSA much higher than real costs). On the other hand, 'benefits' of the partnership should also be equally shared, such as attending (international) training or being interviewed by the media.

Developing a City Strategic Agenda

One of the first activities of the MSF in each of the RUAF partner cities was to develop a City Strategic Agenda on urban agriculture.

These agendas include:

- the *formal decision* to design and adopt a municipal policy and programme on urban agriculture;

- the *city's vision regarding the desired development of urban agriculture*: why do we want to support urban agriculture (for example, for reasons of poverty alleviation, improving urban food security and nutrition, promoting local economic development, improving waste management or a combination thereof). This entails the functions one expects urban agriculture to play in the realization of the city's strategic development plan and municipal policy objectives or the kind of developments in urban agriculture that will be supported or conditioned. This section will also link the urban agriculture agenda to other existing agendas and programmes in the city that are related with one or more of the mentioned policy goals;
- the *key issues:* what are the main issues we will work on (for example, capacity building in urban agriculture, local production and marketing of urban agriculture, access to land or financial resources, sustainable use of wastewater in urban agriculture and strengthening the legal and institutional framework for urban agriculture);
- *identification of the main strategies to be applied for each of the key issues and an assessment of their likely impacts, target groups* (whose behaviour and decisions are to be influenced) and *beneficiaries* (who are intended to benefit from this strategy). In most cases the strategies proposed are not alternatives, but overlap and complement each other. These strategy components, with the associated instruments, will form the basis for elaboration of detailed action plans at a later stage; it is recommended to include, for each main strategy, short *project profiles* for each of the proposed projects and other actions planned (e.g. reformulation of a policy or regulation; integration of urban agriculture in land use zoning, setting up a new funding mechanism for urban agriculture projects) indicating briefly its objectives (expected results), main implementing actors, budget indication and possible source of funding;
- *development of an institutional framework* (what actors should be involved?) and proposed coordination and monitoring mechanisms;
- *identification of available resources* for implementation *as well as potential sources* of additional funding; and
- an initial *time-plan* for operationalization and implementation.

The city strategic agenda thus constitutes a policy document once it is formally adopted by the local government and other stakeholders. A well-defined strategic agenda should include arrangements on how the policy will be translated into concrete actions: how the operational planning and funding of the selected policies and strategies will be organized as well as periodic review and how the implementation and monitoring of these activities will be coordinated.

The development of the City Strategic Agenda on urban agriculture in the RUAF partner cities was organized in a number of steps that may be summarized as follows (although important variations occurred from city to city):

1. First forum meeting: presentation and discussion of the results of the diagnosis, formulation of a *vision* and strategic objectives for the desired development of urban agriculture in the city, identification of key issues, and establishment of *working groups* around each of the key issues.
2. The working groups deepen the analysis of their issue and come up with *proposals regarding effective policy measures and action strategies* related to this issue.
3. Second forum meeting: discussion of the results of the working groups, *prioritization and linking* of the proposed policies and action strategies and identification of additional tasks of the working groups.
4. Working groups further develop the proposals *(main activities, actors, budget)* and make project profiles, the coordinating team integrates the proposals into a draft City Strategic Agenda.
5. Third forum meeting: discussion of a draft City Strategic Agenda, elaboration of agreements regarding the *role, responsibilities and contributions* of each MSF member in the operationalization and implementation of certain parts of the City Strategic Agenda.
6. Fourth forum meeting: finalization and *approval* of the City Strategic Agenda by the forum and its presentation to the Council committee for formal review.

Visioning

Design of an effective city urban agriculture programme is not possible without a clear vision on the desired longer-term development of urban agriculture in the city: What kind of urban agriculture would one like to bring about in the city? What roles and functions should it fulfil and what contributions to which strategic objectives (income, employment, food security, social inclusion, recycling, water management, etc.) would one like to see? What categories of the population should benefit most?

The vision reflects the future situation regarding urban agriculture one hopes to bring about and acts as a stimulating and leading image that orients the further development of the Agenda.

Therefore in one of the first forum meetings in each city such a vision was developed through interaction between all the members of the forum, using questions such as those above.

It is helpful during the vision exercise to remind the participants of the different policy dimensions of urban agriculture (see Chapter 1) which may help the discussion on what the desired focus for the development of urban agriculture in this city should be: mainly with an economic focus, mainly with a social focus, or more with an ecological focus or a specific mixture suited to local needs, priorities and opportunities. For example, a city concerned about growing food insecurity or the exclusion of certain groups of citizens will probably focus more on the social dimension of urban agriculture. Where poverty alleviation and local economic development is a high priority, one will focus more on the economic dimension of urban agriculture and seek

> ### Box 2.9 Cape Town vision statement on and strategic goals for urban agriculture
>
> 'The City seeks to employ all available means to build a prosperous City in which no-one is left out. The City recognizes that urban agriculture can play a key role in strategies for poverty alleviation (food security and nutrition) and economic development (income generation). However, the City is also aware of the numerous negative impacts of urban agriculture on city life. Therefore, the City supports and promotes urban agriculture within the context that it will not degrade the quality of life of citizens, will not impact harmfully on public health, the natural environment and will contribute to the economic and social well-being of people. In order to achieve this it is necessary to create an enabling and regulated environment in which the development and practice of urban agriculture can flourish. To promote "A prosperous and growing urban agricultural sector" in Cape Town, our vision is supported by the following strategic goals:
>
> - to enable the poorest of the poor to utilise urban agriculture as an element of their survival strategy (household food security);
> - to enable people to create commercially sustainable economic opportunities through urban agriculture (jobs and income);
> - to enable previously disadvantaged people to participate in the land redistribution for agricultural development programme (redress imbalances);
> - to facilitate human resources development (technical, business and social skills training).'
>
> *Source:* City of Cape Town, 2006.

to stimulate subsistence farmers to move into the market sector. Cities with a growing waste management problem or flooding problems might want to orient the development of urban agriculture more towards recycling wastes and wastewater, greening the city and creating a better urban living climate (capturing CO_2 and dust, lowering temperature).

Selection of key issues

On the basis of the defined vision, the MSF in the RUAF partner cities continued to define the development of the City Strategic Agenda. Based on the results of the situation analysis summarized in the 'policy narrative', the stakeholders in the forum jointly identified a number of key issues for the development of urban agriculture in the direction indicated by the vision.

Working groups elaborating proposals

Secondly, working groups were formed to analyse each issue more deeply, to define the changes needed, and to work out practical strategies to bring about these changes. Each working group involved the actors with a high 'stake' and/or expertise in that issue.

In some cases the working groups met regularly (e.g. weekly) during a period of months. This system allows the preparation of inputs by each member before meeting as a group (like in the Pikine case presented below and in Belo Horizonte, Brazil). In other cases (like in Bobo

Working groups were formed to analyse each issue more deeply (Accra, Ghana)

Dioulasso, Burkina Faso and Porto Novo, Benin) the working groups prepared their proposals in one or two intensive 3–4 day workshops. The advantage of the latter method is that the City Strategic Agenda is elaborated in a shorter period of time and the intensive workshops are more convenient for stakeholders with numerous work commitments. The disadvantage of this approach may be that there is hardly any opportunity for group members to sort out certain aspects and consult others that are not part of the working group.

Subsequently, RUAF partner IAGU (the African Institute for Urban Management) organized a training and work planning session for the members of the working group and facilitated four meetings held by each working group, applying Local Agenda 21 tools for strategic planning. Each working group analysed one key issue and developed a set of related strategies.

During the forum meeting with all stakeholders which followed the results of the working groups, the various strategies and actions were prioritized and included in the City Strategic Agenda.

Normally the working groups first analysed the issue in more detail and discussed the required changes and identified the policy measures and actions needed to realize these changes. It is of crucial importance that the working groups are well aware that they may propose the use of various types of instruments to bring about the desired changes: legal policy instruments

---

Box 2.10 Development of a City Strategic Agenda on urban agriculture in Pikine, Senegal

The multi-stakeholder forum in Pikine was established in 2006 and involves municipal councillors, urban producers, environmental, planning and agricultural authorities, NGOs and CBOs. Discussing the situation analysis, the forum identified as the main key issues for the development of urban agriculture: 1) Need to enhance access to water, other inputs and equipments; 2) Need to enhance access to and security of land; 3) Need to update present norms and regulations regarding urban agriculture. It was decided to further study and discuss these issues in three working groups that had to come up with policies and action strategies regarding each issue.

The tasks and expected outputs of the working groups were discussed and agreements were made on the required profile of the working group members, their role and responsibilities, the activities to be implemented by the working groups and the profile and tasks of the working group coordinator.

(bye-laws, norms, regulations, ordinances), as well as economic instruments (project funding, subsidies, tax incentives, economic sanctions), educational instruments (public education, training, technical assistance, study visits, etc.) and design instruments (e.g. approaches for slum upgrading that integrate home and community gardening, shift from centralized to decentralized/community-based waste management and reuse). In Chapter 4, 'Municipal policies and programmes on urban agriculture', a variety of policy instruments and measures are presented that could be considered for review or formulation.

After discussion of the initial proposals in the MSF, the working groups further developed these ideas in more detail by developing clear (one-page) *project profiles* for each main action that is included in the City Strategic Agenda, outlining per action: expected project results; proposed activities; partners involved and their roles/contributions; approximate budget per activity line; and potential sources of funding.

Not in all cases did the members of the MSF have all the required expertise or mandate or social basis to develop an adequate strategy and occasionally additional actors – with specific expertise or network – were invited to take part in the working groups.

Approval of the City Strategic Agenda

The results of the working groups were discussed in the multi-stakeholder forum and integrated in the City Strategic Agenda on urban agriculture. The forum approved this Agenda, which included joint agreement on the City Strategic Agenda in the forum and adoption of the Agenda by the individual institutions. The participating institutions committed i) to assist in the further operationalization of the Agenda; and ii) to integrate the Agenda into their institutional programmes and budgets and contribute with their own resources to the implementation of the Agenda in line with their institutional mandate. Such approval was formalized by means of official and signed letters by the directors or heads of the institutions and organizations involved.

The next step was to put the City Strategic Agenda on urban agriculture forward to the Council (or one of its Commissions) in order to be reviewed and formally approved and adopted by the municipality. Adoption of the City Strategic Agenda by the municipality should preferably be formalized by means of a decree or ordinance.

In Villa Maria del Triunfo, for example, the local government committed itself to: 'articulate the City Strategic Agenda to other municipal plans and management mechanisms, such as

The Gampaha City Strategic Agenda

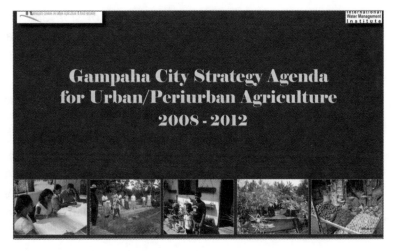

the city's or urban development plan, the economic development plan, zoning and land use plans, as well as other sectoral plans related to urban agriculture' (Municipality of Villa Maria del Triunfo, April, 2007).

Lessons learned regarding establishment of the multi-stakeholder forum and development of the city strategic agenda

Building up ownership and partnerships is crucial for effective functioning of the MSF

In a multi-stakeholder process it is not enough to simply come together and assume that a partnership for urban agriculture development will magically appear. Building further institutional commitment and relations needs time and should be a conscious effort. Building partnerships should be a goal of the MSF in itself. Practically this means bringing it up as an agenda item and discussing it regularly.

Once local ownership of the forum is higher, the degree of implementation of the City Strategic Agenda on urban agriculture will also be higher. Generally, stakeholders will *get and stay involved* if they believe that the issues dealt with are important to them or their organization; if they have something to contribute; if they will be listened to and their contributions will be respected and appreciated; if they feel that their participation makes a difference and has an impact; and if their participation is well organized (including child care, transportation, meals).

Preferably, structures and procedures for participatory decision-making should be clearly defined by the forum. Clear and transparent agreements concerning financial contributions and rewards should be arrived at, including arrangements for transport or arrangements for compensation for loss of income by the farmer representatives in the MSF.

Elections and replacement of staff and 'champions' for urban agriculture in the partner organizations and local authorities may lead to changing policy conditions and changing views on the role of that organization in the development of urban agriculture. It is important to seek to reduce this risk by:

- building of institutional rather than personal relations (although the latter are often the entrance to the former);
- training of several officers (rather than one or two) in each municipal department and other partner organizations so that urban agriculture and the MPAP will be more widely supported and not depend on one or two persons;
- establishing relations with more permanent municipal staff;
- informing newcomers on urban agriculture and the MPAP process;

- strengthening the multi-stakeholder forum and securing its formal recognition and political support (but maintaining an independent position *vis à vis* politicians), so that the forum can give counter pressure for urban agriculture if negative changes in policies and plans are considered as was done successfully by the urban agriculture forum in Harare, Zimbabwe;
- strengthening local farmers' networks that can lobby for the implementation of the City Strategic Agenda on urban agriculture, as was done successfully in Villa Maria del Triunfo;
- informing the wider public on urban agriculture and its importance.

Integration of gender mainstreaming in development of the Strategic Agenda needs continuous attention. The application of gender sensitive tools in the situation analysis (and specifically the participatory analysis of the urban farming systems) provides more detailed information on women's position and roles/tasks in urban agriculture and their specific needs and interests. However, as soon as it comes to policy development and action planning such information is easily lost. Special attention should be given to the integration of gender in the development of the Strategic Agenda and the formulation of policies and projects and the inclusion of gender-affirmative actions.

Implementation of concrete activities early on in the planning process helps to generate dynamism. Implementation of small concrete actions – with high visibility and low risk – during the planning stage greatly enhances the motivation of urban producers and other local actors involved in the process and generates more dynamism ('this is not only about talking and paperwork').

The organization of a demonstration and training on practical technologies that require low space was helpful in enhancing the credibility of the MPAP among the urban poor as well as the local authorities in Serilingampally, India. Also, the experience in Beijing, China (see the 'Networking for policy change in Beijing, China' case study in Chapter 3) shows that small practical projects were crucial in enhancing decision-making by the local government.

Implementation of such small concrete activities also provides an opportunity for learning by doing, and may provide valuable information for further policy development and design of longer-term activities. For the reasons outlined here, RUAF always included a small seed-fund for implementation of some pilot activities in the budget for an MPAP process.

Phase 5: Operationalization

The City Strategic Agenda on urban agriculture provides the vision and main policies and strategies for the development of urban agriculture in the city and commitments by various stakeholders regarding their participation in the operationalization and implementation of the Strategic Agenda.

Credit: Takawira Mubvami / MDP

Specific urban agriculture projects were formulated with local urban actors (Bulawayo, Zimbabwe)

To facilitate implementation of the City Strategic Agenda, the working groups of the MSF continued to function in order, or new ones were formed around the major actions planned:

- to elaborate *operational plans for each project* for which a project profile is included in the City Strategic Agenda;
- to (re)formulate *bye-laws, norms and regulations* regarding urban and peri-urban agriculture;
- to further the *integration of urban agriculture into existing plans* (including city strategic development and land use zoning plans) *and into institutional programmes and budgets.*

Project planning and design

The focus here lies on participatory formulation of specific urban agriculture projects with local urban farmers and other local actors. Projects may include a variety of activities depending on the specific problems and/or potentials to be tackled, for example:

- further studies (e.g. a marketing study), exchange with other cities, documentation of 'good practices' in urban agriculture or establishment of a 'resource centre';
- actions enhancing access to land, like integration of urban agriculture in land use planning, setting up of a 'Land Bank of Vacant Land Areas' suitable for urban agriculture, tax incentives for land owners that lease out vacant land to groups of urban producers;
- participatory development of appropriate technologies for urban agriculture (to develop and test practical solutions for priority problems);
- training and technical assistance for farmers and agro-based small enterprises, farmer field schools and demonstration plots;
- projects enhancing access to water (rainwater harvesting, water-saving irrigation techniques, safe reuse of wastewater, wells);
- projects promoting ecological production practices, maintaining soil fertility, composting and recycling of urban organic wastes, intensification of land use (e.g. production under cover allowing several harvests/year);
- projects aiming at strengthening farmer organizations and their strategic linkages with other organizations in order to get better access to land/water, training and technical support, and to enhance their role in value-adding and marketing;
- projects enhancing access to credit: groups savings and credit schemes, institutional micro-credit systems, and project financing;

- projects improving processing and marketing (micro-enterprise development, establishment of farmers' markets, provision of infrastructure for small-scale packaging and processing and composting sites);
- projects focusing on the development of communication materials to inform and educate the general public and consumers regarding urban agriculture.

Operationalization of the City Strategic Agenda in RUAF partner cities

Some examples of the projects on urban agriculture that have already been developed and implemented by the partners in the MSF in RUAF partner cities are:

- setting up and supporting community gardens and nurseries (e.g. in Bulawayo, Zimbabwe and Bobo Dioulasso, Burkina Faso);
- establishing farmers' markets (e.g. in Villa Maria del Triunfo, Peru);
- promotion of space-confined technologies in school-gardens and high-density low income settlements (e.g. Hyderabad, India and Gampaha, Sri Lanka);
- establishing and strengthening of urban producer organizations (e.g. in Villa Maria del Triunfo, Peru and Beijing, China);
- supporting community-based agro-tourism enterprises (e.g. Beijing and Chengdu, China);
- design and promotion of rooftop gardens (e.g. Bogota, Colombia);
- implementing and monitoring of small-scale wastewater treatment systems for urban horticulture production (Pikine, Senegal);
- development of educational materials on urban agriculture (Accra, Ghana);
- integrating urban agriculture into the city development and zoning plans (e.g. Beijing, China) or into sectoral policy documents (e.g. Ghana, China);
- revision of outdated and/or formulation of new bye-laws and ordinances on urban agriculture (e.g. Accra, Ghana and Bulawayo, Zimbabwe);
- provision of land and equipment for urban agriculture (e.g. Bulawayo, Zimbabwe and Cape Town, South Africa);
- inclusion of urban agriculture in City Master Plan (e.g. Ndola, Zambia and Bobo Dioulasso, Burkina Faso);
- providing economic incentives and inputs for urban agriculture (e.g. Cape Town, South Africa);
- inclusion of urban agriculture curricula in extension institutes and universities (e.g. Pikine, Senegal and Bogota, Colombia);
- inclusion of urban agriculture in the municipal budget (e.g. Cape Town, South Africa and Bobo Dioulasso, Burkina Faso).

The beneficiaries of these projects by MSF partners and supported by RUAF included: widows and refugees from Ivory Coast (Bobo Dioulasso, Burkina Faso); traditional urban farmers (Pikine, Senegal); migrants from rural areas with very limited rights (Beijing, China); inmates from detention centres (Porto Novo, Benin); female-headed households (Villa Maria del Triunfo, Peru); displaced people because of war (Bogota); elderly people with no or low pension (Macaé, Brazil); HIV/AIDS infected and affected people (Magadi, India); unemployed youth (Cape Coast, Sierra Leone); people living with disabilities (Tamale, Ghana); poor women in slum areas (Hyderabad, India).

The above indicates the potential of urban agriculture projects to reach out to the (very) urban poor and constitutes an extremely positive contribution to social inclusion approaches (Cabannes and Pasquini, 2008).

Revision of existing or development of new norms, bye-laws and regulations

This activity includes the adaptation of existing – or the formulation of new – municipal bye-laws, norms, technical quality criteria and regulations on urban agriculture. In several RUAF partner's cities, such as Accra, members of the multi-stakeholder forum have been supportive to drafting legal texts (with the support of officials and/or lawyers) and have presented these to the policy makers, which in most cases were almost integrally adopted by the municipal council.

Policy makers need technical inputs on which to design their policies. Counting with standards, technical norms and quality criteria assists them to revise or design policies related to urban agriculture. The drafting of new policies often includes the development of, for example, guidelines and parameters related to the quality of water to be used in urban agriculture, quality criteria for the use of compost, guidelines for certification of urban agriculture produce, and technical norms for the number of livestock to be held in certain areas in the city, which have a scientific basis and are accepted and applicable for the urban producers (if not, the adherence to such norms will be very low). This requires the participation of several stakeholders in the development of such norms and quality criteria.

Institutionalization

Traditionally, participatory and multi-stakeholder approaches have focused primarily on the communication and planning aspects, and less on the institutional dimension.

The 'institutionalization' of multi-stakeholder planning was understood in RUAF in three ways. Firstly and for all: enhancing the commitment of the organizations taking part in the MPAP process so that they will integrate (components of) the City Strategic Agenda into their institutional programmes and budgets and will contribute to its implementation with their own resources (as far as fitting within their mandate).

Secondly, and in a broader sense: institutionalization meant making participatory and multi-stakeholder processes the 'regular way of doing things' in the organizations taking part in the MSF. This requires:

- *Acceptance of the principles* of participatory planning and decision-making and corresponding adaptations in the institutional structure and culture so that participatory and multi-stakeholder practice becomes a repeatable day-to-day practice and routine institutional procedures. Such principles include: involvement of the direct stakeholders in the planning process; a shifting from a sectoral approach to a more integrated approach considering cross-cutting issues; acceptance of coordinated planning and monitoring based on co-operation and collaboration around key issues.
- *Building up the required technical capacities and expertise* within the organizations needed to implement participatory planning and decision-making processes.
- New *financial mechanisms and resource allocation measures* might be needed as well as new structures to facilitate application of the MPAP approach (an urban agriculture unit, a task force or working group).

To facilitate the above, RUAF gave a lot of attention to capacity development and commitment building and encouraged the local partners in the MPAP process to apply this approach also in other institutional programmes.

Finally, the multi-stakeholder forum on urban agriculture was itself institutionalized. This involved formal recognition by the city government and other key stakeholders and creation of a permanent secretariat for the MSF with a minimum of resources in order to sustain longer-term functioning of planning, coordination and monitoring of urban agriculture.

Specific attention was given by RUAF to ensure the sustainability and consolidation of the urban agriculture policy and programme beyond the period of a given political administration and to plan for future up-scaling of the urban agriculture programme: from working with a

Box 2.11 Institutionalizing and scaling up urban agriculture in RUAF

The RUAF partner IGSNRR in Beijing, together with its extended network partners, supported the enhancement and integration of urban agriculture in the peri-urban planning in Beijing and the design and implementation of the '2-2-1' programme that was established to promote urban agricultural development. The success of this programme strongly influenced the formulation of the national 'reconstruction of the new country side programme' and the uptake of urban agriculture in the new national 5 year plan.

In Amman an Urban Agriculture Bureau was established within the municipality and urban agriculture land use included in land use planning, with 15 per cent of the new development permits to be given out for green and urban agriculture spaces.

In Bulawayo, Zimbabwe and Cape Town, South Africa an Urban Agriculture Unit was established within an existing municipal department and staff and an annual budget were allocated to this unit.

small group of beneficiaries to working with a larger number of people; from working in one or a few districts of the city to working in various districts. One way to enhance the continuity of the urban agriculture programme is by creating an institutional home for urban agriculture within the municipal structure and including it in the city's strategic development plan.

Identifying sources of financing for implementation

However good the City Strategic Agenda may be, without the financial and other resources needed for its implementation, it will remain an Agenda on paper. Implementation delays (as a result of lack of financing or otherwise) will dissipate the interest and enthusiasm of the participating stakeholders, particularly the beneficiaries. The question of financing the Strategic Agenda is therefore an issue that must be addressed from the beginning and throughout the process of strategic planning.

Local partners have financed a water pump to implement one of the activities in the CSA (Freetown, Sierra Leone)

Credit: René van Veenhuizen

When identifying the strategies of the City Strategic Agenda, a rough estimate of costs and indications of possible sources of funding for each main action will be made (as part of the project profiles).

At the operationalization stage detailed cost estimates per activity and year will be made and (realistic!) sources of funding will be specified (as part of the detailed project proposal).

In general, RUAF partners accessed the following sources of finance and other resources:

- foreseen own contributions by the beneficiaries (labour, materials);
- own resources of the organizations participating in the implementation of a specific project;
- local municipal funds / programmes;
- national funds / programmes;
- international projects operating in the country;
- private sector support;
- non-governmental funding organizations and Foundations in the North.

Where possible, all these types of potential resource partners should be involved in the development of the City Strategic Agenda from the beginning.

However, RUAF's experience shows that it is important to stress from the beginning of the strategic planning process that the local partners are responsible for (financing) the implementation of the City Strategic Agenda and to build on the resources and means available in these organizations before looking to additional sources at national or international level. The institutions participating in the MSF should be committed to include identified priority actions in their own *institutional programmes and annual operational plans and budgets.* This often requires explaining to higher level officials in these organizations why the proposed actions are relevant to their institutional priorities.

Also, farmers and community members can and will make investments in project implementation. For this to occur, the initiative to be financed should be among their priorities, they must be involved in a meaningful way in its planning and implementation and they must have the confidence that reliable and useful outputs will occur.

One should also seek to involve local financing institutions (banks, credit cooperatives, mini-credit programmes) and to convince them to include a credit line for urban producers and/or to adapt their conditions if needed. Experience shows that it is important not to make the implementation of the City Strategic Agenda dependent upon one main funding source only: in such cases, the urban agriculture programme has been in danger of being halted after a change in local government.

Lessons learned regarding operationalization

Project planning should go hand in hand with reformulation of bye-laws, norms and regulations and other policy measures. In RUAF the tendency in most multi-stakeholder forums was to focus in this phase on detailed project planning and implementation. Therefore, it is important that during operationalization the coordinating committee asks sufficient attention for the operationalization of other components of the Strategic Agenda like the revision of norms and regulations, integration of urban agriculture into land use zoning and city development plans.

When working on the latter, it is important to make sure that sufficient attention is given to the development of facilitating policies that use legal instruments as well as economic, educational and design instruments. The legal measures often have the tendency to become restrictive (you are not allowed to ....) and reactive (if you don't adhere to this norm, you will be sanctioned) which in some cases is necessary but often not very effective to realize the desired changes as indicated by the vision included in the City Strategic Agenda. Economic incentives, educational measures, or design measures might be much more effective. Often a combination of legal and other instruments leads to a strong and effective 'package' of policy measures that will effectively facilitate the development of a safe and sustainable urban agriculture (see further Chapter 4).

Differentiation of the policy measures for different types of agriculture is important. Many policy documents on urban agriculture hardly differentiate between different types of urban agriculture and apply the same policy measures for various types of urban agriculture existing in a city, often with the exception of livestock production. Differentiation of the policy measures for the different types of agriculture (according to main product, level of technology and scale) is important since each type of urban agriculture has its specific characteristics, risks, development potentials and support needs and hence requires different intervention strategies for its development. Also, differentiation for different parts of the city is important: certain types of urban agriculture may be acceptable in certain locations (e.g. in the city centre or in an ecologically sensitive area) while others are not, or only under certain conditions.

Phase 6: Implementation, monitoring, adaptation and innovation

During implementation of the City Strategic Agenda, the coordinating committee will periodically meet to coordinate activities, review progress and monitor the results that have been achieved. It is of crucial importance that during the design stage clear agreements are made regarding how the implementation will be coordinated and monitored.

The whole forum will meet once a year to reflect on the process in motion, to review the results obtained, to discuss additional actions needed and to decide on adaptations in the agreed strategies.

When implementing the Strategic Agenda, building in effective monitoring and evaluation is very important. Monitoring and evaluation allows the demonstration of progress, efficiency and the results obtained by an urban agriculture project or policy which enhances accountability and provides a basis for decisions on replication or up-scaling). It also allows for the review and – where needed/possible – the adaptation/improvement of strategies that were chosen to realize the desired changes indicated by the City Strategic Agenda. It also enables one to keep track of the impacts of the MPAP on policy change and on the livelihoods of different stakeholders that are involved (impacts), enables the communication of successful efforts to a wider public and creates opportunities for further change.

Moreover, if the monitoring and evaluation is done in a participatory way, it enhances 'ownership' and co-responsibility among beneficiaries and other stakeholders in the MPAP and encourages learning and capacity development.

To this effect, three modes of monitoring and evaluation were applied by RUAF: built-in, outcome and impact monitoring.

Built-in monitoring. In all main activities implemented by RUAF partners, a monitoring component is built in, in order to be able to measure *progress* (did we do what we planned to do), *process* (how did we do it) and the *direct results or outputs* obtained (number of people trained and number of gardens established). Discussion of the results of the built-in monitoring in the MSF coordination committee helps to review the progress made, to discuss solutions for problems and new challenges or opportunities encountered and to learn from each other's experiences.

Outcome Mapping. One main aim of the MPAP is to facilitate capacity development at the local level and to stimulate local partners to make changes in their existing policies, to integrate urban agriculture into their programmes and to initiate action projects with and for the urban poor interested in or engaged in farming. It is expected that by doing so, the MPAP will make a longer term contribution to development, since the capacity and motivation in MSF partners is enhanced in this way, leading them to mobilize their resources to implement actions with the intended ultimate beneficiaries on a continuing basis.

Outcome Mapping is a method used to monitor the *changes in the behaviour* (policies, actions, relations, communications) of the groups and organizations directly involved in the MPAP process. Such changes can be logically linked to the MPAP process (although they may not be necessarily directly caused by them). Outcome mapping generates feedback on the effectiveness of the applied strategies and helps in identifying mechanisms for improvement (Earl et al., 2001). Furthermore, the outcome mapping activities stimulate the capacity development process.

In RUAF, Outcome Mapping was carried out as follows:

- During the formulation of the City Strategic Agenda, each of the partners in the MSF formulates an 'outcome challenge' for their organization describing the changes in behav-

Outcome mapping drafts are discussed in MSF meetings, Freetown

Credit: René van Veenhuizen

iour of the organization that they intend to realize (changes in their policy, programme, cooperation) based on the vision/strategies for the development of urban agriculture defined in the City Strategic Agenda. Also, 'progress markers' are defined (indicators to monitor the degree of change achieved).
- In a meeting of the MSF these drafts are discussed and approved and changes are made if needed.
- At least annually each boundary partner is requested to mark the progress made for each progress marker and to analyse the factors that contributed to or hampered the desired change.

- The results of this exercise are presented and discussed during a meeting of the multi-stakeholder forum in order to draw some lessons and to identify possible improvements in the strategies and the coordination mechanism of the MSF.

Impact monitoring. This concerns the measurement of the impacts of the MPAP and implementation of the City Strategic Agenda at target group level (changes in the livelihood situation of the people impacted by the interventions undertaken by the partners in the MSF to implement the City Strategic Agenda).

Easy-to-measure and realistic indicators have been defined to monitor the impacts of the urban agriculture projects and other policy measures undertaken.

Credit: IWMI India

Impacts were measured at the household level, Gampaha

Indicators included:

- increased levels of nutrition and food security;
- increased income and micro-enterprise development;
- enhanced access to and security of land;
- improved gender relations;
- strengthening farmer organizations;
- social inclusion of marginal groups;
- improved access to productive resources (land, water);
- enhanced recycling of urban wastes and urban greening.

The impact monitoring allows the stakeholders to keep track of the impacts of the activities implemented in relation to a wide number of urban issues, and evaluate the degree to which these correspond with the objectives of the City Strategic Agenda. It also enables communication of the results obtained to a wider public and funding sources, and creates opportunities for further change.

Updating the City Strategic Agenda

It is expected that the MSF in RUAF partner cities will revise and update the City Strategic Agenda every three to five years, by defining priorities for the coming years and eventually including additional policy goals and strategies. During the implementation of the City Strategic Agenda new strategic needs or opportunities for development of urban agriculture will emerge that can be taken up in the City Strategic Agenda. In other cases, monitoring and evaluation showed that the initial Agenda mainly focussed on certain types of urban agriculture (for example, the promotion of home and community gardening) and needed to be broadened to also include strategies for the development of other types of urban agriculture.

Lessons learned with regards to implementation, monitoring and evaluation and adaptation/innovation of the City Strategic Agenda

Monitoring and evaluation activities are an integral part of any MPAP and should not be considered as isolated activities to be done only at a certain stage or at the end of the process. A budget should be set aside for this purpose from the start of the process.

Monitoring is a sensitive subject that often raises resistance in partner organizations and among staff. Overcoming such resistance through open dialogue on the sense and nonsense of monitoring is crucial for its success. Most organizations taking part in the MSF will have their own monitoring and evaluation systems and are often not much inclined to take additional measures for the sake of a collaborative process like the MPAP and MSF on urban agriculture. Staff will be inclined to see M&E as 'more work' and their bosses as 'more costs' and 'external evaluation', which they both might not appreciate.

In order to arrive at a meaningful and cost effective system that yields meaningful results and leads to improved management and learning, the MPAP facilitators will have to make the effort to get to know the existing M&E systems and make optimal use of the information generated by such systems. Adding certain elements should be discussed and agreed in the MSF and staff of the individual organizations need guidance in the implementation of such additional elements. Universities or research centres participating in the MSF can play an important role in the evaluation of impacts and in drawing lessons learned.

Additional specific technical training is required for successful project implementation. The implementation of the projects identified in the City Strategic Agenda often required previous training of the staff of the MSF partners listed to implement such projects. This sometimes required substantial additional resources (staff time and funds). Such additional training activities might be incorporated in the City Strategic Agenda and local research and extension organizations and NGOs should be mobilized to provide such training (as done, for example, by AREX and SNV in Bulawayo, Zimbabwe, the Department of Horticulture in Hyderabad, India, or the Department of Agriculture in Beijing, China).

Future perspectives

In promoting multi-stakeholder policy development and action planning on urban agriculture, RUAF has aimed to build participatory governance (in the city and the institutions involved), to empower urban producers and to create an enabling policy and institutional framework for urban agriculture (the immediate objectives of an MPAP process). The expectation is that this will lead to poverty reduction, enhanced food security, more (self-)employment and better environmental management and recycling in the cities concerned.

The effects of the recent food and economic crisis, growing energy and water crisis and ongoing climate change are felt strongly by an increasing number of urban poor. Adequate responses are urgently needed. Urban agriculture can play an important role in responding to these challenges, especially if urban agriculture is made part of a comprehensive approach to sustainable urban development characterized by an emphasis on multi-stakeholder involvement, decentralized and flexible approaches, participatory planning and management of spaces and services, a pro-poor focus and optimal use of locally available resources.

This chapter has described the principles, phases and challenges of a Multi-Stakeholder Process developed for urban agriculture. The following chapters will illustrate several case studies from RUAF partner cities and describe in more detail possible policy measures for urban agriculture that can be applied to further develop and promote urban agriculture.

References

Arnstein, S.R. (1969) 'A ladder of citizen participation', *Journal of the American Planning Association* 35: 4, pp. 216–224.

Cabannes, Y. and Pasquini, M. (2008) *Mid-term review Cities Farming for the Future*, unpublished.

Cabannes, Y., Dubbeling, M. and Santandreu, A. (eds.) (2003) *Guidelines for municipal policy making on urban agriculture*, Policy Brief 2: Urban agriculture and citizen's involvement, IPES/UMP-LAC, Quito-Ecuador.

City of Cape Town (2006) *Urban Agricultural Policy for the City of Cape Town.* Available from: http://www.capetown.gov.za/en/ehd/Documents/EHD_Urban_Agricultural_Policy_2007_8102007113120_.pdf

Earl, S., Carden, F. and Smutylo, T. (2001) *Outcome Mapping: Building Learning and Reflection into Development Programs,* International Development and Research Centre (IDRC), Ottawa.

Gonzales, N., Salvo, M. and Prain, G. (2007) 'Innovations in producer-market linkages: Urban field schools and organic markets in Lima', *Urban Agriculture Magazine* 19: 46–8.

Hemmati, M. (with contributions from F. Dodds, J. Enayati and J. McHarry) (2002) *Multi-Stakeholder Processes for Governance and Sustainability: Beyond Deadlock and Conflict,* Earthscan, London, UK.

International Water Management Institute (2006) *Declaration for the promotion of urban and peri-urban agriculture in Serilingampally, Hyderabad,* IWMI South Asia Regional Office, Hyderabad, India.

Mougeot, L.J.A. (ed.) (2005) *AGROPOLIS: The Social, Political and Environmental Dimensions of Urban Agriculture*, Earthscan, London.

Municipality of Villa María del Triunfo, IPES and RUAF (2006) *Villa María, Sembrando para la vida*, Lima, Peru.

Municipality of Villa María del Triunfo (2007) *Ordinance no 021*, Villa María del Triunfo, Lima, Peru.

Partners and Propper (2004) *Verslag Afronding 'initiatieffase' opstelling regeling burgerparticipatie gemeente Westervoort*, Internal Report to the Municipality of Westervoort.

UN Habitat and UNEP (1999) *Institutionalising environmental planning and management process*, Sustainable Cities Programme, UN Habitat and UNEP, Nairobi.

Wilbers, J. and De Zeeuw, H. (2006) 'A critical review of recent policy documents on urban agriculture', *Urban Agriculture Magazine* 16: 3–9.

Chapter 3
CASE STUDIES

Introduction

In Chapter 2 the principles, process and methodology for multi-stakeholder policy formulation and action planning (MPAP) on urban agriculture were discussed. This chapter presents seven case studies that illustrate how the MPAP process has evolved in selected RUAF partner cities, the local stakeholders involved, challenges encountered and results obtained. These cases highlight how the general approach developed a specific form and dynamic under the influence of the local conditions and interactions between participating organizations in each city.

Starting in 2005, the RUAF Foundation has supported an MPAP process on urban agriculture in 20 cities in 17 countries (Fig. 3.1). In 18 of the 20 cities a multi-stakeholder forum (MSF) on urban agriculture has been established, involving 272 organizations (an average of 15 organizations per MSF) which clearly shows the interest of the various stakeholders in these cities to actively contribute to the development of safe and sustainable urban agriculture in their city. In all cities a City Strategic Agenda on urban agriculture has been published, and in most cases the Agenda has been formally approved by the City Council or a Council Commission and is being integrated within formal policies, bye-laws and regulations. Urban agriculture is now integrated within the City Master or Development plan in nine cities and

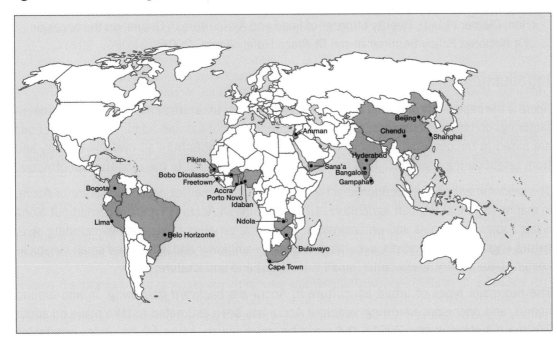

RUAF
partner cities

in six cities this process is ongoing. In 13 cities an (urban) agriculture department or unit is coordinating the implementation of the City Strategic Agenda while in five cities urban agriculture is coordinated by another department (e.g. Parks or Social Development).

The participatory evaluations held in the RUAF partner cities at the end of the CFF programme (December 2008) indicate that, as a consequence of the MPAP process and the development of a City Strategic Agenda on urban agriculture, the communication and cooperation between local authorities, civil society organizations and other local stakeholders in urban agriculture have improved, the participation of urban farmer groups in planning and decision-making processes has been strengthened and the services provided to urban producers have improved in most of the RUAF partner cities.

Gradual institutionalization of urban agriculture in Accra, Ghana

Theophilus Otchere-Larbi and Olufunke Cofie

> 'There is need to support and regulate the practice of urban and peri-urban agriculture to make it more efficient and sustainable to contribute to urban food security and poverty reduction in our cities.'
>
> (Hon. Clement Eledi, Deputy Minister of Food and Agriculture in Ghana, on the occasion of a National Policy Seminar at the M-Plaza Hotel, Accra, 2006).

Introduction

Accra is the capital city of Ghana and is the country's most urbanized city. Most industry, manufacturing, commerce, business, cultural, educational, political and administrative functions are based in the conurbation Accra-Tema, attracting migrants from all over the country and from neighbouring countries. This has contributed a great deal to the urbanization of Accra.

The predominant primary economic activity, which is the smallest economic sector of Accra, is marine fishing and urban agriculture. Urban farming in Accra is typically carried out along water bodies and drains and on backyards, producing varieties of vegetables including okra, garden eggs, tomatoes, carrots, cucumber, cabbage, cauliflower and lettuce and small-livestock-keeping (like poultry, grass-cutter, small ruminants) and aquaculture.

The two major types of urban agriculture in Accra are *backyard gardening*, in and around homes, and *open-space farming*, which in Accra has been estimated to take place on about 700 ha (Obuobie et al., 2006); the majority under maize, some 50 ha under vegetables (rain-fed) and 250 ha under mixed cereal-vegetable systems, of which some 100 ha are irrigated vegetable production in the dry season. It was estimated in the exploratory survey that was implemented by IWMI/RUAF (Cofie et al., 2005) that about 1,000 farmers were involved in rain-fed and irrigated urban agriculture on plot sizes that range between 0.01–0.02 ha per farmer, but which reach 20 in the peri-urban areas. There are different tenure arrangements for the use of the urban open spaces. In general, no farmer owns the land that is cultivated and very few of them pay a fee. Most of the cultivated open spaces belong to public or private institutions. The farmers use various sources of water. Most of the open-space farmers use water from drains, streams/rivers, and if available, from pipe-borne water and hand-dug wells.

Credit: IWMI Ghana

Irrigated vegetable farming in Accra

In spite of its benefits, such as employment and access to food in Accra, urban and peri-urban agriculture is faced with challenges. The increasing land value in Accra results in a changing use of land from agriculture to more commercial and economic purposes. Next to limited access to land, urban producers are also faced with limited access to water resources, contamination of crops from poor quality water and improper use of pesticides, lack of an institutional framework and the lack of farmer organization to facilitate advocacy and lobbying.

Urban and peri-urban agriculture and related issues in Accra fall under the jurisdiction of different levels and types of authorities. Smallholder agriculture development is highlighted in almost all major policies, programmes and projects such as the Food and Agriculture Sector Development Policy, the Ghana Poverty Reduction Strategy, and the Decentralization Policy, which provide opportunities for better integration of urban agriculture within the overall city's development policies and programmes.

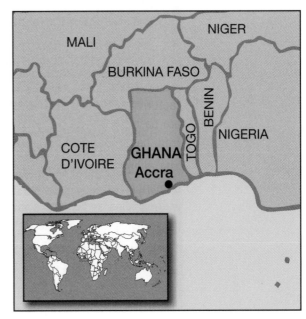

The MPAP process

RUAF started its activities on urban agriculture in Accra in 2000 with the IWMI office in Ghana as its main partner. In 2005, several key institutions were brought together to start a multi-stakeholder planning process on urban agriculture in a MPAP team. A first step was to create the needed local ownership, commitment and inclusive consensus. Regular consultations were made with the local partners through office visits, telephone calls and meetings, which required continued engagement and follow-ups to explain and discuss the process and to arouse interest. The initial focus was on lead stakeholders, including the Accra Metropolitan Food and Agriculture Department, the Planning and Coordinating Unit of the Accra Metropolitan Assembly (AMA), the Accra Metropolitan Health Department, the Department of Geography and Resource Development of the University of Ghana and the Science and Technology Policy Research Institute (STEPRI). Other stakeholders were identified and engaged as the process gained momentum. A major challenge during this phase was finding ways and means to identify and involve representatives of vulnerable and marginalized groups who were typically not well organized in order to be truly 'inclusive'. Beyond having a representative from one vegetable farmers' group, and another livestock farmer, other groups' representatives were not included in the initial steps of the process.

By the end of 2005 a 'Multi-stakeholder Agreement' was signed with a core team of nine stakeholder institutions. This agreement highlighted what the various partner institutions agreed to do together, what resources they wished to contribute and how urban agriculture could be brought into the development agenda. In order to assure that the representatives attended the meetings regularly, early notices were given and reminders sent to members a few days prior to the meeting. Meeting venues were also rotated among institutions to ensure active participation and interest.

The members of the core team conducted the situation analysis, which involved the gathering of key data, gaining an understanding of the policy and institutional context, and the identification

Box 3.1 Decentralization

The Multi-stakeholder Policy formulation and Action Planning (MPAP) approach is well adapted to the decentralization and multi-stakeholder processes in local governance in Ghana. The decentralized planning in Ghana involves a change from the top-down approach of planning to a bottom-up approach under which the jurisdiction of local development planning is assigned to the Metropolitan Municipal and District Assemblies (MMDAs) and, requiring participatory approaches with the identification of the community's problems, forming the basis of prioritization of development efforts. Political decentralization started in Ghana in 1988 when 110 MMDAs were established, which was further expanded to 138 in 1994 with the establishment of the sub-metropolitan district councils, urban, zonal and town councils and unit committees. The MMDAs have further been increased to 170 since 2008, including 6 Metropolitan, 40 Municipal and 125 District Assemblies. The major intention to decentralize has been to share power with the districts as a means to advance participatory democracy and collective decision-making, and the restructuring of power relations between the centre and the MMDAs, in addition to other societal stake-holding sectors. In line with this power sharing initiative, the National Development Planning Commission (NDPC) introduced a new decentralized planning system in 1994. The main objective was to establish efficient political, planning and administrative institutions at the MMDA level, which would enjoy popular support from local communities, and to facilitate the mobilization of support and resources for district development.

of problems and development potentials in urban agriculture and the interventions required. Lack of data and unreliability of data posed challenges in this phase of the process. These challenges, in certain cases, were solved through primary data collection. In other cases, projections and adjustments were made using available data. For example, recent satellite maps of Accra were not available and there was a lack of data on existing farmer groups. These situations meant that more time was required to undertake primary data collection and analysis. After data collection, a synthesis document, containing the key issues on urban agriculture, was used to inform a larger group of stakeholders and to advance the planning process with the stakeholders (Cofie et al., 2005).

AWGUPA members
after a meeting

Credit: IWMI Ghana

A three-day multi-stakeholder forum for action planning was held in November 2005. Up to 55 participants were at the forum and included both technical staff and directors of public institutions, farmer group representatives, NGOs and political heads of the AMA and adjoining

Box 3.2 The Accra Working Group on Urban and Peri-urban Agriculture (AWGUPA)

Membership in 2009:

Decentralized departments of the **Accra Metropolitan Assembly**: Department of Food and Agriculture, AMA Planning and Coordination Unit, Public Health Department, and Town and Country Planning Department, Parks and Gardens Department, Department of Cooperatives;

University of Ghana: College of Agriculture and Consumer Sciences, Department of Geography and Resource Development;

Council for Scientific & Industrial Research: Science and Technology Policy Research Institute (STEPRI); Water Research Institute (WRI);

IWMI-Ghana;

Environmental Protection Agency;

Directorate of Agricultural Extension Services;

Enterprise Works, Ghana (NGO);

General Agriculture Workers Union;

Dzorwulu Vegetable Production Society;

La Livestock Farmers Association;

Ecumenical Association for Sustainable Agriculture and Rural Development (NGO);

Heifer International Ghana (NGO);

ActionAid, Ghana (NGO).

districts. This large-scale consultation aimed to mobilize a wide range of stakeholders and deepen their knowledge and understanding of the importance of urban agriculture in urban economic development. In addition, the forum sought to agree on common problems and potentials for urban agriculture, and to subsequently identify priority issues for intervention and mechanisms for addressing them. The Forum was further used to draw legitimacy from the expressed collective will of the participating stakeholders and individuals to develop a City Strategic Agenda on urban agriculture in Accra.

At this forum the composition of the core MPAP team was expanded into a 15-member Working Group; the Accra Working Group on Urban and Peri-urban Agriculture (AWGUPA). Its mandate was to further elaborate a detailed Action Plan and to operationalize the agreements reached at the multi-stakeholder forum, and to develop the identified strategies further (AWGUPA, 2006). AWGUPA prioritized eight policy and technical issues for intervention in a short- to medium-term (3–5 years) vision on the desired development in Accra: the City Strategic Action plan on Urban and Peri-urban Agriculture.

The Ministry of Food and Agriculture (MoFA) chairs and facilitates the AWGUPA. The progress of institutionalization is monitored through outcome journals and capacity gaps are addressed in capacity building events. Other events of 'reaching up' (upscaling) and 'reaching out' (outscaling) included policy seminars and study visits IWMI/RUAF continued to support the process, as a member of AWGUPA and to further mainstream the process.

Following the first multi-stakeholder forum a policy seminar was held in December 2005 during which people in key policy making positions discussed and endorsed a Statement of Consensus. In support of this statement, the Deputy Minister of Food and Agriculture, pronounced the institution of an award for the 'National Best Urban and Peri-urban Farmer' during the annual National Farmers' day celebration which started in full operation in 2006.

City Strategic Agenda

The City Strategic Agenda (CSA) on urban agriculture was developed by AWGUPA as mandated by the forum. The following main issues were identified to guide the work in Accra in the forthcoming years:

- policy and legislative support for urban agriculture;
- education and public awareness on urban agriculture and urban food safety;
- standards and quality assurance of products;
- the promotion of urban agriculture (micro-)enterprises;
- capacity building of farmers and farmer associations: the formalization of farmer associations;
- development of collaborative projects and programmes among key actors in Accra;
- improvement in post-harvest handling and in marketing;
- improved access to land (temporal arrangements).

Yearly work plans are being agreed upon to operationalize this agenda. The CSA is also used to source for funding or to integrate priority issues into specific institutional development agendas (Adzorkor Doku, 2008).

Under the CSA, AWGUPA implemented a number of activities. A first major activity was under the (RUAF co-funded) project 'Promoting Public Education and Policy Support for Urban and Peri-Urban Agriculture in Accra', which aimed to improve public awareness and perception of urban agriculture and stimulate participatory city governance. Next to this project, farmers have been provided with extension information on good agricultural practices, on improved post-harvest handling strategies, on environmental sanitation and personal hygiene.

Based on a review of urban agriculture-related policies in other cities, a draft guideline for strengthening and supporting urban agriculture in Accra was produced. Finally, the AWGUPA facilitated stakeholder involvement in the review of the bye-laws related to urban agriculture which have been presented to the AMA for adoption.

Results and outcomes

The AWGUPA has been officially recognized by the Ministry of Food and Agriculture and the Accra Metropolitan Assembly.

Credit: René van Veenhuizen

Capacity building of farmers

Credit: Philip Amoah / IWMI Ghana

Training relates to better production, marketing and consumption practices

Awareness on urban agriculture has been created in Accra Metropolitan Assembly. The Assembly adopted a motion to develop an institutional policy on urban agriculture for metropolitan Accra.

The Ministry of Food and Agriculture, stimulated by the experiences gained in the multiple stakeholder planning process in Accra, has integrated urban and peri-urban agriculture as a component in the Food and Agriculture Sub-sector Development Policy II (FASDEP), and is now expecting the city governments (metro, districts and municipalities) to develop specific programmes to support urban agriculture. Also, the Ministry of Food and Agriculture has approved and instituted an award system for the Best National Urban Farmer.

Some NGOs and worker unions (e.g. Enterprise Works, the Ghana Agricultural Workers Union) have also taken up urban agriculture as an issue in their extension and training programmes.

Some university departments (e.g. the Department of Geography and Resource Development and Department of Agricultural Economics of the University of Ghana) have included urban agriculture in their curricula as from 2007.

The Environmental Protection Agency now considers urban agriculture in its hitherto strict regulatory processes and supports the realization of the City Strategic Agenda on urban agriculture.

Lessons learned

The MPAP process is unique in each city context and involves a lot of learning while doing. It therefore requires adequate monitoring, documenting, reviewing, and disseminating experiences to a wide range of stakeholders. This is very demanding and requires expertise in facilitation. The selection and application of different tools and methods to promote this joint learning is crucial. Methods and tools used under the process in Accra included the Internet, a bibliographic database, flyers, newsletters, posters, workshop reports, project updates, packaging of information into CD-ROMs and videos. It was observed that not all stakeholders have adequate access to the Internet. This was partially circumvented through distribution of hard copies of information materials through postal and personal deliveries, as well as during meetings.

The full participation and cooperation of stakeholders is required (Accra, Ghana)

Credit: René van Veenhuizen

The MPAP requires time. The process depends on building consensus through broader consultations. Achieving the expected changes in municipal and institutional policies, in a short period of time, has appeared to be quite a challenge in Accra. The process is still ongoing and requires regular consultations (through office visits, telephone calls and reminders, for example) and combination of both formal and informal relations to obtain the full cooperation of stakeholders and to establish relations beyond technical issues, such as inviting stakeholders to a variety of events. These occasions were also used to show appreciation to stakeholders and to celebrate the successes of the project.

In addition, cultural standards in dealing with the elderly and hierarchies tend to hinder open and frank discussions. This requires active facilitation.

Beyond technical knowledge on the subject itself, the group members' knowledge on working as a team, participatory processes and principles and conflict management, needed to be developed. Members of AWGUPA also required skills in management, leadership styles and project management, and in policy formulation, advocacy and lobbying for policy change, as well as on understanding the policy-influencing process itself (of which they were a part). In addition to the MPAP framework, further tailor-made training on these issues has been organized.

The process is dependent on both individual and institutional interests and commitment. It is difficult to differentiate the level of participation as arising from individual versus institutional interest and commitment. Motivation is key for the members who are overburdened with other institutional responsibilities. Some persons expect monetary benefits, especially when they are not yet convinced of the benefit of the process to their own work. Also, members are more committed if they are assessed on their performance in the MPAP as part of their institutional performance assessment criteria.

The implementation of the MPAP requires an anchor institution to spearhead the process, and a facilitator within that institution to get and keep things moving. In Accra, despite the inputs provided by a number of institutions, no institute took up this function until 2008 when IWMI handed the facilitative role to the AMA-MoFA. One reason is that members of AWGUPA were afraid that other institutional assignments would not allow them to fully participate in the process, since representation in AWGUPA was no official task for their own institution, and thus did not relieve them of other functions.

The MPAP approach can be used to affect a paradigm shift in the thinking and planning of agricultural development in the city. However, to ensure that the participatory decision-making process and policy formulation is widely understood, accepted and integrated, there is a need for steady and progressive institutional changes and adaptations, which modify attitudes, institutional structures and organizational behaviour.

References

Accra Metropolitan Assembly (AMA) (2000) *Accra Metropolitan Assembly Report*.

Accra Working Group on Urban and Peri-urban Agriculture (AWGUPA) (2006) *Strategic Action Plan for Urban Agriculture in Accra*, IWMI-RUAF, Accra.

Adzorkor Doku, E. (ed.) (2008) *A Strategic Agenda for Urban and Peri-urban Agriculture in Accra, Ghana*, IWMI-RUAF, Accra.

Cofie, O. Larbi, T., Danso, G., Abraham, E., Kufogbe, S.K., Henseler, M., Schuetz, T., and Obiri-Opareh, N.A. (2005) *Narrative on Urban Agriculture in Accra Metropolis*, Accra RUAF Programme, IWMI, Accra.

Obuobie, E., Keraita, B., Danso, G., Amoah, P., Cofie. O., Rashid-Sally, L., and Drechsel, P. (2006) *Irrigated Urban Vegetable Production in Ghana: Characteristics, benefits and risks*, IWMI-RUAF-CPWF, Accra.

Networking for policy change in Beijing, China

Cai Jianming

Introduction

Beijing lies in the northern tip of the North China Plain and has a moderate continental climate with average annual rainfall of about 500 mm. It covers an area of 16,808 km² and has a permanent population of 16.95 million in 2008 (Beijing Statistics Yearbook 2009). Metropolitan Beijing has experienced rapid economic growth during 2005–2008 averaging 15.05 per cent per annum (Beijing Statistical Yearbook 2006, 2009). The rapid urban growth (2.82 per cent annually during 2005–2008) has brought along some new challenges: a sharply increasing disparity between urban and rural incomes (now 3:1), a vast inflow of migrants (it is estimated that there are some 4 million migrants in addition to the registered population), rapid loss of farmland and a quick deterioration of the urban environment. Currently, Beijing faces a shortage of arable land and a shortage of water.

To help cope with these problems and to make the city more liveable and sustainable, the Beijing government – in cooperation with other stakeholders – is actively promoting the development of agriculture in the peri-urban zones of Beijing as part of the national 'Reconstruction of the Countryside' policy.

This takes place along two major lines: modernization of agriculture and the development of multi-functional agriculture. The modernization policy seeks to promote the intensification of agricultural production (using greenhouses, irrigation and improved technology) and diversification from grains to vegetables, herbs, animal products, flowers and horticulture.

Credit: Lu Mingwei / IGSNRR

The Beijing Government is actively promoting peri-urban agriculture

Various types of capital-intensive agriculture are being stimulated.

The multi-functionality policy seeks to enhance the multiple roles of urban and peri-urban agriculture, by combining agricultural production with other functions of urban- and peri-urban agriculture such as social inclusion of migrant farmers by employment creation in peri-urban horticulture, ecological improvement through stimulation of agro-forestry (wind breaks, dust and CO_2 capture, land and water management), and local economic development by exploring agro-tourism and other services to urban citizens by the peri-urban villages.

Beijing urban residents experience farming in Crab Island agro-tourism park, Chaoyang, Beijing

A key element in the city's efforts to develop peri-urban agriculture is the '2-2-1 Action Programme on Urban Agriculture', a comprehensive programme that was initiated by the Beijing municipal government in April 2004 (http://www.agri.ac.cn/JingJiaoDT/Zonghe/200501/1552.html). Based on this programme, a number of specific policies were issued by the municipal and district governments of Beijing, including a zoning plan indicating the desired type(s) of agricultural activities in each of the peri-urban regions, regulations to protect ecologically sensitive areas, support to capital-intensive agriculture, provision of credit to farmers, encouragement of the development of cooperatives, and improved support to farmers (through, for example, extension, improved seeds, branding, marketing and certification).

Grape harvest festival in Daxing district, Beijing

Due to the implementation of these policies, Beijing has experienced a fast growth and rapid change in its urban agriculture development. Farmers' income has more than doubled (2.67 times) in the last 10 years from 1998 to 2008 (Beijing Statistical Yearbook 2009). The RUAF supported Multi-stakeholder Action Planning and Policy influencing process played a big role in the above described process, which involves a wide spectrum of stakeholders. RUAF supported this process in four districts of Beijing, but with strong linkages with – and effects on – the metropolitan level.

Box 3.3 Agro-tourism

In the late 1990s, some local governments realized the potential of traditional harvest festivals, such as the Watermelon Festival in Daxing and Peach Festival in Pinggu, to attract many visitors and stimulate agro-tourism. After 2002, with strong support from governments, local farmers were supported more intensively to develop (profitable) recreational opportunities for urban citizens such as fishing, sightseeing, 'pick your own fruits', meal preparation and lodging facilities. By 2007, some 1,032 agro-tourism parks and 630 agro-tourism villages had been developed, of which 65 were high-level resorts. Altogether, these parks and resorts received over 26 million guests in 2007, and earned a total gross income of RMB 1.8 billion (investigation data by Beijing Agro-tourism Association in 2008). The prospects for further development of recreational agriculture in Beijing are promising since the income and leisure time of the urban population is growing alongside an interest in outdoor recreation and the environment.

The MPAP process

As indicated above, in the political context of China it is not straightforward to bring various stakeholders together in one platform and to jointly develop a City Strategic Agenda related to peri-urban agriculture, as was taking place in other cities.

After a stakeholder analysis, the Institute of Geographical Sciences & Natural Resources Research (IGSNRR), which is part of the Chinese Academy of Sciences, organized a working group on urban agriculture in 2005 that involved, next to IGSNRR, the following key institutes: Beijing Rural Economic Research Centre, which is a think tank to the municipal agricultural commission, Beijing Agriculture College, China Agriculture University, the Agricultural Promotion (extension) departments of Huairou and Chaoyang Districts, the Beijing Green Vegetable and Fruit Cooperative, and town officials from Chaoyang and Shunyi districts responsible for the improvement of livelihood of migrants farmers in the area.

The working group conducted a series of surveys and analysis to develop potential development strategies for urban agriculture in Beijing, and assisted different levels of government (municipal, district, and village level) in identifying important issues, formulating policy suggestions, assisting in zonification and the development of concrete projects with urban producers' groups.

Due to the existing political context and the need to show the potentials of urban agriculture in practice in order to be able to convince high-level policy makers, the emphasis was put on practical pilots and 'learning by doing' in four districts of Beijing which were chosen for their differences in location and physio-geographic condition.

In Beizhai, which is part of the Huairou District of Beijing, farmer-based agro-ecotourism has been supported, with the aim to improve the public's awareness and perception of urban agriculture and thereby further enhance its development. A comprehensive master plan for Beizhai village has been developed in a participatory manner, based on the MPAP process, which included various stakeholders, like local villagers, village committees, the township government, municipal authorities, academic institutions and tourism organizations.

In addition, attention has been given to the situation of migrant farmers in Beijing. Three villages located in the Chaoyang and Shunyi Districts of Beijing were selected as study sites. The main constraints facing migrant farmers were identified and policy proposals were developed.

Farmer-led cooperative development was addressed by RUAF in supporting the Huairou Green Vegetable and Fruit Cooperative. This

Credit: IGSNRR

Farmer-led cooperative development is supported

cooperative started in 2004 and now consists of 1,108 household members distributed over nine townships. RUAF assisted the Cooperative to strengthen its internal structure, to diversify into mushroom production, introduce innovative water-saving techniques and to develop market chains for organic products.

In Shunyi, IGSNRR/China and a local NGO, Shunyi Sannong Association, established a platform for policy makers, farmers and researchers, which supports local farmers and informs researchers and policy makers and the wider public about current and future issues related to peri-urban agriculture.

In addition, the working group assisted in the development of a series of standard quality criteria for the classification of agro-tourism parks and villages and the creation of demonstration zones on urban agriculture next to the main highways of Beijing.

Next to the working group, a Beijing level informal network (the multi-stakeholder forum (MSF)) was also initiated, bringing together different actors involved in peri-urban agricultural development, such as farmers, entrepreneurs, farm-cooperatives, universities, research institutes and government departments. The MSF, other than in the other RUAF supported cities, rarely met in plenary and did not jointly develop a City Strategic Agenda on urban agriculture. Rather, the partners in the RUAF working group kept the participating institutions informed and visited them regularly. In this way the exchange between the stakeholders was realized and shared views were developed even though these were not formally expressed in larger meetings.

In this way the informal MSF network was very important in facilitating information exchange and dialogue between the various stakeholders and influencing policy development.

The RUAF working group, together with the MSF network partners, supported the enhancement and integration of urban agriculture (especially its multi-functional form) in the peri-urban planning of Beijing and in the national 5 year plan. The informal RUAF platform was able to make suggestions for policies and to persuade the Beijing government and several district governments, such as in Huairou, Chaoyang and Shunyi districts, to support peri-urban multi-functional agriculture and to adopt a number of basic principles for the development of peri-urban agriculture, as is reflected in the new policy of Beijing regarding the development of its peri-urban areas. These include the following directives:

- The development of urban agriculture in each district or county should comply with the requirements of the Beijing municipal master plan and related zonification (indicating the preferred types of agriculture according to the ecological characteristics of each region).
- Agricultural production is more closely linked to (regional, national and international) market demand and diversification and modernization of production systems.
- Resources, particularly land and water, are more efficiently used and better managed.
- Agricultural production is integrated with ecological and social services and multi-functional urban agriculture, particularly agro-tourism, is stimulated.
- A major role is given to farmer cooperatives in the development of peri-urban agriculture in Beijing.
- Cooperation (between departments; public–private; between different levels) is stimulated and diversity allowed at different levels (village, district and city).

Results and outcomes

Policy awareness on the importance of – and need for support to – peri-urban agriculture has been enhanced.

The '2-2-1' programme that was established for promoting urban agricultural development in Beijing, and which was supported by IGSNRR/China in design and implementation, has been institutionalized as a regular department called the Beijing New Countryside Development Office.

The investment of the Beijing Government in peri-urban agriculture has substantially increased over the past four years (2.26 times from 2005 to 2008, Beijing Statistical Yearbook 2009). RUAF activities in Beijing have contributed to the introduction and further operationalization of the new national 'New Countryside' policy. Since the municipalities (either on provincial level or district level) are the main driving forces for planning and investment in the peri-urban areas, the RUAF focus on peri-urban producers fitted in well, and the application of the MPAP approach introduced a form of coordinated inter-institutional planning that is quite rare in China. RUAF introduced and further stimulated new development models, like small farmer – and community-based – agro-tourism (in contrast to the very large-scale enterprise-based agro-parks) and the stimulation of farmer-led cooperatives for intensive market-oriented horticulture and/or agro-tourism (as an alternative to the former state-led cooperatives). RUAF activities have also stimulated the development of a new zoning plan for peri-urban Beijing, including various types of urban agriculture, and contributions to the further development of the 'new countryside reconstruction' policies of the Beijing Agricultural Bureau.

The Huairou Green Vegetable and Fruit Cooperative is now relatively successful in terms of its income (as compared to similar cooperatives). RUAF encouraged the cooperative to orient their production more to market demand and to diversify its activities. Huairou district government has been convinced that mushrooms can be a promising product in the Beijing market and in 2008 designated mushrooms as one of the future pillar agro-products for the district and has put a mushroom-growing stimulation policy in place.

Mushroom production in a greenhouse (Beijing, China)

RUAF activities also have led to more attention for the important role of migrants in food production for Beijing and the need for more social and technical support for the more than 300,000 migrants working as small-scale vegetable producers in the peri-urban areas (these migrants have no working and residence permit and thus lack access to health, education and technical support services).

A national network (the Chinese Urban Agriculture Association) was established in 2006 with the help of IGSNRR/RUAF and acts as the national platform for exchange of experiences among Chinese cities (currently over 20 large cities are participating), universities and national agencies (like the Ministry of Agriculture and Ministry of Sciences and Technologies) that are actively promoting urban and peri-urban agriculture. This network on peri-urban agriculture has been established in Beijing, enables frequent communications between urban agriculture practitioners, policy makers and researchers via personal contacts, periodic meetings and workshops. The network is expanding to other cities including Shanghai, Chengdu, Nanjing, Wuhan, Tianjin, Harbin, Zhengzhou, Lijiang and many more.

More attention is now given to the important role of migrants in food production

With support from the national network, a new Department of Recreational Agriculture under the Ministry of Agriculture was set up in 2007, which will be the main policy making and regulating unit regarding urban agricultural development in China, including funding support for many related projects.

Based on the experiences gained in the '2-2-1' programme the Beijing Agricultural Bureau, supported by RUAF (through its regional partner IGSNRR) and the Beijing Agro-Tourism Association, drafted the Beijing Urban Agriculture Policy Guidelines, which were recently submitted for approval as a municipal bye-law (some of the contents can be reviewed from the website at http://news.sohu.com/20100127/n269858548.shtml). These guidelines contain the views of the Beijing municipal government on the comprehensive development of agriculture in the peri-urban areas of Beijing, addressing its multi-functional character.

As the 11th five-year plan is approaching its end, the RUAF–China network is now seeking to influence the 12th five-year plan (2011–2015). This five-year plan will see a much more integrated development of urban and rural areas, in which urban and peri-urban agriculture will be an important strategy.

Lessons learned

The MPAP proved to be a useful approach for the promotion of urban agriculture development, since it facilitates the expression of different viewpoints and opportunities by the different stakeholders and consensus building towards decision-making. Moreover, every stakeholder has the responsibility to make a contribution in this policy-influencing process by elaborating the same issues from their specific perspective, even if this collaboration may not lead to an official agreement. This process is very important in allowing experimentation in a strictly planned economy.

As a new approach in China, the MPAP basically remained informal and in most cases was restricted to a series of bilateral discussions between institutions involved in the MSF network, because this was the preferred style of operation and because it proved to be effective in reaching consensus. IGSNRR/RUAF subsequently disseminated these agreements to the larger group of stakeholders in the informal network. In this way, innovation and experimentation was made possible while staying aligned with official city planning and the city strategic vision of official city development policies.

The role of the working group was essential in bringing together active partners that adapt, facilitate and promote urban agriculture. In this sense, the cooperation between IGSNRR and the Beijing Rural Economic Research Centre as well as between universities such as China Agriculture University and Beijing Agriculture College was important for the success of RUAF-China. There is, however, a need for better process documentation and information exchange with similar processes.

The MPAP can be time-consuming and as the country is experiencing a fast growth and rapid transition, most local governments lack the patience to go through this process, and tend to support arguments in favour of quick decisions. Changes can take place overnight, therefore practical decisions need to be made based on 'learning by doing' and the link to practical pilot projects is therefore paramount.

More research is needed on the impacts of urban agriculture and its development needs to be more closely monitored. This information is key for decision-making at higher levels.

The organization of urban producers (including migrants) in farmer-led agro-enterprises and cooperatives and their involvement in the MPAP process at local levels needs to be stimulated, so that these organizations can influence policy making. This voice has been relatively weak in the MPAP process in the country so far. Moreover, such organizations can play a key role in the development of sustainable multi-functional peri-urban agriculture in China.

Selected publications

Beijing Municipal Bureau of Statistics & Beijing General Team of Investigation under the National Bureau of Statistics (2006, 2009) *Beijing Statistical Yearbook*, Beijing, China Statistics Press.

Cai, J., Liu, S., Yang, Z., Yuan, H. and Fang, J. (2006) 'The Beijing Urban Agriculture Policy Guidelines: A milestone', *Urban Agriculture Magazine* 16: 32–4.

Fang, J., Yuan, H., Liu, S. and Cai, J. (2006) 'Multi-functional agrotourism in Beijing', *Urban Agriculture Magazine* 15: 14–15.

Feifei, Z., Wang, G. and Cai, J. (2007) 'Different types of agricultural cooperatives with peri-urban farmers in China: two cases', *Urban Agriculture Magazine* 17: 35–7.

Feifei, Z., Cai, J. and Liu, G. (2007) 'Emerging migrant farmer communities in peri-urban Beijing', *Urban Agriculture Magazine* 18: 25–6.

Feifei, Z., Cai, J. and Wenhua. J. (2007) 'Innovations in greenhouse rainwater harvesting system in Beijing, China', *Urban Agriculture Magazine* 19: 20–21.

Guo, H. (ed.) (2006) *Theory and Practice of Agro-tourism & Rural Tourism*, China University of Mining & Technology Press, Xuzhou.

Qi, R., Guo, H. (2006) *Development of Agro-tourism*, China Tourism Press.

Wenhua, J. and Cai, J. (2008) 'Adapting to water scarcity: Improving water sources and use in urban agriculture in Beijing', *Urban Agriculture Magazine* 20: 11–13.

Joint action planning on urban agriculture in Bulawayo, Zimbabwe

Takawira Mubvami and Percy Toriro

'Key stakeholders have met for the first time, who realized that urban agriculture plays a critical role in food security for the urban poor and in local economic development' (J. J. Ndebele, Head of Town Planning and Local Development Control, Bulawayo City Council).

Introduction

Bulawayo is the second largest city in Zimbabwe with an estimated population of 2 million people. Located in the southwest of the country, Bulawayo is the hub of the Matabeleland

region. The region receives relatively little rainfall. Once Zimbabwe's industrial hub, the city has lost most of its major industries, through outright closure or relocation to the capital city, Harare. Bulawayo receives less than 800 mm of rainfall per year in the summer season (from November to March). Maintaining a sufficient water supply has always been a challenge. The city's supply dams rarely fill up and water levels go down during the dry season, making them insufficient to meet demand.

Poverty levels in Bulawayo have increased as a result of the recent political and economic crisis, resulting in high unemployment (estimated at 80 per cent) and a high poverty level (around 60 per cent of the population is under the poverty line). Urban agriculture has become an important activity for many people in Bulawayo. Those engaged in urban agriculture seek to supplement their meagre incomes and/or to produce for their own consumption.

Credit: MDPESA

Urban agriculture has become an important activity for the poor in Bulawayo

Since 1996 the city council has recognized the importance of urban farming and is seeking

to increase the area under urban agriculture activities and the intensity of production per given area in a manner that will not harm the environment. Policy guidelines were adopted in 2000, which aim to identify suitable land and allocate it to disadvantaged households (i.e. women heading a household, elderly people without a pension and unemployed youth), to promote the productive use of (treated) wastewater and to support urban producers with proper extension services and financing. However, up to 2005, only a few activities had been implemented (other than allotting the Gum Plantation, see below). Various reasons were identified, including the lack of coordination, the fact that urban agriculture had no specific institutional home and the lack of involvement of the producers and civic society organizations in policy design and implementation. With the assistance of RUAF through its regional partner, MDP, this situation changed drastically from 2005 onwards.

The MPAP process

The MPAP process in Bulawayo is led by a core team consisting of some municipal departments (Health; Town Planning; Housing and Social Welfare), a number of NGOs (SNV; World Vision), the Environmental Management Agency (a government department), the national agricultural extension service (AGRITEX), the national Department of Physical Planning, the Zimbabwe Open University of Bulawayo, farmer representatives and Agribank. The core team, led by the Chief Town Planner of Bulawayo City Council, guided the implementation of the MPAP process, which started in April 2005 with a visit of the core team to urban agriculture sites in Bulawayo.

The first urban agriculture stakeholder forum in September 2005 was attended by over 50 representatives of various stakeholder groups, including local and central government officials, NGOs, farmers' associations, researchers and members of the business community. The Forum agreed to guide the further development and implementation of a City Strategic Agenda on urban agriculture. It was also agreed that the forum would report to the Council committee on Town Lands and Planning, and that the forum would be chaired by a councillor from this committee.

The forum created a number of sub-committees to study the actual situation in the city regarding urban agriculture (where are the urban producers located? What are their main problems and constraints? What can be practically done to improve production?). Also, a review of the actual policy on urban agriculture was made and the reasons why it was not implemented were analysed.

Based on the situation analysis, the following priority issues were identified by the multi-stakeholder forum as the main areas for action in the City Strategic Agenda on urban agriculture:

- the identification of peri-urban land on the edge of the city for (permanent) use in urban agriculture. The land is to be demarcated into 200 m² plots for use by poor urban households;
- in relation to the above: the resuscitation of derelict boreholes in the city. Tens of boreholes were once drilled as part of a drought disaster management programme, but are now all out of order;
- the development of training materials and provision of technical assistance to the urban producers;

Working groups focused on each of the key issues related to urban agriculture

Credit: MDPESA

- strengthening the organization of the producers and the management of the community garden at Gum Plantation and improvement of the infrastructure and production practices. The Gum Plantation is a municipal land area of around 450 ha that had been allotted in small plots to poor urban households in 1998, where the municipality started to provide treated wastewater for irrigation. However, the allotment was hardly organized, production methods rather rustic and one-sided and the provision of wastewater was erratic and inefficient;
- the revision of urban agriculture related bye-laws;
- provision of support to the small-scale urban producers to diversify their production and to market their produce;
- the identification of sources of funding for the implementation of the prioritized activities.

The multi-stakeholder forum created new working groups to work on each of the key issues identified related to urban agriculture development, and to make recommendations to the forum regarding actions to be included in the Bulawayo Strategic Agenda on urban agriculture.

The Bulawayo City Strategic Agenda on urban agriculture (CSAU) was accepted by the forum in 2007 (Bulawayo Core Team, 2007). The central aim of the CSAU is the development of urban agriculture that is vibrant, diversified and environmentally sustainable for subsistence and commercial purposes.

The City Strategic Agenda

The various organizations participating in the forum individually or in sub-groups developed specific projects and other actions to implement the City Strategic Agenda, including the following:

The municipal policy on urban agriculture in Bulawayo was revised and officially adopted by the Council in December 2007. Various stakeholders participated in the revision of the policy and its approval, which facilitated the involvement of these actors in the implementation of the policy.

- Municipal bye-laws related to urban agriculture have been revised and are awaiting final approval by the city council. The urban producers actively participate in the revision of the bye-laws, which enhances their acceptance by the direct stakeholders.
- The national agricultural extension organization AGRITEX, which until 2005 did not give much attention to urban agriculture, made extension staff available for training of urban producers in appropriate methods of mushroom production, horticulture and poultry keeping and continues to contribute to capacity development for urban producers. Training packages were developed in conjunction with the Khami School Leavers Training Centre in Bulawayo and the Open University of Zimbabwe differentiating between the resource-

poor urban producers (mainly operating small plots in home- and community gardens) and those who have more resources (e.g. owners of a well).

- Being members of the forum and actively involved in the multi-stakeholder planning process, various NGOs became active in Bulawayo and have started urban agriculture projects (using their own resources). For example, World Vision has drilled about 22 boreholes in the low-income residential areas, around which new allotment gardens were organized for poor urban households and SNV has played a critical role in the strengthening of farmer organization and management in the Gum Plantation by organizing training for farmer leaders and assisting in the organization of the Gum Plantation Management Committee. The Institute of Water and Sanitation Development carried out research and provided training regarding the safe reuse of treated wastewater. MDP supported the participatory design and implementation of diversification and marketing projects (new horticulture crops, herbs, mushrooms, beekeeping, and poultry).

Results and outcomes

An Urban Agriculture Unit within the Town Planning Section of the Engineering Department was established, creating an institutional home for urban agriculture within the municipality. The two staff of the unit play an important facilitating role and enable effective coordination between the various municipal departments as well as between municipality and other organizations involved in urban agriculture in the city (e.g. NGOs, AGRITEX, urban producer groups).

The 2000 policy has been revised. The policy now distinguishes and encourages both 'off-plot' (in open fields) and 'on-plot' agriculture (around the house) and promotes safe use of wastewater, water-efficient use of wells and water harvesting for urban agriculture (both gardening and aquaculture). Also, new bye-laws on sustainable crop cultivation and livestock practices have been defined whereby earlier prohibitive measures, where possible, were replaced by measures that allow urban agriculture under the condition of sustainable resource use. For example, legislation used to prohibit planting within 30 m of a stream in order to protect watercourses from pollution by agrochemicals and prevent soil erosion. Now, cultivation of crops within 30 m of streams is allowed under the condition that ecological production practices and adequate soil and water management practices are applied. Also, the regulations regarding the keeping of small livestock within the city have been revised, removing unnecessary restrictions and adding supportive actions.Urban agriculture has also been integrated within the Bulawayo Master Plan 2006–2015, which marks its recognition as a permanent land use. The establishment of the multi-stakeholder forum and the joint formulation of the City Strategic Agenda on urban agriculture enabled the shift from a well intended, but not implemented, 2000 policy on urban agriculture, to a new situation in which both governmental and several non-governmental organizations became actively involved and used their own resources to put the policy into practice (whilst further improving it). Next to the organizations already mentioned (like SNV, World Vision and AGRITEX) new organizations have now also been attracted (such as OXFAM-UK and Action Aid) due to the clear agenda and dynamism generated by the multi-stakeholder forum and the coordination it provides. Also, the municipality now included urban agriculture in its annual budget (which was not the case in earlier years, despite the adoption of the 2000 urban agriculture policy).

Access to land and water for food production has improved

As a result, the projects that could be implemented have yielded important results. Access to land and water for food production by poor urban households has been further improved. In total 31 irrigated community gardens are functioning now in Bulawayo of which nine are directly supported by the Social Services Office of the Department of Housing and Community Services, totalling 25 ha, where over 5,000 households grow vegetables predominantly for domestic consumption and 22 are supported by World Vision (18 ha 1,500 households).

Credit: MDPESA

These households gained access to municipal land, were given access to water (through the establishment of boreholes) and were provided with basic training in horticulture, water management, nutrition and organization of the garden.

The organization of the urban producers (1,100 households) at Gum Plantation has been strengthened and their level of participation in decision-making has improved. The farmers are now also represented in the forum.

Over 600 households at the Gum Plantation substantially improved their access to irrigation water tanks to improvement of the infrastructure related to the provision of treated wastewater and related training, enabling year-round production of vegetables and a substantial increase in production and food security.

They also diversified their production; 170 households have shifted to organic gardening methods and have started marketing organic vegetables, raising their income by about 50 per cent. Twenty farmers have started beekeeping as a way of diversifying their activities. Another 20 farmers have initiated mushroom production, while again another 25 farmers have initiated the production and marketing of herbs, raising their income by 50 per cent or more.

The experiences gained in Bulawayo have also attracted the attention of policy makers at a national level, leading to a request to MDP/RUAF to assist in the organization of a national policy seminar on urban agriculture on this issue. The Ministry of Agriculture has established a working committee, involving MDP/RUAF and members of the Harare forum on urban agriculture, to develop a national policy on urban agriculture. Further, AGRITEX (the national agricultural extension agency) has appointed a coordinator on urban agriculture and trained its staff in urban agriculture with the support of MDP/RUAF. Also, the Ministry of Local Governments is supportive.

A memorandum of understanding is to be signed by mid-2010 between Bulawayo City Council and Johannesburg Metropolitan Municipality to formally agree on a partnership on urban agriculture.

Lessons learned

The MPAP process is a tool that is convincing to policy makers. Multi-stakeholder processes were not entirely new to them, but the packaging (specifically for urban agriculture and with clear links to pertinent urban issues) and the process and methodologies used by RUAF have made it easy to convince the authorities and other stakeholders of the need to jointly define and implement a Strategic Agenda on Urban Agriculture.

What turned out to be of specific importance is that RUAF showed how urban agriculture could contribute to the policy priorities defined by the Council itself (food security, local economic development and reuse of wastewater). It also proved important to agree on a clear process for design, approval and implementation, with the multi-stakeholder forum reporting directly to a municipal planning committee, which in turn reports to the full municipal council.

Learning from the experiences gained in other cities is a very effective way to inform policy makers. The Urban Agriculture Policy and Legislation Seminar, held in November 2005, was successful because of the presentation of experiences from other cities in Zimbabwe and beyond (Cape Town, Lusaka, Maputo and others). Various participants highlighted that they had learned, and even those participants who were doing well admitted to having learned new issues from other cities' or countries' experiences.

The earlier 2000 policy had been largely crafted by only a small committee within the city council, which was one of the main reasons for the limited degree of implementation of the 2000 policy. Central to the MPAP process was the promotion of a wider dialogue on urban agriculture policy formulation and action planning. The broad-based participation of a wide array of urban agriculture stakeholders in the development of the Strategic City Agenda on Urban Agriculture, the revised policy and the new bye-laws on urban agriculture have been crucial for the success of the new policy. Moreover, the participation of urban producers and civil society organizations as well of national departments, has laid the basis for an effective implementation of the policy through the design and implementation of urban agriculture projects and the mobilization of resources from/by various actors.

References

Bulawayo City Council (2000) *Summary of Draft Report on Urban Agriculture in Bulawayo – Issues and an Inception of Policy Guidelines for its Sustainable Development*

Bulawayo Core Team (2006) *Urban Agriculture Baseline Survey for Bulawayo City Council*, MDP/RUAF, Institute for Water and Sanitation Development, Bulawayo.

Bulawayo Core Team (2007) *Bulawayo Urban Agriculture Policy Narrative*, MDP/ RUAF, Harare.

Bulawayo Core Team (2007) *Urban Agriculture Strategic Agenda for the city of Bulawayo*, MDP/RUAF, Harare.

Steering committee of the Bulawayo Urban Agriculture Multi-Stakeholder Forum (2007) *Urban Agriculture Policy for the City of Bulawayo*, MDP/RUAF, Bulawayo City Council, Harare.

From rehabilitation to development in Freetown, Sierra Leone

Olufunke Cofie, Marco Serena and Theophilus Otchere-Larbi

'By 2011, urban and peri-urban agriculture in Freetown will be recognized as significantly contributing to the achievement of urban food security, reducing urban poverty, and its activities well integrated into the municipal planning process for a vibrant, clean, green and beautiful city' (FUPAP, 2008).

Introduction

Sierra Leone experienced a civil conflict between 1991 and 2002, as a result of which many persons fled to the Greater Freetown Area (GFA). During and after this unfortunate period, urban agriculture became an important livelihood strategy. It is increasingly being recognized as a reliable coping mechanism for redressing food shortages and gaining income and employment.

The Greater Freetown Area covers about 8,100 ha, and it is estimated that up to one quarter of the country's population, around 1 million people, reside in Freetown (Government of Sierra Leone, 2006). Sierra Leone is one of the poorest countries in the world. GFA's population increased by 65 per cent between 1985 and 2004 with more women than men, particularly in the active age group of 15 to 64 years (a similar gender pattern is observed in the labour force). Unemployment in GFA (about 52 per cent) is below the national average of 66 per cent, particularly among the youth. Net migration for GFA declined in 2004 (about 47 per cent) (Government of Sierra Leone, 2006).

Despite abundant natural resources and the favourable agricultural climate, the country's economy went through a decline since the early 1980s, attributed to a variety of factors, foremost of which is the recently concluded decade-long civil war (1991–2002). More than 2 million people were displaced, and major activities, such as farming, mining, and forestry, were disrupted. Also, people flooded into Freetown. After the war, a significant number of persons displaced from the rural areas preferred to permanently stay in the city in the expectation of finding a job and better living conditions. The increased urban population created high demand for food and put pressure on urban facilities and services.

Signing the City Strategic Agenda in Freetown

Many urban poor, including migrants and internally displaced persons, and many youngsters and women, developed a keen interest in urban agriculture as an option for ensuring a food supply. They took up the cultivation of leafy vegetables and, within and near Freetown, the processing and marketing thereof. This involved: packaging vegetables; preparing fast food; transport; and retailing. These factors contributed to a significant expansion of urban and peri-urban agriculture as an essential coping strategy for providing a vital supply of food to the expanding urban population.

Urban agriculture is widespread in Freetown; agricultural activities have been identified in all eight administrative zones. Most agricultural activities are observed in the Western Area and Eastern Area of the city. Agriculture is also widely practised in peri-urban areas, in combination with forestry

Urban agriculture is widespread in Freetown

activities on the verge of the peninsula forest and in larger plots towards the periphery of GFA.

The most commonly cultivated crops are exotic vegetables (cabbage, lettuce, carrots, spring onions, tomatoes, beans, etc.) and local vegetables (potato leaves, spinach, cassava leaves, etc.) and different sorts of fruits. These are consumed on a daily basis and as perishables, cannot withstand long-haul transportation. They are usually harvested and sold at the market on the same day. Poultry (mainly free range) and pigs are the main types of animals raised. Processing and marketing are marginal activities, but these are also growing and are stimulated under present agricultural policies. Most urban producers sell a large part of their produce in order to generate a basic income. Urban and peri-urban agriculture contributes substantially to the local economic development of Freetown and the country as a whole. In the situation analysis undertaken in 2007 (Cofie and Larbi, 2007), it was estimated that urban agriculture provides full or part-time employment to over 1,800 people in urban Freetown. Women constitute approximately 80 per cent of the urban producers and they also do most of the marketing. Men provide assistance mainly in the preparation of land, such as initial land clearing, building the irrigation channels in the swampy areas, and supplying the money needed to buy inputs. A significant proportion of male urban producers are also engaged in other activities, such as working in the civil service or the artisan sector. A portion of the income generated from these other livelihood activities is often re-invested in the agricultural activities.

Urban agriculture is situated in private (e.g. residential) and public or institutional lands, often with complex land tenure arrangements. Most institutional lands are leased, while private and public open space lands are seasonally rented. Land is a primary constraint, agricultural land use being in competition with housing, commercial and industrial land uses. Use of external inputs, like fertilizers, is generally low, and animal manure (from piggeries and poultry units) is mainly applied. Rainwater, streams, pipe-borne water, household wastewater and groundwater are common sources of water in crop and livestock activities. Apart from rainwater, most water sources are contaminated by human and animal excreta, as well as by domestic and industrial effluents. A number of institutions, such as the Ministry of Agriculture, Forestry and Food Security (MAFFS), the National Association of Farmers of Sierra Leone (NAFSL) and Freetown City Council (FCC) provide agricultural extension services (mainly on crops) to farmers. Almost all urban farmers belong to a farmers' association or a community-based organization, except those individuals who farm the backyards of their homes.

Next to land, another major constraint is pests and diseases. Thieves are also a problem. Further, the high price of seeds, and the shortage of water and animal feed, are constraints to urban farming. These constraints are less important as we move from the centre to the periphery of GFA, while marketing becomes more of a constraint for farmers located further away from the centre. Urban farmers in Freetown are often in competition with importers of vegetables and animal products (Cornell University and NUC, 2006; Winnebah and Cofie, 2007) hence they require capacity strengthening in critical aspects of urban agricultural production and marketing.

The MPAP process

In 2006, RUAF partner IWMI launched the 'Freetown Urban and Peri-Urban Agriculture Project' (FUPAP) in Freetown, Sierra Leone, with the goal to support city authorities in recognizing the benefits of urban agriculture, while addressing its challenges in order to contribute to urban poverty reduction, food security and improved urban environmental management. The multi-faceted nature of urban and peri-urban agriculture in Freetown, and the many ongoing activities which are not interlinked, called for a multi-stakeholder intervention.

The launching of FUPAP

The MPAP approach brought together major stakeholders in urban agriculture for joint situation analysis, decision-making, planning and implementation of related projects in Freetown. The FUPAP core team was constituted in 2006. MAFFS chaired FUPAP, and additional facilitation was provided by Njala University. Other institutions that participated in the FUPAP multi-stakeholder team were: FCC, NAFSL, the Department for Environmental Health, the Commission for Environment and Forestry, Western Area (Rural) Council, Waterloo, LEXES, Care, World Vision and Ministry of Lands and Country Planning. Although initially part of the MPAP training, most NGOs did not participate actively in the MPAP process because they were more active in the rural provinces. Several of them joined FUPAP again later on when government and international donor attention for the process and urban agriculture grew.

The FUPAP team jointly implemented the situation analysis. The report (FUPAP, 2007b) on the situation analysis presented the presence and location of different types of urban and peri-urban agriculture in Freetown, profiled all institutional stakeholders and analysed the existing policies affecting urban agriculture. The main constraints identified in the situation analysis were: access to land and security on tenure, access to clean water for irrigation, inadequate and untimely supply of farm inputs, and limited agricultural extension services.

City Strategic Agenda

The multi-stakeholder forum on urban agriculture was established in 2006. During its first meeting the Forum discussed the findings of the situation analysis and discussed the desired development of urban agriculture in Freetown and agreed on a number of key issues for intervention.

During 2008 the FUPAP core team further developed these issues, which resulted in the Freetown City Strategic Agenda (CSA) on Urban and Peri-urban Agriculture (FUPAP, 2008). The CSA analyses the various key policy issues for the development of sustainable urban agriculture and outlines the main strategies concerning each key issue. It also includes the main actors involved and responsible for each action and the actual or potential sources of funding.

Credit: Theopilus Larbi

Farmers collaborating with FUPAP partners in the pilot project

As part of the design process, the FUPAP partners successfully implemented a pilot project on 'value addition to urban and peri-urban products towards increased marketability'. Two communities in Congo Water and in Potor Levuma participated in this project and received basic farm inputs, such as tools, fertilizers and seeds, capacity building on integrated pest management (IPM), postharvest techniques, safe handling of vegetables, and processing. Further, irrigation facilities were improved or installed, such as wells and treadle pumps.

The City Strategic Agenda for Freetown defines policy issues and strategies for seven specific areas:

- provision of adequate and reliable quality farmland for urban agriculture;
- promotion and public awareness on the contribution of urban agriculture to food security and sound environmental management;
- capacity building of farmers and farmers' associations (both human and materials);
- availability of year-round good quality irrigation water;
- value addition to products towards improving marketability;
- creation and regulation of guidelines and policies conducive for efficient, sustainable urban and peri-urban agriculture;
- strengthening extension services and M&E as a tool for efficient urban agriculture production.

The CSA was agreed by the MSF at a meeting in November 2008, and formally endorsed by the Deputy Mayor of Freetown in April 2009.

The multi-stakeholder forum, created during the FUPAP implementation, was institutional-ized in 2009 as the Freetown Urban and Peri-urban Agriculture Platform (FUPAP). The new FUPAP is chaired on a rotational basis by MAFFS, FCC and the new member, the Western Area Rural District Council (WARDC). FCC and WARDC are the two local authorities in GFA. The three rotating chairs are also members of the FUPAP Steering committee, which took over the role of the FUPAP core team. Other members of this steering group are NAFSL, The Department of Agricultural Research, Ministry of Health and Sanitation, Ministry of Lands and Country Planning, Njala University, Youth organizations, like SLYO, and the NGOs COOPI, Concern, Friends of the Earth and Heifer. The FUPAP meetings are organized every three months. A work plan has been agreed by FUPAP for the years 2009–2010. An inventory on access to land, both for GFA and Western Area is ongoing.

Results and outcomes

One of the principal outputs of the process was the agreed Five Year (2009–2013) Freetown City Strategic Agenda on urban agriculture. Several of the activities included in the CSA are actually under implementation with active support from national government and international donors. FUPAP had the merit of putting urban food production and marketing in and around Freetown, and its multiple impacts, on the agenda of local and national authorities and of international support organizations operating in Sierra Leone.

The multi-stakeholder forum on urban agriculture, in which the major institutions and NGOs participate, has played, and continues to play, an important role in the discussion of issues related to urban agriculture and the coordination of planning and implementation of actions to promote the development of safe and sustainable urban agriculture.

Partially as a consequence of this, the European Union decided to provide funding to ad-dress food security in and around Freetown and to implement important activities included in the City Strategic Agenda. A consortium made up of Italian NGO COOPI, ETC/RUAF, Sierra Leone National Association of Farmers and Sierra Leone Youth Empowerment Organization will, in coordination with other FUPAP members, implement the 4-year project (2009–2012) co-funded by the EU. The project aims to stimulate innovation in urban agriculture in GFA through support to urban subsistence farmers, emerging commercial producers and to youth interested in agricultural production, processing and marketing. A second grant was awarded by the European Commission to the Irish NGO Concern Worldwide and to the German NGO Welthunger Hilfe for similar activities that will be implemented in close cooperation with the project mentioned above and with the FUPAP.

Attention to youth involvement is very important in the development process of Sierra Leone, and urban agriculture has been recognized as a key way to provide employment for youth. Various stakeholders, coordinated under FUPAP, have started to work with groups of vulner-able youth on commercial agricultural activities in the city, including value chain analysis

Credit: René van Veenhuizen

Meeting of farmers to discuss progress in the RUAF project

and business development, group strengthening and participatory life skills training ranging from communication, leadership and decision-making to conflict management and literacy and numeracy.

As a consequence of these developments, the reconstituted FUPAP has expanded to include several other actors, mainly international and national NGOs, youth serving agencies and youth umbrellas and organizations operating in Freetown and in Western Area.

In the new 'National Sustainable Agriculture Development Plan' and the 'Sierra Leone Chapter of the Comprehensive African Agriculture Development Plan' that was signed in September 2009, sustainable urban agriculture processing and marketing are seen as key activities in Freetown and GFA.

In addition, there is interest from MAFFS and FAO to include urban agriculture as part of their strategy and to expand activities to secondary cities in Sierra Leone. This has resulted in the inclusion of urban agriculture and the MPAP approach in the national curriculum on Farmer Field Schools, which will be used to train MAFFS extension workers across the country, starting in 2010.

The EU-supported preparation of a new Freetown Master Development Plan paves the way for negotiating solutions to long-standing constraints to urban farmers, such as enhanced access to land and more security of land use, prevention of land, water and soil pollution by other urban uses and enabling the use of urban organic wastes as fertilizer in agriculture.

The mapping of vacant urban spaces suitable for urban agriculture that was undertaken by FUPAP in Freetown as part of the situation analysis (Forkuor et al., 2007) is currently expanded to the Western Area and linked to the current GIS land mapping undertaken by the Ministry of Land, which provides an opportunity to address the issue of integration of urban agriculture in the urban land zoning and the legal protection of urban agriculture sites. The FUPAP will assist in the further development of the Master plan in terms of seeking suitable areas and types of urban agriculture.

Njala University, a major agricultural training institution, and member of FUPAP, has incorporated urban and peri-urban agriculture into its curriculum. At Fourah Bay College, a research programme on urban agriculture is ongoing and the researchers have agreed to collaborate with Njala University and the relevant line ministries to promote the development of urban agriculture in Freetown.

Urban agriculture is now also seen as being fully part of the national development strategy and this opens several opportunities for urban farmers – especially for small-scale enterprises run by unemployed youth and poor women engaged in value addition and marketing of agricultural produce – including financing, technical support, research and extension services, and assistance for business planning and development.

Lessons learned

Urban agriculture in Greater Freetown has been recognized as a main source of livelihood for disadvantaged communities, and an appropriate strategy in augmenting food production not only during crisis periods, but also in the subsequent rehabilitation and local economic development. It significantly contributes to food security and employment creation, particularly for youth, which is crucial for Sierra Leone in the current development process.

Further development of urban agriculture is now on the political agenda and is seen as pivotal in the achievement of food security and income generation by the urban poor and as an important way to build resilience of the city and its inhabitants to future shocks (like the current food and economic crises).

Credit: René van Veenhuizen

Urban agriculture is recognized as a main source of livelihood (Freetown, Sierra Leone)

The multi-stakeholder process for action planning and policy development for urban agriculture has managed to include the major stakeholders. The joint situation analysis, dialogue and decision-making has greatly contributed to the clarification of the actual and potential role of urban agriculture, joint identification of key issues and coordinated planning and implementation of policies and programmes. A challenge during the initial stages of the MPAP process is to enhance the commitment of the members and to actively involve all stakeholders in the planning and implementation of the City Strategic Agenda, which requires time and regular consultations with stakeholder representatives through both formal and informal relations. The implementation of the MPAP process requires an anchor institution to spearhead the process, which in Freetown was MAFFS. Also, a committed facilitator is important; in the case of FUPAP, this role was shared initially by representatives from MAFFS and Njala University and subsequently taken on by MAFFS.

In addition, it is important to ensure funding for the activities that are agreed by the partners in the CSA. It is crucial to start implementing small activities at an early stage, mobilizing the resources from the participating actors. At a later stage, the interest and contributions by international donors (especially the EU and FAO) allowed the implementation of larger projects. But without the initial efforts by the FUPAP members based on their own resources and the efforts to integrate urban agriculture into policies at city and national level, such international funding probably would not have materialized.

As each city is unique, the development and institutionalization of urban agriculture requires that a link be made to pertinent urban policy issues. In the case of GFA, rehabilitation, food security and youth employment were and are important entry points.

References

Cofie, O. and Larbi, T. (ed.) (2007) *Exploratory Study Report on UPA in Freetown, Sierra Leone*, IWMI/RUAF Project Report.

Cornell University and Njala University College (NUC) (2006) *Food Security in Freetown: The Role of Urban and Peri-urban Agriculture*. Final Technical Report submitted to the International Development Research Centre, Ottawa.

Forkuor, G., Barber, Larbi, T. and Cofie, O. (2007) 'Freetown Land Use Mapping', in O. Cofie and T. Larbi (ed.) *Exploratory Study Report on UPA in Freetown, Sierra Leone*, IWMI/RUAF Project Report.

FUPAP (2007a) *Action Plan on Urban and Peri-urban Agriculture for Food Security, Livelihood Support and Green City*, IWMI/RUAF, Freetown.

FUPAP (2007b) *Urban Agriculture in Freetown: Status, Opportunities and Constraints, Policy Narrative*, IWMI/RUAF, Freetown.

FUPAP (2008) *Urban and Peri-urban Agriculture in Freetown: A Five Year Rolling Strategic Agenda (2009–2013)*, IWMI/RUAF, Freetown.

Government of Sierra Leone (2006) *2004 Population Census*, Statistics Sierra Leone, Freetown.

Winnebah, T.R.A. and Cofie, O. (2007) 'Urban farms after a war', in Worldwatch Institute, *State of the World: Our Urban Future*, pp. 64–5, Worldwatch Institute, Washington, D.C.

Building synergies to promote urban agriculture in Gampaha, Sri Lanka

Priyanie Amerasinghe

Introduction

The City of Gampaha is a rapidly growing city in the Western Province of Sri Lanka. It is located in Gampaha District, the second most populous district in the country, home to 12 per cent of the total population of Sri Lanka. A decade ago, the landscape of Gampaha was dominated by agriculture. With good soil conditions and a surplus of water the agricultural economy has been booming. Today much of the city area is being taken over by buildings. Rapid urbanization has posed a number of problems, including congestion, increased waste and environmental pollution, reduced drainage and increase in food prices.

Gampaha City reported a total population of over 300,000 inhabitants in 2001 (DCS, 2001), a number that has since increased. An additional 100,000 people travel daily to the city for schooling and work. Gampaha is one of the districts with the lowest poverty indicators (8.7 per cent) (DCS, 2008). However, its reduction over time is low (only 2 per cent since 2002) and is believed to be associated with rapid industrial development in the district, and rising urban poverty (Sunday Times, 2008; DCS, 2008).

Credit: IWMI India

Multi-stakeholder forum meeting in Gampaha

Agriculture in Gampaha benefits from a tropical climate with an average annual temperature of 28°C and an annual rainfall of 2,400 mm. Paddy cultivation has always taken a prominent place in and around the city, although many fields have been abandoned, due to high input costs and lack of labour. In order to safeguard the country's food security, however, the national government has prohibited the sale of agricultural land for construction and has ordered, by presidential directive, the revitalization of agricultural lands back into paddy cultivation or their conversion into production of vegetables, fruits and commercial crops like manioc (Ministry of Agricultural Development and Agrarian Services, 2007). As part of the national 'grow more food campaign' (Api Wavamu Rata Nagamu) incentives are being given to farmers to take these paddy lands into cultivation again.

Since the year 2000, the Western Province Department of Agriculture has been promoting and establishing home-gardens and Family Business Gardens in Gampaha (Ranasinghe, 2009) to meet the nutritional needs of the population, to generate income for underserved communities and to contribute to the greening of the city. With the city's increased waste generation at 55 tonnes per day, the city has launched a successful recycling programme and generates compost

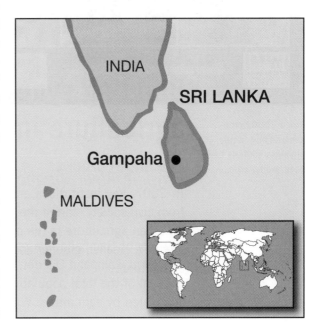

Credit: IWMI India

Since 2000 home-gardens and family business gardens have been promoted

to be used in floriculture and home gardens. Awareness and educational programmes in schools on home gardening and food security are being implemented with a view to ensuring a clean, green and food secure city for the future. School gardens are also being promoted, and serve as models to encourage students to participate in agricultural activities from a young age. It is estimated that at least 1,100 families living within the city limits are involved in home gardening, while an additional 25–30 are estimated to practise more commercial (small-scale) forms of agriculture (Personal communication, Department of Agriculture, 2009).

Urban agriculture is mentioned in three national (agricultural) policy documents, related to the establishment of city home gardens and supporting women in cities to develop capacity for such activities. In this context, several promotional activities, including awareness and training programmes, have been developed by the Department of Agriculture under different funding schemes. However, this has never been done in a comprehensive way, and many issues unique to urban agriculture have never been addressed, including the need for limited-space growing techniques, recycling of household waste and water, and disease and pest problems.

The MPAP process

In 2007, key institutions and stakeholders from the city and provincial governments and from civil society started the process of further analysis of the forms of, and actors involved in, urban agriculture in the city, with the support of IWMI/RUAF. Their overall vision was to 'create a cleaner, greener and more food secure city by promoting and strengthening urban agriculture'.

Stakeholder inventory and awareness. Given the unique requirements of city farming, the need for a multi-stakeholder approach was endorsed by the stakeholders involved (in 2007, when Gampaha city was selected as a pilot city). This was aimed especially towards strengthening multi-sectoral cohesion, avoiding duplication of activities and competition for resources, and building on the diverse capabilities of the different organizations involved. The MPAP process was introduced at a time when each of the sectors were separately discussing issues such as food security and waste management, with the health department observing nutritional disorders and disease aspects, the educational

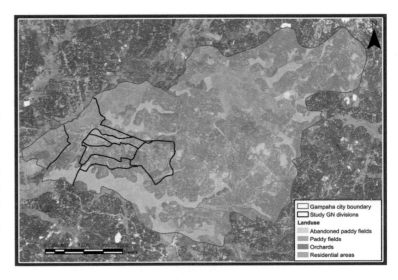

Map of Gampaha showing land-use patterns

sector thinking of how to engage youth in agriculture, the water department looking at conservation and recycling, the municipality aiming to reduce waste collection by promoting recycling of household waste and the Department of Agriculture promoting home gardens. The MPAP was the first attempt to take joint action on urban agriculture activities.

A policy awareness and partners' orientation workshop was organized in May 2007, where eight organizations agreed to collaborate on the situation analysis and suggest further action planning for urban agriculture. The representative members, forming the *Nagarika Haritha Balakaya* or 'Urban Green Force', were nominated by their respective heads of department, namely the provincial departments of Agriculture, Animal Husbandry, Health Services and

Haritha Balakaya – The Urban Green Force

Education, the central government managed department of Agrarian Development and Botanical Gardens, the Municipal Council and the city Sanasa Bank.

Identifying constraints and opportunities to urban agriculture development. The situation analysis, comprising land use mapping, participatory farming system analysis and critical policy review, was implemented in six of Gampaha's 33 GN (*Grama Niladhari*) divisions (the smallest administrative unit), namely Medagama I, II, III, IV and Bendiyamulla North and East. The analysis highlighted several constraints to further development of urban agriculture, including: inadequate capacity and knowledge

Credit: IWMI India

on appropriate urban agriculture production systems and technologies (like low-space/no-space technologies for production on very small areas of land and new production systems like floriculture and mushroom cultivation, including pests and diseases management):

- lack of good seeds and seedlings for all types of crops;
- lack of capital to start-up agricultural activities: such as cultivation material and inputs;
- low entrepreneurial skills among farmers;
- lack of proper drainage and irrigation for paddy cultivation, as Gampaha is prone to flooding;
- limited knowledge and lack of interest in recycling household waste; and
- limited knowledge on daily nutritional requirements and low cost home-grown products.

Opportunities included the availability of (abandoned areas of) land, the presence and commitment of municipal and provincial government services to support urban agriculture and the presence of a national policy framework promoting such development.

The results of this situation analysis were presented and shared with a broader audience in the form of a policy briefing document in December 2007. This laid the basis for further action planning in 2008.

Building the institutional framework. The Urban Green Force met once every month, and was chaired by the Mayor of Gampaha. This direct involvement of the Mayor and various municipal departments proved to be very beneficial, as municipal facilities and services could now be better coordinated and directly made available through the forum for the benefit of Gampaha's citizens. As a result of stakeholder analysis and awareness raising, new stakeholders became involved in the process, including NGOs, schools and private enterprises. A larger multi-stakeholder forum was set up that currently meets every three months.

In addition, a high level steering committee has been formed with the heads of the core forum member institutions, in order to assure commitment, liaise between the project activities of the different institutions, and discuss the future development and uptake of urban agriculture programmes in their respective institutions.

A City Strategic Agenda. One of the first activities of the Urban Green Force comprised the elaboration of a City Strategic Agenda on urban agriculture (City of Gampaha, 2007). Four major objectives were identified to which the Strategic Agenda should respond:

1. promote and support a culture of sustainable urban agriculture in Gampaha municipality;
2. revitalize the (abandoned) paddy farming systems and develop strategies to improve productivity with innovative farming practices that harmonize with nature and improve access to paddy lands for those who are keen on farming;

3. reduce environmental pollution and health concerns by proper management of city infrastructure for drainage; and

4. strengthen marketing of urban agriculture production – both within the city as well as outside the city.

For each of these objectives, different interventions and activities were outlined, responsibilities were clarified, and local as well as external funding sources were indicated. The agenda was formally accepted by the MSF steering committee in April 2009.

Project and policy formulation and implementation

The MSF members have actively supported project and policy formulation and implementation of the following activities mentioned in the City Strategic Agenda.

Training. The Department of Agriculture (Extension) Gampaha has trained over 30 community leaders, drawn from each of the six Divisions, in crop management and household organic waste recycling. These leaders together with agriculture extension officers supported community groups in policy implementation. The extension officers visited the participating households and farming sites regularly.

Establishment of home gardens. The multi-stakeholder forum developed the project 'Greening of Gampaha City through Urban Agriculture'. Home gardens were established in 500 households (75 low-income and 425 low- to middle-income households) in the six administrative divisions. All households (in total 2,000 persons) received training on home gardening including land preparation, use of low-space requirement technologies, planting and pest management. Extension support was provided by the Department for Agriculture Extension.

Composting at household level. In an attempt to manage the vast amounts of waste being generated in the city, the Central Environmental Authority, the Western province waste management authority and the municipality, launched a programme *Kunu Kasalata milak* or 'Money for your waste'. The programme included segregation of waste at household level, waste collection, home composting of biodegradable waste and biogas production. Over 4,000 composting bins were distributed to city homes and around 60 per cent of recipients are making compost at home now, which has

Containers and tiers are used to produce vegetables in home gardens

Credit: IWMI India

Credit: IWMI India

The programme has contributed to the city's waste management

resulted in the reduction of waste collection by nearly 10 tonnes per day.

Support services. The Department of Agriculture supported the above mentioned projects. For instance, a sales outlet for input materials was established in six of the divisions and six demonstration plots were established on municipal council sites, at the Sanasa society, at a hospital and at three schools (to showcase organic production and waste recycling methods, and advertise the above mentioned projects).

Value-chain development. Starting in 2009, the programme has expanded its focus from home gardening to other more commercial forms of urban agriculture. Market analysis has indicated the potential for commercial chilli growing. As from 2009 some 100 families have started to produce high quality green chilli (*Capsicum annuum*) variety MI2 and *Veraniya*, applying eco-friendly agricultural practices, to supply to the Gampaha vegetable market as well as to the export market. Seeds and technical advice are provided by the Department for Agriculture Extension in Gampaha. The Gampaha City Bank (Sanasa City Bank and People's Bank) provides financial advice and will grant loans to farmers. Farmers will in future be trained in technical and marketing aspects as well as supported to strengthen their recently formed business association.

Upscaling project activities to other administrative divisions and cities. The Western Province is currently funding similar home gardening and composting programmes in the 27 remaining administrative units in Gampaha city. It is expected that in total, an additional 1,600 households will benefit from this city-wide programme. Additionally, the programme will be expanded to other cities, including districts of Colombo and Kalutara.

Results and outcomes

The urban agriculture programme has contributed positively to household food security, savings and nutrition. Findings for the initial projects in the six divisions show a high percentage of women (63 per cent) engaged in kitchen garden activities. An increase in vegetable consumption has also been observed, which is linked to the increase in the number of types of vegetables grown in the gardens (from 6 to 11 types). In addition, average household savings of 15 per cent (by growing food for home consumption) have been observed, and 8 per cent of the participating households registered increases in their cash income of 1–5 per cent, through the sale of crops.

The project has also sparked off healthy social trends such as the exchange of surplus produce with neighbours and improved social interaction, all of which had been rare occurrences in the past.

Moreover, the programme has contributed to the city's waste management. Daily, 10 tonnes of waste is now being recycled in the form of compost, thereby reducing costs for waste collection for the municipality. This compost is made available to farming households through sales outlets set up in 6 of the 33 divisions. Savings are now used by the municipality for funding welfare activities, such as housing loans and educational loans. In this sense, the MPAP has enforced/improved the ongoing initiative of the different departments, by facilitating joint analysis, planning and liaising activities.

Continuation of planning and activities in Gampaha is guaranteed by the formalization of the forum and the City Strategic Agenda and the formation of the high-level steering committee. Efforts taken by the Western Province Department of Agriculture to upscale activities within Gampaha and to other cities form a good example.

Gampaha National Campaign to Motivate Domestic Food Production

The process and experiences in Gampaha have directly contributed to the promotion of urban agriculture at provincial and at national level, and has provided examples of initiatives that can be developed to increase domestic food production as promoted by the national government in its 'National Campaign to Motivate Domestic Food Production 2007–2010' (see Box 3.4).

Gampaha's experiences and results are mentioned in a cabinet paper. Both the Chief Secretary of the Western Provincial Council as well as the Presidential Task Force for Domestic Food Production, have given special recognition to the RUAF-supported Gampaha programme for its achievements and its operationalization of the national strategy on food production (personal letter to IWMI/RUAF by the Chief Secretary of the Western Provincial Council, dated April 16, 2009) and have praised the programme for providing evidence of impacts and outcomes. This recognition has been a boost to the Gampaha stakeholders, and further strengthens them in their commitment to continue better serving their city communities.

Box 3.4 Sri Lanka's National Food Security Policy

The President of Sri Lanka, Hon Mr Mahinda Rajapaksa, has launched the National Campaign to Motivate Domestic Food Production calling for the cultivation of every inch of suitable land. It is his conviction that sustainable development of the country can only be ensured through the enhancement of local food production, including urban and peri-urban agriculture. He stresses the need for reversing the trend of abandoning farmland, for modernization of agricultural practices – through applying agro-ecological production principles and through collaboration between all government sectors, civil society organizations and communities in enhancing both rural and urban food production.

Some of the strategies that are promoted include:

- the establishment of rural and urban home gardens, school gardens, home gardens and model farms on office premises and on premises of private institutions;
- increasing the use of fallow lands for food production and enhancing the productivity thereof;
- the production and utilization of organic manure;
- the promotion and dissemination of environmentally friendly agro-technologies;
- enhancing the marketing of agricultural products;
- improving input-supply, post-harvesting, farmer organization, awareness-raising and publication.

For the time being the policy document provides general guidelines and statements on each of these issues.

Lessons learned

The key to the success of the programme has been in building the right synergies in the administrative set-up. The Provincial administration has been instrumental in facilitating the interaction between the stakeholders, and for effective action planning of activities, without which this programme would not have been successful. Establishing good working relationships with the municipal council and departments of agriculture and agrarian services were key to the outcomes observed. Further, the leadership role and participation of the Mayor, of the municipal council, and the positive support from other departments has allowed for swift decision-making, for optimizing the use of municipal resources and services and for enhancing the confidence of the community in programme formulation and implementation. It also facilitated linking of urban agriculture activities to other municipal programmes like the city's solid waste management programme and household composting scheme, allowing for increasing the efficiency and effectiveness of programme implementation and for cost-savings. Compost produced in the solid waste management programme could now be directly applied in the urban agriculture programme and by recycling waste at home the waste collection costs were brought down significantly. However, in order not to be dependent on municipal support, the challenge remains to strengthen civil society participation in the multi-stakeholder forum, including participation of the urban producers themselves – as is illustrated by the experience in Lima (see the following Case Study in this chapter) .

Sponsorship from higher-level government, such as the Chief Secretary of Province and Western Provincial Department for Agriculture has allowed for quick upscaling of initial project activities at both the local as well as provincial level. The Department of Agriculture has played a crucial role in facilitating and guiding uptake at national level policy formulation and implementation.

In order to contribute to both the country's as well as the city's policy goals of enhancing local and domestic food production the development of different types of urban agriculture remains crucial. Where home, school and institutional gardens will contribute to enhancing food security and nutrition at household level, the development of more commercial urban agriculture will contribute to income and job creation as well as food security at city and national level thus reducing dependence on food imports and making concrete steps towards enhancing the country's food sovereignty.

References

City of Gampaha (2007) *City Strategy Agenda for Urban and Peri-urban Agriculture 2008–2012*, City of Gampaha, Gampaha District, Sri Lanka, IWMI/RUAF, Sri Lanka.

Department of Census and Statistics (DCS) (2001) *Poverty Indicators, Household Income and Expenditure Survey – 2000,* Department of Census and Statistics, Ministry of Finance and Planning, Sri Lanka.

DCS (2008) *Poverty Indicators, Household Income and Expenditure Survey – 2006/07*, Department of Census and Statistics, Ministry of Finance and Planning, Sri Lanka.

IWMI (2008) *Situation analysis of urban agriculture in Gampaha: A concept document:* 'Towards a Firm Urban Development through Urban Agriculture', IWMI/RUAF, India.

Ministry of Agricultural Development and Agrarian Services (2007) *Let Us Cultivate and Uplift the National: National Campaign to Motivate Domestic Food Production 2007–2011*, National Government of Sri Lanka, Colombo.

Ministry of Agriculture and Livestock (2003) *National Policy on Agriculture and Livestock 2003–2010*, Ministry of Agriculture and Livestock, Colombo.

Ranasinghe, T.T. (2009) *Manual of low/no-space agriculture-cum-Family Business Gardens*, IWMI/RUAF, Sri Lanka

The Sunday Times (2008) 'National poverty lines declining', *Financial times*, Sri Lanka, available from: http://sundaytimes.lk/080518/FinancialTimes/ft319.html [last accessed 25 March 2010].

Enhancing urban producers' participation in policy making in Lima, Peru

Gunther Merzthal and Noemi Soto

'Urban agriculture is a permanent and legitimate activity in our district and a strategy for poverty alleviation and local economic development' (Municipal Council, Villa Maria del Triunfo).

Introduction

Agriculture is practised widely in the low-income districts of Lima, the capital of Peru. This sector of the economy was little known or understood until a couple of years ago, despite the significant contributions that urban and peri-urban agriculture make to household income and food security. Urban agriculture was not given attention in municipal policy making and planning and the voices of local producers were not being heard.

Promoting participatory design and implementation of plans and projects

The municipality of Villa Maria del Triunfo is located at the southern outskirts of Lima and has a population of almost 360,000. Over 57 per cent of the residents live in poverty and 15 per cent of the population suffers from malnutrition, with children mainly affected. In response, the municipality started an urban agriculture programme in 1999 to improve urban food security. The authorities of Villa Maria del Triunfo incorporated urban agriculture within the city's Integrated Development Plan (2001–2010) and created a Municipal Urban Agriculture and Environmental Protection Programme (PAU). However, this urban agriculture programme did not provide adequate guidelines for implementation since it was not based on a solid analysis of the state of agriculture in the city. Also, urban producers did not participate sufficiently in the process, which meant that their needs and priorities were not taken into account. Further, limited human and financial resources were available from the municipality for programme implementation.

Credit: IPES

To fill these gaps, the Municipality of Villa Maria del Triunfo conducted a multi-stakeholder policy formulation and action planning process from 2005 to 2007, with the support of IPES/RUAF. Action-oriented research was implemented to: i) analyse the contribution of urban agriculture to household livelihoods and the urban environment in the district; ii) develop a better understanding among decision-makers and other actors of the significance of local food production and its potential impacts; iii) revise the municipality's urban agriculture policy; and iv) formulate a Strategic Action Plan for Urban Agriculture (Merzthal et al., 2006).

Villa Maria has poor soil quality and an annual rainfall of only 25 mm per year. Despite these difficult growing conditions, over 500 family and community gardens have been established and are supported by the urban agriculture programme. In addition, many landless families living in the city's poor hillside settlements keep small animals for occasional sales or home consumption. The production of vegetables, birds, guinea pigs, rabbits and pigs also provides a source of food and income, which is vital to these low-income families.

Despite difficult growing conditions there are over 500 community gardens

Multi-stakeholder policy formulation and action planning

The Multi-stakeholder Policy formulation and Action Planning (MPAP) process in Villa Maria consisted of four stages:

1. Strengthening local capacity
Decision-makers, municipal and NGO staff, and university representatives participated in awareness raising activities, policy seminars and exchange visits to other cities with experience in urban agriculture. This helped them to gain a better understanding of urban agriculture and its effect on food security, incomes and a greener urban environment and reinforced their commitment to the multi-stakeholder planning process. In addition, staff were trained in the MPAP methodology and process.

Credit: IPES

Credit: IPES

Further action planning

2. Situation analysis

A participatory analysis of urban agriculture was implemented as a basis for further action planning.

Local stakeholders were identified and mobilized. The legal and normative frameworks impacting urban agriculture were studied. The existing urban farming systems and their (potential) impacts were analysed. Available open spaces were also identified and mapped. Results of the diagnosis were published in 2006 in the form of a short policy brief called 'Villa Maria: farming for life' (IPES and Municipality of Villa Maria del Triunfo, 2006) which outlined the principle obstacles and opportunities for the further development of urban agriculture in the district.

3. Action Planning

By the end of 2006, a multi-stakeholder forum on urban agriculture (MSF) had been formed, in which 20 institutions, including the local government, development NGOs, community-based organizations, private sector organizations, international agencies and urban producer groups participated. Key issues for the development of urban agriculture were identified and working groups formed to develop a five year Strategic Action Plan and a set of policy guidelines on urban agriculture (Urban Harvest, 2007).

The plan was formally approved by all stakeholders and implementation started at the end of 2007.

Box 3.5 Strategic plan on urban agriculture (2007–2011)

The Villa Maria Strategic Plan on Urban Agriculture views urban agriculture as an important factor in the creation of a healthy, productive and food secure city and identifies six key areas for the development of urban agriculture:

1. Strengthening the awareness of the urban population on the benefits of urban agriculture;
2. Development of technical and organizational capacities of urban producers;
3. Improving access to and the rational use of water for urban agriculture;
4. Improving local production systems and the marketing of food products;
5. Strengthening the institutional and normative framework for development of urban agriculture in the district;
6. Facilitating access to information on and financing for urban agriculture.

Source: IPES and Municipality of Villa Maria del Triunfo, 2006.

4. Implementation

A pilot project was implemented directly following the formulation of the Strategic Plan, in order to keep the farmers and other forum members motivated, and to further build effective partnerships. The pilot project consisted of setting up a demonstration and learning centre, involving 12 producer families directly (through improved production and commercialization of their produce) and a larger number of households indirectly (through participation in the training and demonstration activities). The centre, which covers an area of 4000 m², includes a composting area, a nursery and a research and training area where improved dry-land horticulture production methods are demonstrated. Over 15 types of aromatic and medicinal plants and vegetables are currently being produced and the Centre is frequently visited by other urban producers from the city. In addition to this RUAF-funded project, several other activities were implemented under the strategic plan and are outlined below.

Credit: IPES

The pilot project engaged 12 families in improved production and commercialization

Operationalizing the strategic plan into projects and policies

With some financial support from IPES/RUAF, the multi-stakeholder forum was able to mobilize almost US$200,000 from local sources during 2007 and 2008 to implement several of the other priority actions mentioned in the strategic plan, including:

1. Strengthening and formalizing an urban agriculture producers' network

The organization of urban producers and the strengthening of their capacities is an important prerequisite to their effective participation in the multi-stakeholder forum and decision-making processes. That is why the urban producers in Villa Maria were assisted to organize themselves at the neighbourhood and district level and received training in organic crop production methods, nutritional awareness, personal relations, organizational management and policy lobbying methods. Practical information materials were produced in collaboration with the National Agricultural University La Molina. The producers' organization, which obtained legal status in 2008, played a critical role in lobbying for continued political support for urban agriculture, after the elections (Mayor and municipal council) in 2006.

2. Marketing of urban agriculture produce

A market study was conducted to identify (actual and potential) local marketing venues (such as farmers' markets, direct sales to consumers visiting the gardens and to the city's communal food-kitchens), unmet demand for specific products and their profit potential. The market study was used by IPES and the technical municipal staff to develop a production schedule and marketing plan for the various community gardens, taking into account the small size of production units (100 m²). Also, a logo for the organic vegetables was developed with the farmers that is linked to social certification and regular quality control, which has raised consumer awareness and trust in these products. The production and marketing of the vegetables generates an additional monthly income of around US$30/family.

3. Setting up of five community garden units

In collaboration with Red de Energía del Peru (an electric utility company), which also provided financial support, the UN Food and Agriculture Organization, and the Municipality five community gardens have been established on vacant land located under electric power lines involving 45 families (225 people). Gardens are fenced, a small covered area for training, meetings and sales has been constructed and water-tanks have been positioned (water is provided at reduced tariffs by the Municipality). Terraces have also been built, where needed. Lessons learned during the pilot project described above were applied.

4. Support to peri-urban producers in improving their value chains

Next to the more social forms of urban agriculture as promoted through the community gardens, another pilot project was implemented with peri-urban producers in Villa Maria to analyse and develop more commercial forms of urban agriculture. With support from IDRC Canada, a peri-urban producers' organization (with 59 members) has been supported to improve the production and marketing of *Aloe vera*. The technical and organizational capacity of the producers was strengthened in Urban Producer Field Schools. In addition, the project supported the organization to secure access to land.

5. The organization and institutionalization of an 'urban agriculture week'

In August 2007, the first annual urban agriculture week was organized to enhance public support for urban agriculture. Each year, during one week, urban gardens can be visited, short workshops are organized, videos are shown, and a variety of local products are sold.

6. The elaboration of a municipal ordinance on urban agriculture

IPES/RUAF assisted the municipality and the multi-stakeholder forum to draft a municipal ordinance on urban agriculture. The ordinance recognizes urban agriculture as a permanent and legitimate activity in the district, allocates financial and human resources to a municipal sub-department for urban agriculture; provides for the inclusion of urban agriculture into land use plans; and specifies that technical assistance be provided to producers (see Box 3.6).

Box 3.6 Municipal ordinance of urban agriculture

The ordinance recognizes urban agriculture as a permanent and legal activity in the city and as a municipal strategy to combat poverty and enhance local economic development.

The ordinance specifically seeks to:

- promote the participatory design and implementation of specific plans and projects for urban agriculture, and links these with the existing comprehensive city plan, the economic develop-ment plan, the urban development plan and other sectoral plans;
- promote and strengthen the organization of urban farmers;
- encourage the creation and strengthening of multi-stakeholder and multi-institutional spaces for networking and consensus building in favour of urban agriculture;
- provide sufficient human and financial resources to strengthen the municipal sub-department for urban agriculture;
- include urban agriculture in land use plans and promote the productive use of vacant spaces and access to land for the poorest residents of the city;
- promote access to finance for urban producers and provide technical support and follow-up;
- promote the consumption of safe, healthy, pollutant free food from urban crop cultivation, animal husbandry and food processing activities.

7. Formulation of legal instruments to secure access to land for community gardens
The municipality has legalized access by urban producer groups to public (municipal) land for the development of community gardens. This has been carried out under a municipal authorization for land use based on the Municipal Urban Agriculture Ordinance mentioned above.

Results and outcomes

There is currently a wide consensus among urban producers, decision-makers and other stakeholders that 'urban agriculture land use' is legitimate, sustainable and should be actively supported and maintained. Formerly vacant land areas located under high-voltage power lines or on steep slopes have been transformed into productive green spaces, contributing not only to greater food security and increased income, but also to a more liveable urban environment.

The municipal ordinance has given legitimacy to urban agriculture and facilitated integration within the cities' Economic Development and Land Use Plans. The urban agriculture pro-gramme is now a permanent structure under the Department for Local Economic Development with three permanent staff and an annual budget of US$55,000.

The multi-stakeholder process facilitated the production of a five year Strategic Plan that responds to the real needs of the population. Some 570 poor farming families and over 20 local organizations have participated actively in the process of designing, planning and implementing strategic activities on urban agriculture. There is now an active and formally

Credit: IPES

**Multi-stakeholder forum
meeting**

recognized urban farmers' network in Villa Maria which is able to lobby and advocate for support and funding, for example, through the local Participatory Budgeting process.

The multi-stakeholder forum continues to operate with a secretariat rotating among its members. It thus assures continuous dialogue among involved stakeholders and oversees the implementation and monitoring of the Strategic Plan for Urban Agriculture. The forum is fundamental to the mobilization of resources for the plan's implementation. It also regularly updates the Strategic Plan to ensure its relevance to the viability of urban agriculture in a dynamic social, economic and political environment.

The experiences gained in Villa Maria del Triunfo are shared with other districts of Lima. IPES/ RUAF is currently conducting an MPAP process in Villa El Salvador, building on the lessons learned in neighbouring Villa Maria del Triunfo as well as in a similar process supported by CIP-Urban Harvest in Lurigancho Chosica, another district of Lima. These experiences also have lead to the development of proposals for a comprehensive urban agriculture programme for metropolitan Lima.

Lessons learned

Continued awareness raising and information dissemination amongst decision-makers and other stakeholders concerning the potential of urban agriculture to alleviate hunger and poverty is key to promoting and institutionalizing urban agriculture friendly policies. Strategies could include the organization of policy seminars, exchange visits, fairs and field days, such as those organized during the urban agriculture week.

In order to enhance the development of concrete activities, it is essential to provide an institutional home for urban agriculture and to incorporate urban agriculture in the existing legal and normative frameworks and the development and land use plans of the city. Specific policies (municipal ordinances, laws, regulations) for urban agriculture should also be developed that facilitate and regulate its practice.

Lastly, consolidated and strong producers' organizations are better equipped to speak clearly and in unison with local authorities and to overcome inevitable changes in the level of political support for urban agriculture. The organization and empowerment of urban farmers in Villa Maria proved vital to sustain the multi-stakeholder planning process when political changes took place after municipal elections. It is necessary to strengthen the organizational, managerial, technical and networking capacities of urban producers.

References

Merzthal, G., Prain, G., and Soto, N. (2006) 'Integration of urban agriculture in municipal agendas: Experiences from Lima, Peru', *Urban Agriculture Magazine* 16: 27–31. Available from: http://www.ruaf.org/node/1090 [last accessed 25 March 2010].

Merzthal, G. (ed.) (2006) *Identificación y mapeo de suelos potenciales para la agricultura urbana en Villa Maria del Triunfo*, Municipality of Villa Maria del Triunfo, IPES and RUAF, Lima.

Merzthal, G. and Santandreu, A. (2006) *Análisis situacional de la agricultura urbana en Villa Maria del Triunfo*, Municipality of Villa Maria del Triunfo, IPES and RUAF, Lima.

Urban Harvest (2007) 'Getting agriculture on the municipal agenda in Lima', in C. Barker, G. Prain, M. Warnaars, X. Warnaars, L. Wing and F. Wolf (eds), *Impacts of Urban Agriculture – Highlights of Urban Harvest Research and Development, 2003–2006*, pp. 34–6, International Potato Center (CIP), Lima, Peru. Available from: http://www.uharvest.org/ [last accessed 25 March 2010].

IPES and Municipality of Villa Maria del Triunfo (2006) *Villa Maria sembrando para la vida. Situacion, limitaciones, potenciales y actores de la agricultura urbana en Villa Maria del Triunfo* (Villa Maria: farming for life: Concerted Strategic Plan for Urban Agriculture in Villa Maria del Triunfo. Available from: http://ipes.org/index.php?option=com_content&view=article&id=172&Itemid=104 [last accessed 25 March 2010].

The integration of food production in Sana'a urban planning, Yemen

Salwa Tohme Tawk, Ziad Moussa and Layal Dandache

'If you plant, you will never be poor nor miserable, you retain your dignity' (Ali ben Abi Zayed, a philosopher from the 18th century).

Introduction

Sana'a, the capital of the Republic of Yemen, is situated on a plateau 2,000 m above sea level, and has an estimated population of 1.7 million (based on figures from the 2004 census), which is projected to double by the year 2010. Agriculture forms an important part of the Yemen economy despite the lack of arable land (3 per cent of total land area), scarcity of water, periodic droughts and difficult terrain. Employment in the agricultural sector accounts for more than 64 per cent of the workforce.

Traditionally, Yemen has been famous for its coffee but currently the main cash crop is qat, a mild stimulant chewed by most Yemenis on a daily basis, but which is not exported in significant amounts since it is highly perishable. Qat plays a major role in the Yemeni economy; it accounts for around 6 per cent of GDP, 10 per cent of consumption, one-third of agricultural GDP, and provides employment for one in seven working Yemenis. As the predominant cash crop, the income it generates plays a vital role in urban and rural economies. But it also depletes scarce water resources and has replaced essential food crops and agriculture exports. Some 72 per cent of Yemeni males reported that they chew qat, compared to 33 per cent of females. Further, because qat has become so important in Yemeni life, some of the poorest people will willingly forgo food in favour of buying qat. In addition, commercial farming of fruits and vegetables provides a level of production to nearly satisfy domestic demand.

The geographical area of the Municipality of Sana'a has dramatically expanded in recent decades to accommodate the population increase. However, a large number of citizens (9,770 as estimated in 2007) still work on 9,300 ha of agricultural land in the city. The same 2007 census showed that more than 37,500 tons of vegetables (leek, coriander, radish, onions and tomatoes), forage (alfalfa, maize, and barley), fruits (grapes, berries, nuts, peaches and apricots), qat and other seasonal grain crops were produced on 7,700 ha. The historic city still contains 21 ha of orchards and vegetable farms (like the *Almaqashim* or the mosque gardens),

Urban agriculture in the city centre of Sana'a

Credit: J.W. Harmmeijer

(Barcelo, 2004) which supply the population with part of its local food needs. The livestock population in the city comprises around 4,500 head of cows and 110,000 head of sheep and goats besides camels, donkeys, poultry and bees. In addition, there are large areas within military camps that are cultivated by the armed forces to contribute to their fresh food supply, which are not included in the census.

Sixty one per cent of agricultural activity is concentrated in the directorate of Beni-Harith, while the remaining 39 per cent is distributed among ten other directorates in different neighbourhoods and peripheries of the city. The size of land holdings range between 0.25 and 7 ha;

85 per cent of which are private properties, while the rest is owned either by the public or *Waqf* (religious community). The main source of irrigation is groundwater, which is used mainly for horticulture and qat production. The production of cereals and forage is rain-fed. Another water source specific for Sana'a is greywater from the mosques to irrigate the *maquashim* or mosque gardens. More than 100 community gardens exist within the fortified wall of old Sana'a (which is now classified as a UNESCO World Heritage site).

Credit: Salwa Tohme Tawk

61 per cent of agricultural activity is concentrated in the Beni-Harith directorate

Agriculture constitutes an essential part of urban livelihoods, supplying food for consumption and income, and involving the whole family. Women, who account for 27 per cent of the urban agricultural permanent workers, usually keep the animals and participate in planting, harvesting and post-harvesting activities as well as marketing via direct sale in the field or in nearby public markets. Sana'a is the cradle of one of the most ancient urban agriculture systems in the world so the overall policy environment is quite supportive to urban agriculture activities. The ancestral city centre of Sana'a, including the *Maquashem* has been declared a UNESCO world heritage site and the conservation plans of the city include the rehabilitation and conservation of these gardens. The expansion of the city, which has intensified significantly over the last two decades, has led to human settlement and agricultural activities in flood prone areas (seasonal torrential flooding also known as '*Sayl*') and has led to the first attempts by the Municipality of Sana'a to regulate urban agriculture in the city.

Multi-stakeholder policy formulation and action planning

Supported by RUAF/ESDU, and in cooperation with Sana'a municipality represented by the Public Department of Gardens and the Bureau of Agriculture, the non-governmental organization YASAD (Yemeni Association for Sustainable Agriculture and Development) initiated the MPAP in 2007. A core team of seven persons was formed to implement and coordinate the process and a multi-stakeholder forum on urban agriculture was established including representatives from non-governmental organizations, research institutes, producer organizations and various municipal and ministerial departments (agriculture council, public gardens, public works) and the Sana'a Watershed Management Project, funded by the World Bank, the National Council for Urban Planning, individual urban farmers, the Association for the Conservation of Gardens in Old Sana'a, the Agricultural University of Sana'a and the Agriculture Cooperatives Union.

Credit: Salwa Tohme Tawk

YASAD initiated the MPAP in 2007

Further, a policy narrative was developed, based on the situation analysis (YASAD, 2007), and served as a basis for the development of the Sana'a City Strategic Agenda on urban agriculture. During the writing of the policy narrative, in early 2008, Yemen was very badly hit by the world food crisis and urban agriculture became an important issue. YASAD managed to extend the process across the 10 districts of Sana'a and the Ministry of Agriculture also became particularly interested in the MPAP and linked it to the 'Green Belt Initiative', which aims to increase the planted surfaces in Greater Sana'a and in peri-urban areas by 20 per cent (Albalagh newspaper, 2008). This increased the possibility of acquiring additional funding.

The results of the situation analysis and policy narrative were presented at an initial meeting of the multi-stakeholder forum (MSF) which took place in September 2008. During this meeting the value of urban agriculture was recognized as an important entry point for poverty alleviation and achieving food security in Yemen in general and in Sana'a in particular; and significant attention was received from the press (Al Thawra et al., 2008). The MSF formulated a vision statement for the development of urban agriculture indicating its historical role and importance in Sana'a and focusing on food security and water optimization. The MSF was well attended with representatives from almost all relevant line ministries and different services of the Sana'a municipality, the Sana'a Farmers' Unions and researchers from the University of Sana'a. Civil society organizations were underrepresented, however, and there was a lack of gender balance (although this needs to be understood within the Yemeni context).

The first meeting of the MSF marked the start of the preparation of the Sana'a City Strategic Agenda on urban agriculture. This development was guided by three working groups on: media, technical aspects and legal aspects. These working groups elaborated on: water availability and more efficient use of irrigation water; agriculture extension and development services; empowering women in agriculture production and in relevant institutions; the reformulation of laws and regulations in order to preserve agricultural activities and enhance access to land and, more specifically, access to land for grazing. The results were shared with a broader group of stakeholders during consultative meetings and were presented and discussed in a second MSF meeting in December 2008, leading to the adoption of the Sana'a City Strategic Agenda on urban agriculture.

The City Strategic Agenda

The Sana'a City Strategic Agenda on urban agriculture (CSA) links the work of the MSF to existing or planned initiatives targeting poverty reduction (through the Social Fund for Development and European Union funded projects), as well as the 'Green Belt Initiative' championed by the Ministry of Agriculture (YASAD, 2008). The CSA was agreed by the multi-stakeholder forum in Sana'a in March 2009, and includes the following strategic lines:

Credit: Salwa Tohme Tawk

- increase water availability and more efficient use for agricultural purposes (including water harvesting and improving the quality of recycled grey and wastewater);
- improve the agriculture extension and development services with regard to agriculture inputs, veterinary advice, efficient forage production;

The CSA links poverty reduction efforts with the Green Belt initiative

- empowering the role of women in different agricultural activities (generating income, alleviating poverty and access to food);
- (re)formulating laws and regulations, so that agricultural activities can be preserved and access to land is enhanced specially for grazing pastures (YASAD, 2008).

Results

Urban agriculture has strongly returned to the development map of Sana'a. Previously, the main focus of the municipality was to preserve the ancestral community gardens of Sana'a purely for conservation purposes (through the UNESCO World Heritage Classification). With support from RUAF, urban agriculture in Sana'a has been linked to other important city issues like food security and poverty alleviation.

Urban agriculture has repeatedly been featured in radio shows and in the press. This has helped to promote urban agriculture in the city and with key persons in the public and private sector, who have become familiar with and aware of urban agriculture.

All related municipal departments and Committees of the Municipality of Sana'a (Agriculture, Public Gardens, Public Works) actively participate in the MSF and contribute to the situation analysis and the development of the CSA. Cooperation has been enhanced, both between these institutions and with other stakeholders.

Credit: Salwa Tohme Tawk

**An urban farmer sells
dried beans and grains
on the street in Sana'a**

Also, urban farmers have been encouraged to organize themselves. They now participate in an increasing number and are more active in the MSF. Furthermore, their lobbying capacities have been supported, which is essential for participatory and inclusive decision-making processes.

Laws and regulations related to urban agriculture have been analysed and suggestions for change have been made in coordination with the municipal and legislative institutions concerned. This will support the revision of the Master Plan of Sana'a in 2010. A major recommendation by the MSF to this revision is the preservation of the remaining agricultural land and the need for spatial urban development towards the arid plateaus surrounding the city, rather than on prime agricultural lands as has been the case so far.

Moreover, the Municipality of Sana'a has provided a public space, which will be used as a demonstration plot for teachers and school children to learn how to implement small school gardens at their premises, while also encouraging parents to grow crops at home.

The 'Green Belt Initiative' in Sana'a has been revived under the MSF. This initiative seeks to increase the planted areas of Sana'a by 20 per cent (and involves various line ministries as well as community-based organizations). This initiative is now also a national example for other cities such as Aden, Taez or Hadramout. IFAD and UNESCWA (the UN Economic and Social Commission for Western Asia) support this initiative. Integration of urban agriculture in the greenbelt will also help to improve access to land (urban agriculture is currently practised mainly on lands owned by religious institutions or large landlords).

The MSF is serving now as a key interlocutor for major donors, such as the World Bank. Based on the CSA, a proposal has been developed to support and develop urban agriculture in Sana'a, and the Bank has earmarked US$1 million for this purpose. In addition, the Bank is planning to replicate these experiences in two other cities in Yemen, and has invited RUAF to assist in the development of a regional programme on urban agriculture in the Middle East (that will include Yemen, Egypt, Jordan and Syria). This will be the first substantial urban agriculture programme to be financed by the World Bank. Also, the Social Fund for Development of Yemen awarded the MSF a grant in 2009 to equip a meeting room with furniture, a portable computer and audio-visual equipment. Currently, both parties are looking at the possibilities for financing CSA activities related to female empowerment and food security. In addition, contacts have been established with other donors for potential support in the execution of the CSA in 2010.

Lessons learned

The MSF on urban agriculture is a continuous platform for action planning, facilitating the input of financial and human resources and the involvement and interaction of local stakeholders. The Sana'a platform has also supported the inclusion of urban agriculture in the policy agenda of the local government leading to further institutionalization. Also, the MSF has managed to engage most of the national key players, including a large number of policy makers.

The challenge is to maintain a balance between policy makers and other stakeholders. The organization of urban farmers is important. The lobbying capacities of this group must be increased in order to create an active, participatory and inclusive decision-making process.

The lack of gender balance in Sana'a remains a concern. In the Yemeni cultural setting, women are rarely allowed outside the house without the presence of a male chaperon (*Muharram*) and the mixing of males and females in public meetings is not a common practice. The involvement of a female social researcher of YASAD has facilitated gender mainstreaming, since she was able to encourage participation while maintaining and respecting tradition and culture. The situation analysis that was carried out included a study on gender in urban agriculture in Sana'a. Participatory Rapid Appraisal (PRA) methods were applied, which allowed generated attention for the mainstreaming of gender issues in the Sana'a City Strategic Agenda on urban agriculture (Al Jundi, 2008). It further made the women who participated more aware of the potential role they can play in their communities. It is recommended that gender mainstreaming should be given special attention in all activities that will be organized as a follow up to the CSA. Since women are responsible for the bulk of food production, enhancing their decision-making power in household expenditures will improve the food security and increase the diversity of diet within the poorest category of the population.

There is growing support from key policy makers for the integration of urban agriculture in the Green Belt and old Sana'a, but the sustainability of urban agriculture will depend on political and financial support from additional initiatives. The RUAF initiative combined with the hard work of local stakeholders can form the foundation upon which to further build urban agriculture activities.

References

Al Jundi, R. (2008) *Gender and Urban Agriculture: The Case of Sana'a – Yemen*, Environment and Sustainable Development Unit of the American University of Beirut, Lebanon.

Al Thawra, Al Jumhuriya, Yemeni News Agency (2008) Article on the MSF meeting, 26th September, 2008.

Albalagh newspaper (2008) *Green Belt initiative and funding*, 24 June 2008, issue 785.

Barcelo, M. et al. (2004) « Les jardins de la Vieille Ville de Sanaa » in arabic, translated by Frédéric Pelat et Amin al-Hakimi and Social Fund for Development in 2007, French Centre for Archaeology and Social Sciences.

Central Statistical Organisation, Ministry of Planning and International Cooperation (2004) *Final Results, the General Population Housing and Establishment Census 2004*, First Report.

Central Statistical Organisation, Ministry of Planning and International Cooperation (2007) *Statistical Yearbook* 2007.

YASAD (2007) *Towards the Promotion of Urban Agriculture in Sana'a: An Exploratory Study*, Environment and Sustainable Development Unit of the American University of Beirut, Lebanon.

YASAD (2008) *Sana'a City Strategic Agenda on Urban Agriculture*, Environment and Sustainable Development Unit of the American University of Beirut, Lebanon.

Chapter 4
MUNICIPAL POLICIES AND PROGRAMMES ON URBAN AGRICULTURE: KEY ISSUES AND POSSIBLE COURSES OF ACTION

'Local governments should show a clear commitment to the development of urban agriculture, mobilising existing local resources, integrating urban agriculture in the municipal structure, expanding it nationwide, and allotting funds from the municipal budgets for carrying out urban agriculture activities.' Quito Declaration, signed by 40 cities (UMP-LAC, 2000).

Introduction

Chapter 1 showed that urban and peri-urban agriculture can make important contributions in responding to various important challenges that cities are currently facing. The size and urgency of these challenges require innovative solutions and the promotion of safe, sustainable and multi-functional urban and peri-urban agriculture is certainly one of them.

Once governmental authorities and support institutions (public, non-profit, private) better understand urban agriculture and the contributions it can make to their policy goals and to addressing key urban challenges, they are likely to seek to facilitate its development by means of proactive policies and intervention strategies.

Farmers are involved in decision making (Lima, Peru)

Such policy development starts from the recognition that:

- Urban and peri-urban agriculture are an integral part of the urban socio-economic and ecological system. Urban agriculture is a dynamic, although largely informal, economic sector that quickly adapts to changing urban conditions and demands and involves large numbers of urban poor.

- Urban and peri-urban agriculture have an important role to play in strategies that seek to address key urban challenges such as rising urban poverty, increasing food insecurity, growing fresh water scarcity, the need to adapt to climate change and growing urban waste disposal problems.
- A number of health and environmental risks are associated with urban and peri-urban agriculture that need to be properly attended. Simply prohibiting urban agriculture, or just tolerating urban agriculture without taking proper guiding measures, have proven to be ineffective policies for the reduction of such risks. Pro-active policies are needed to optimize the benefits of urban agriculture whilst reducing associated public health and environmental hazards, mainly resulting from improper management and/or improper location of urban agriculture.
- Urban and peri-urban agriculture constitute an important safety net for the urban poor in times of economic or food crisis. However, support to urban and peri-urban agriculture should go beyond periods of crisis and should be made a component of more comprehensive strategies to build sustainable and resilient cities that are socially inclusive, food-secure, productive and environmentally healthy.

Policies and interventions on urban agriculture may be oriented towards various development perspectives or visions (as discussed in Chapter 1):

Policies and programmes need to be differentiated for the various zones of a city

- the social perspective, with an emphasis on subsistence-oriented urban agriculture with strong impacts on food security and social inclusion of disadvantaged groups;
- the economic perspective with an emphasis on poverty alleviation and local economic development through stimulation of market-oriented types of urban agriculture;

- the ecological perspective with an emphasis on the ecological roles of (especially multi-functional types of) urban agriculture, productive reuse of urban wastes, city greening, adaptation to climate change (by reducing energy use, enhancing storm water infiltration and capturing CO_2).

When developed in a participatory way, these policies and programmes will respond to the local conditions and priorities and result in a specific mix of the three perspectives that is typical for the respective city. It is important to note that policies and programmes need to be differentiated for the main types of agriculture and for different zones of the respective city.

This chapter will describe the various policy instruments and intervention strategies that city governments may apply to promote and regulate the various types of intra- and peri-urban agriculture. A series of key issues for the development of safe and sustainable urban agriculture is presented. For each of these key issues a number of recommended policy measures and courses of action are discussed that have arisen in the multi-stakeholder processes implemented in the 20 RUAF partner cities (as discussed in Chapters 2 and 3). That is to say that the suggested policy measures and action strategies are based on the practical experience of local governments and their partners that has been gained over the last 5 years.

Policy instruments

Cities (and national governments) generally have four types of policy instruments to support urban agriculture development. Contrary to what is generally believed, legislation is just one of the instruments. Others include: economic, communicative/educative and urban planning and design instruments. Each instrument is based on a specific assumption regarding how the behaviour of actors in society can be influenced, and will be described in more detail below.

Legal instruments

The logic underlying legal instruments is that actors (such as citizens, industries or public institutions) can be forced to adopt a certain desired behaviour through legal norms and regulations (such as laws, bye-laws or ordinances) and that it is possible to control whether these actors adhere to the given rules and norms. Actors who do not adhere to the rules will be sanctioned. This policy instrument is especially useful in cases when: 1) The desired

Actors may sign an agreement to adhere voluntarily to certain norms and regulations

behaviour cannot be realized in another way; and 2) The rules can easily be controlled. In addition, legal instruments are used in case the other instruments (economic, educational and design) require an adequate legal basis. As such, the urban agriculture programme in Governador Valadares (Brazil) or Lima (Peru) were formalized by law (Governador Valadares, 2003; Merzthal and Soto, 2006).

Application of legal instruments is, however, not without some common challenges. An increasing number of laws, bye-laws or regulations may lead to contradictions (what is allowed or promoted in one law or regulation may be prohibited or restricted in another). This situation

Credit: IWMI India

often occurs in relation to urban agriculture due to its multi-sectoral character. For example, a city can have a formal policy that supports urban agriculture while at the same time, the same city's environmental or health regulations still prohibit or severely restrict it.

Moreover, the mechanisms to enforce legal instruments are often weak due to the related costs or lack of political will, leading to a low level of control and sanctioning of undesired behaviour or to unequal treatment of the various actors. This leads to a situation in which some actors' activities are sanctioned while others are not. Such a situation (prohibited in law, but tolerated in practice) is quite common where urban agriculture is concerned, especially in cities in sub-Saharan Africa.

An alternative legal instrument to issuing general bye-laws, norms and regulations, is a contract or covenant. In this case, the government and certain actors sign an agreement in which the community actors (e.g. urban farmers' organizations) agree to adhere voluntarily to certain norms and regulations, often in exchange for certain support by local government or other organizations (for example, access to municipal land, obtaining a license for a farmers' market and technical support). Whereas a municipal bye-law or ordinance generally contains do's and don'ts that apply to all citizens, the covenant is an agreement made voluntarily between local government and specific actors in a city that applies only to those groups. This makes it possible to establish more specific norms and regulations for specific situations or specific groups of actors.

Economic instruments

The logic behind the application of economic instruments is the assumption that community actors will adopt a certain desired behaviour if this gives them some economic gains (or losses if they continue with the undesired behaviour). Local governments, for example, may grant tax incentives or subsidies if actors adopt the desired behaviour, or levy special taxes for undesired behaviour (similar to a levy on cigarettes or alcohol). Such economic instruments also need a legal basis, but the essential element is not the law itself but the economic incentive or loss that encourages (or is supposed to encourage) certain behaviour.

Several municipalities grant tax exemptions to land owners who allow poor urban farmers use of vacant private land. For example, the municipality of Governador Valadares (Brazil) exempts private landowners from progressive property taxation if their lands are put to productive use (Governador Valadares, 2004). Other cities have reduced the tariffs for irrigation water or provide incentives for composting and reuse of household wastes. Economic support can also be given through supply of irrigation water, tools, seeds and compost to urban farmers.

This policy instrument is especially useful in cases when the economic incentive is easily recognizable and substantial enough to have an effect and is directly related to the desired/undesired behaviour (as in the case above: leasing vacant private land to urban poor).

Challenges related to the application of this instrument include the fact that: 1) The costs of the policy measure may become unfeasible when many actors make use of it; and 2) Levies and subsidies can enhance social inequity if there is no way to ensure that a community's most vulnerable groups are the ones that benefit primarily from the economic incentive.

Communicative / educative instruments

The assumption behind the use of communicative/educative instruments is that people will adopt a certain desired behaviour if they are well informed about the positive effects of the

Credit: IPES

Actors adopt certain behaviour if this benefits them economically

desired behaviour as well as the negative effects of the undesired behaviour. Persuasive tools can include media programmes, extension visits, training courses, leaflets and websites.

Such instruments can be applied to make people understand the importance of the desired change and to assist them in the change process. Well-known examples include media-campaigns to discourage smoking or to promote the use of condoms to combat HIV/AIDS. In relation to urban agriculture, a municipality may provide technical training to urban farm-

People need to be well informed about the positive effects and desired behaviour

ers, or provide education on healthy food, food growing and food preparation to schoolchildren and parents.

Communicative/educative instruments are often used as a complementary approach to other policy instruments, since the lack of an adequate communication and education strategy may strongly reduce the effectiveness of the other policy instruments. In this context, the importance of designing and implementing a strategy to communicate municipal urban agriculture policies and policy instruments to the target group should also be emphasized.

Credit: IPES

The design of a neighbourhood may prompt people to act in a desired way

Credit: Joanna Wilbers

Urban design instruments

The logic behind urban design instruments is that actors will adopt a certain desired behaviour if their physical environment has been designed in such a way that they are more easily prompted to act in a certain way. For example, if public dustbins are widely available, people will generally throw less litter on the street. Examples related to urban agriculture include zoning (setting aside and protecting certain areas of the city for agriculture); combining or separating certain land uses depending on the degree of conflict or synergy between them; and the inclusion of space for home or community gardening in social housing and slum upgrading projects. Several cities have already included land designated for urban agriculture in their urban land use plan or social housing schemes.

Current situation regarding use of policy instruments for urban agriculture

A review of existing policy documents on urban agriculture (Wilbers and De Zeeuw, 2006) reveals that many cities still mainly use legal instruments, which often have a 'reactive character'. This means that action is taken only in the form of sanctions in case the community actors do not follow legal rules and regulations properly. In such cities urban agriculture is often restricted or at best tolerated if the capacity of the city to enforce the existing regulations is too limited.

On the other hand, many examples of the use of economic, educative and design instruments can be found, often in cities that apply a more proactive, enabling and development-oriented approach to urban agriculture. As stated above, economic, educative and design instruments have to be combined with supporting legal instruments in an effective 'package' of policy measures in order to arrive at a development-oriented policy on urban agriculture.

In Kampala, Uganda, urban agriculture recently has been formally accepted as a legal form of urban land use and urban agriculture has been included in the city's poverty alleviation and social development strategy. However, the policy relies mainly on legal instruments: city ordinances on urban agriculture, fish, livestock and meat, which restrict unwanted behaviour by establishing a system of licences, regulations, control and sanctions (Azuba and McCans, 2006; IPC, 2007). While these restrictions make sense from a health and environmental point of view, they need to be combined with complementary policy measures to support and stimulate urban agriculture (e.g. training, marketing support and access to land) and to ensure that the urban poor will benefit from this policy and not just see their opportunities restricted by the new ordinances. Kampala city council is actually developing such complementary programmes.

In Rosario (Argentina) the emphasis is mainly on economic and communicative/ educative instruments (Municipality of Rosario, 2002). Rosario has chosen an approach that focuses on stimulating good behaviour through positive incentives including property tax exemption for landowners, provision of seeds, water and tool sheds, farmer education and technical assistance. All of these incentives are financed and supported by the municipality or collaborating organizations.

The second approach is more programme-oriented, enabling, while the first approach is more regulatory and restrictive. Combined use of the various policy instruments probably leads to the best results.

Courses of action for municipal policy making on urban agriculture

The Multi-stakeholder processes in the 20 RUAF partner cities show that urban policy makers can substantially contribute to the development of safe and sustainable urban agriculture. A number of important areas for policy intervention could be distinguished:

- creation of a conducive policy environment and formal acceptance of urban agriculture as an urban land use;
- enhancing access to vacant open urban spaces and the security of agricultural land use;
- enhancing the productivity and economic viability of urban agriculture by improving access of urban farmers to technical assistance, markets and credit;
- promoting social inclusion and gender equity;
- taking measures that prevent/reduce health and environmental risks associated with urban agriculture; and
- inclusion of urban agriculture in local climate change adaptation and disaster risk reduction strategies.

Systematization of the experiences gained in the various RUAF partner cities, complemented by experiences of other cities, has led to the identification of recommendable policy measures and strategies in each of these areas of intervention that might be considered when developing urban agriculture policies and programmes in other cities.

Selection of certain policy measures or actions by a specific city will depend on the characteristics of the city, the priorities and strategies defined in the dialogue between the stakeholders and the assessment of costs and benefits related to implementation of certain policy measures and actions.

Creation of an enabling policy environment

Integration of urban agriculture in city development plans. Formal acceptance of urban agriculture as an urban land use and its integration into municipal city development and land use plans and policies, is a crucial step towards effective regulation and sustainable development of urban agriculture in a city. For this purpose, the city of Ndola (Zambia) included urban and peri-urban agriculture in its Strategic Development Plan 2005–2015; Amman (Jordan) integrated urban agriculture within its new Master Plan; Bogota (Colombia) recently integrated urban and peri-urban agriculture within its Economic, Social and Environmental Plan 2008–2012, while the city of Bobo Dioulasso (Burkina Faso) integrated urban agriculture within its Schéma Directeur d'Aménagement et d'Urbanisme (RUAF Foundation, 2009b).

Revision of existing policies and regulations. Another important step cities could make is to review existing policies, bye-laws, norms and regulations influencing urban agriculture, in order to identify and subsequently remove unsubstantiated or unnecessary legal restrictions that may exist and to integrate more adequate measures to effectively stimulate and regulate the development of sustainable urban agriculture.

Kampala (Uganda), Dar es Salaam (Tanzania), Havana (Cuba) and Harare (Zimbabwe) are examples of cities that revised or are revising their bye-laws and regulations in order to replace colonial bye-laws and international sanitation standards that were seen as excessive, unenforceable or inappropriate to local conditions (Azuba and McCans, 2006; Jacobi et al., 2000; Ministerio de la Agricultura y Grupo Nacional de Agricultura Urbana de Cuba, 2004; Mutonodzo, 2009).

Urban farmers agree to take action

Credit: IPES

'Our bye laws were outdated', admits Winnie Makumbi, former Kampala City Minister of Social Improvement, Community Development and Antiquities. 'They failed to recognize that many residents derive their livelihoods from urban farming. We realized it was up to us as political leaders to initiate the policy changes that would support urban farming practices' (RUAF Foundation, 2009a).

Adequate institutional arrangements. To enable such policy revision and/or the formulation of new policies and programmes on urban agriculture, municipal authorities may select the department that will act as lead agency and/or establish an interdepartmental committee on urban agriculture. They may also invite relevant local actors to take part in a multi-stakeholder platform on urban agriculture (or 'food policy council') that will jointly analyse the presence, role, problems and development perspectives of urban food production, distribution and consumption in the city-region and coordinate the process of municipal policy development and action planning. Also, inclusion of urban agriculture in the municipal budget is crucial. Next to funds to finance the urban agriculture programme, also the means for the functioning of the coordination department, interdepartmental working group and the multi-stakeholder platform have to be included.

Cities like Nairobi (Kenya) and Accra (Ghana) created a municipal agricultural department (IPC, 2007; RUAF Foundation, 2009b). In Villa Maria del Triunfo (Lima, Peru) an urban agriculture sub-department was created under the Department of Economic Development (Merzthal and Soto, 2006). In 2001, the city of Rosario (Argentina) made its Secretariat of Social Promotion responsible for the coordination of the new Urban Agriculture Programme (Terrile and Lattuca, 2006). In Cape Town (South Africa), an inter-departmental working group was established in 2002 to coordinate the activities of the various municipal and Provincial departments active in this field (town planning, health, finance) and to facilitate integrated policy development (Visser, 2006; City of Cape Town, 2006), while in Bulawayo (Zimbabwe) an Interdepartmental Committee on Urban Agriculture was created in 2007 to coordinate the activities of various municipal departments (Mubvami, 2006).

Multi-stakeholder platforms on urban and peri-urban agriculture have been established in various cities in the last few years, in which municipal departments, NGOs, farmer groups, private enterprises, financial institutions, community organizations and universities are collaborating in the development of urban agriculture policies and programmes on urban agriculture and urban food security, in various cases with support of the RUAF Foundation (see the cases presented in the preceding chapters) but also many others on own initiative and without external support.

In North America (e.g. Toronto and Vancouver in Canada and Portland and Chicago in the USA) and Europe (e.g. in London, UK and Copenhagen, Denmark) more and more 'food policy councils' are being established involving business and community groups in the development of policies and programmes that promote urban food security and facilitate the development of equitable urban food systems (see Toronto Food Policy Council, 2009; Mendes, 2006; Cooley, 2006).

Measures to enhance access to vacant urban land and land tenure security

Increased access of the urban poor to land and water and especially enhanced security of land use needs to be given proper attention. City governments may facilitate access of urban producers to available urban open spaces in various ways. Below, a number of such measures are presented.

Demarcation of zones for urban agriculture and integrating these into city development and land use plans. Dar Es Salaam and Dodoma (Tanzania), Dakar (Senegal), Maputo (Mozambique), Bissau (Guinea Bissau), Pretoria (South Africa), Kathmandu (Nepal), Accra (Ghana) and Beijing (China) are examples of the many cities that have demarcated zones for urban agriculture as a form of permanent land use (Dubbeling, 2004; Mbaye and Moustier, 2000; Fang et al., 2005). These zones are intended to support agriculture and/or to protect open green areas from being built upon, to create buffer zones between conflicting land uses (e.g. between residential and industrial areas) or to reserve inner city space for future uses. In Beijing (China), specific urban agricultural types and activities are promoted in various (peri-)urban zones of the city. In Ho Chi Minh City and to a lesser extent in Hanoi (Vietnam), areas in and on the periphery of the city are also set aside for aquaculture (Bunting, et al., 2006).

Such urban agricultural zones are more sustainable if located in areas that are not well suited for construction or where construction is not desirable, such as flood plains, under power lines, in parks or in nature conservation areas. The City Master Plan of Setif (Algeria) includes the creation of a green strip west of the city on the flood-prone fields of the Boussellam wadi valley (Boudjenouia et al., 2006). Zoning in itself is, however, not sufficient to maintain these open spaces. Political will from, and proper control by, the local authorities coupled with practical, technical and financial support for the urban producers in these zones – to stimulate the development of sustainable and multi-functional agriculture in these zones – is very important.

Access to land can be facilitated in various ways

Making an inventory of the available vacant open land within the city. Contrary to common belief, surprisingly high amounts of vacant land can be found even in highly urbanized areas that may be used for agriculture on a temporary or permanent basis. In the city of Chicago (USA), researchers identified 70,000 vacant lots. Various cities, like Cienfuegos (Cuba), Piura (Peru) and Dar es Salaam (Tanzania) have made an inventory of the available vacant open land within the city (using methods like community mapping and/or GIS) and analysed its suitability for use in agriculture, which creates a good starting point for enhancing access, especially of the urban poor, to land for urban farming (Socorro, 2003; Dongus, 2001).

Credit: René van Veenhuizen

Temporary leasing of vacant municipal land. Various cities, like Havana (Cuba), Cagayan de Oro (the Philippines), Cape Town (South Africa), Lima (Peru), Bulawayo (Zimbabwe) and

Governador Valadares (Brazil) have formulated a City Ordinance that regulates the (temporary) use of vacant municipal land by organized groups of urban producers (Potutan et al., 2000; Holmer et al., 2003). The vacant land (including land that is earmarked for future use but is still temporarily available, underutilized land around public facilities or road verges or land that is not fit for construction, such as flood zones, land under power lines or buffer zones) is leased for the short or medium term to organized groups of urban poor for gardening purposes (in the form of multi-annual specific leaseholds or occupancy licences). Often, the contract with the farmers includes conditions and eventually some restrictions regarding the required land, and crop and waste management practices. However, often those in need of land are not aware of such opportunities so information campaigns are an important accompanying measure.

If preparation of formal land lease contracts is too time and labour consuming, civil society organizations may liaise between the city (as land owner) and community gardeners who want to use the land. This is done for example in Amsterdam (the Netherlands), where the local Association of Gardeners (7,200 members) rents over 250 ha of municipal land from the city. The Association then rents garden-plots to individual members. This income allows the association to maintain fences and other infrastructure and to provide certain services to its members (such as training events and waste disposal) (Wilbers, 2005).

Promoting use of vacant private lands. The City of Rosario (Argentina) provides a tax reduction to land owners that lease their land to urban producers (levying municipal taxes on land laying idle might be a complementary measure) and created a Land Bank which brings those in need of agricultural land in contact with landowners in need of temporary or permanent users (Municipality of Rosario, 2003). Also, the city of Cagayan d'Oro (the Philippines) assists urban poor associations to establish allotment gardens on privately owned land. Other examples of tenure agreements between urban producers and owners of private or semi-public estates with idle areas can be found in Accra-Ghana (hospital grounds), Harare-Zimbabwe (golf club), Santiago de Chile-Chile (school yards), Dar es Salaam-Tanzania (university campus) and Port-au-Prince-Haiti (church grounds).

Taking measures to improve the suitability of available areas of land. The City of Cape Town (South Africa) not only provides access to vacant land but is also assisting urban gardening groups in removing debris from that land, ploughing it, delivery of compost, etc. (Visser, 2006). In New York (USA) community groups and volunteers, with the help of the Department of Sanitation, clean out derelict open spaces in their neighbourhoods in order to start community gardens there. A study by Pothukuchi (2006) revealed that the opening of a community garden leads to an increase of the prices of residential properties within 300 m of the garden, and that the impact increases over time, with the greatest impact being in the most disadvantaged neighbourhoods.

Providing assistance to reallocation of urban producers that are poorly located (and where their farming activities may cause serious health and/or environmental risks). For example, in Jakarta (Indonesia) 275 dairy cattle farmers with over 5,500 cows have been reallocated from the inner city (where they caused disease and waste problems) to a peri-urban area (Purnomohadi, 2000). Cape Town (South Africa) is planning a similar action creating new livestock kraals in the peri-urban area for the intra-urban herd owners.

Including space for individual or community gardens in new public social housing and slum upgrading schemes. Cities like Vancouver (Canada), Colombo (Sri Lanka), Kampala (Uganda), Rosario (Argentina), Dar es Salaam (Tanzania) and Chicago (USA) are experimenting with the inclusion of space for home and/or community gardening in new public housing projects and slum upgrading schemes. In Belo Horizonte (Brazil), spaces for home gardens or community gardens, street trees for shade and fruits and 'productive parks' were included in the 'Villa Viva and Drenurbes' housing schemes (Governador Valadares, 2003).

Promotion of multifunctional land use. Under certain conditions urban farming can be combined with other compatible land uses. Farmers may provide recreational services to urban citizens, receive youth groups to provide ecological education, act as co-managers of parks and their land may also be used as water storage areas, nature reserves, firebreak zones and flood zones, for example. By doing so the management costs of such areas may be reduced, and protection against squatting and re-zoning may be enhanced.

In Bangkok (Thailand), for example, aquaculture in urban or peri-urban lakes or ponds is combined with recreational activities like angling, boating, or a fish restaurant (Bunting et al., 2006). In Calcutta (India) the maintenance of the wetlands, agriculture and aquaculture are combined with wastewater treatment and reuse. The Municipality of Beijing (China) is promoting the development of peri-urban agro-tourism both in the form of larger agro-recreational parks as well as family-based agro-tourism through which farmers diversify their activities by offering services to urban tourists (food, accommodation, sales of fresh and processed products, functioning as a tourist guide and horse riding). The local government further made agro-tourism part of municipal and district level planning by: establishing an agro-tourism association and information dissemination service; assisting interested farmers with business planning, tax exemptions and funding of infrastructure development; and providing subsidized water and electricity (Fang et al., 2005).

Other municipalities like Pretoria (South Africa) and Rosario (Argentina) entered into a partnership with producers to manage municipal open green spaces, thus saving the municipality considerable maintenance costs.

Measures to enhance the productivity and economic viability of urban agriculture

The potential for improving the efficiency of various urban farming systems is high. The urban agriculture sector tends to be highly dynamic, in part because of its proximity to urban consumers, but its development is restrained amongst others due to urban farmers' limited access to training and extension services. Agricultural research and extension organizations and other support organizations (i.e. credit institutions) have – until recently – given relatively little attention to agriculture in the urban environment. And where this has happened, most attention has been given to the larger scale, capital intensive and fully commercial farmers, especially peri-urban irrigated vegetable production, poultry and dairy production.

Credit: MDPESA

Providing technical advice from extension services

Important measures that can be taken by municipal governments to enhance the productivity and economic viability of urban agriculture include the following:

Provision of training and extension services to urban producers. Governmental organizations, educational institutes, NGOs and the private sector can be stimulated by the municipal government to provide training, technical advice and extension services to urban producers, with a strong emphasis on ecological farming practices, proper management of health risks, farm development (e.g. intensification and diversification), enterprise management and marketing. Cost-sharing systems (farmers, municipality, government organizations and private enterprises) are needed to ensure the sustainability of such activities.

For example, the Cape Town policy on urban agriculture (South Africa) calls upon the services of the research, training and support organizations in and around the city to provide the urban farmers with training on business administration, technical skills and marketing (Visser, 2006). The Botswana policy paper (Hovorka and Keboneilwe, 2004; Keboneilwe, 2006) on urban agriculture assigns a critical role to farmer education through the production of books, brochures, posters and community-level demonstration projects and advocates the integration of urban agriculture into the formal training and education system (such as agricultural colleges and technical schools). In Chicago (USA), the Food Policy Council is the platform where the municipality and NGOs, for example, Heifer and Growing Power, coordinate their activities regarding capacity building and training activities for community gardeners.

Strengthening farmers' organizations. Most urban farmers are poorly organized and usually operate informally. They therefore lack sufficient access to decision-making processes and power to be able to voice their needs. This limits the representation of their interests in urban policy making and hampers their participation in development programmes. Well-functioning farmers' organizations can negotiate access to land, adequate tenure arrangements and access to credit. Such organizations may also take up roles in farmer training and extension, infrastructure development, processing and marketing and control/certification of the quality of marketed products. In Bangkok (Thailand), for example, associations of aquaculture farmers have been instrumental in negotiating fair prices for producers or negotiating contracts directly with wholesalers and retailers.

More efforts are needed to identify existing farmers' organizations and informal networks of (various types of) urban farmers, to analyse their problems and needs, and to find effective ways to help them develop further. Municipalities may stimulate their own departments, as well as universities, NGOs and CBOs present in the city, to actively support capacity development of farmers' organizations and to strengthen the linkages between these farmers' organizations and private enterprises, consumer organizations and support organizations.

The PROVE programme of Brasilia FD (Brazil) has stimulated urban producers to establish producer associations and their capacities have been enhanced to gradually replace the government officers in their supporting role (Homem de Carvalho, 2005). In Rosario (Argentina) the Municipal Urban Agriculture Programme supported the establishment of the Urban Producers Network and helped to establish working relations between urban producers and various government and non-governmental organizations. In Beijing (China), agricultural cooperatives have been created, often closely linked to village-level management, which facilitate capacity building and joint marketing (Liu et al., 2003).

Available technologies have to be adapted for urban agriculture

Credit: IWMI India

Development of appropriate technologies. Urban agriculture is performed under specific conditions that require technologies that differ from those used in the rural context. Such specific conditions include limited availability of space and the high price of urban land, proximity to large numbers of people (and thus a need for safe production methods), use of urban resources (organic waste and wastewater) and possibilities for direct producer–consumer contacts. Most available agricultural technologies have to be adapted for use under these conditions whilst new technologies have to be developed to respond to specific urban needs (such as non-soil production technologies for use on roofs and in cellars and the development of safe and economic practices for reuse of wastewater).

Municipalities can provide budget and expertise for local technology development, and/or to stimulate research organizations and universities to put urban agriculture issues on their research agenda and to undertake participatory action-research with urban producers. Also, more coordination between research institutes, agricultural extension organizations, NGOs and groups of urban farmers could be promoted. Further, special attention should be given to the introduction of ecological farming practices (such as integrated pest and disease management, ecological soil fertility management and soil and water conservation), space intensive and water saving technologies, health risk reducing practices and the creation of farmer study clubs and field schools that actively engage in the technology development and assessment process.

The national urban agriculture programme in Cuba undertakes a large amount of practical research to develop technology that is appropriate for urban conditions including agro-ecological production methods that do not harm the environment (Ministerio de la Agricultura y Grupo Nacional de Agricultura Urbana de Cuba, 2004). The Botswana policy paper (Keboneilwe, 2006) on urban agriculture urges research and extension institutions to develop and disseminate technologies among small-scale urban farmers. The following technologies are mentioned: 1) Adaptable cultivars (e.g. cabbage, tomato, onion); 2) Water saving techniques (e.g. drip irrigation system or micro-irrigation system); and 3) Appropriate production practices (e.g. hydroponics, concrete benches, protected agriculture). In Gampaha and the Western Province (Sri Lanka) 'no-space and low-space' technologies are being developed and disseminated to households that lack access to land (RUAF Foundation, 2009b; and the 'Building synergies to promote urban agriculture in Gampaha, Sri Lanka case study in Chapter 3).

Enhancing access to water, inputs and basic infrastructure. Access to a year-round supply of low cost water is of crucial importance in urban agriculture as well as access to (composted or fresh) organic materials and other sources of nutrients (like wastewater). Municipalities can play an important role in enhancing access of urban farmers to water and production inputs. The city of Bulawayo (Zimbabwe) provides treated wastewater to poor urban farmers in community gardens (Mubvami, 2006), while the city of Tacna (Peru) has agreed to provide urban farmers with its treated wastewater in return for their assistance to maintain public green areas. The City of Gaza (Palestinian Authority) promotes the reuse of 'grey' household water in home and community gardens (Laeremans and Sourani, 2006). Mexico City (Mexico) promotes systems for rainwater collection and storage, construction of wells and the establishment of localized water-efficient irrigation systems (e.g. drip irrigation) to stimulate production and to reduce the demand for potable water (Silva-Ochoa and Scott, 2002). The municipality of Cape Town (South Africa) assists community garden groups with basic infrastructure (a fence, a tool shed, a tank and hoses for irrigation) and allows them to use up to a certain amount of piped water daily free of charge (Visser, 2006). They have also transferred an old industrial site and building to Abalimi (an NGO that supports 3,000 urban producers) to be converted into a place that includes a packaging shed for green vegetables, demonstration ground for ecological production technologies and a training centre. The city of Havana (Cuba) facilitates an adequate supply of quality seeds, natural fertilizers and bio-pesticides in small quantities to urban farmers through a network of local stores and is supporting the establishment of decentralized low-cost facilities for compost production and the installation of composting toilets (Ministerio de la Agricultura y Grupo Nacional de Agricultura Urbana de Cuba, 2004).

Enhancing access of urban farmers to credit and finance. Improvement of the access of urban farmers to credit and finance (with an emphasis on women-producers and resource-poor farmers) is very much needed. Municipalities can stimulate existing credit institutions to establish special credit schemes for urban producers (e.g. by creating a guarantee fund) or to allow the participation of urban producers in existing credit schemes for the informal sector. In Brasilia FD (Brazil), the PROVE programme provides urban producer associations with a nonmonetary guarantee in the form of 'Mobile Agro-industries' (metal frames that can be transported on a truck). Since these frames are mobile and durable, they can be used as collateral for a commercial loan (Homem de Cavalho, 2005).

The inclusion of urban agriculture in the municipal budget is also an essential component in the promotion of urban agriculture activities. In many cities, the City Council allocates resources to support its policy and programme on urban agriculture (infrastructure development, training, marketing support, start up kits, etc.).

Marketing of surpluses by poor urban farmers needs to be facilitated

Facilitating direct marketing by urban farmers. Due to the informal status of urban agriculture and the usual exclusive focus on food imported from rural areas and from outside the country, the creation of an infrastructure for direct local marketing of fresh urban-produced food and local small processing of locally produced food has received little attention in most cities. However, some municipalities do facilitate the marketing of surpluses by poor urban farmers by providing them access to existing city markets, assisting them in the creation of farmers' markets (infrastructure development, licences, control of product quality), authorising food box schemes and/or supporting the establishment of 'green labels' for ecologically grown and safe urban food. An example is how the Budapest municipality (Hungary) assisted Biokultura,

Credit: IPES

the local organization of urban and peri-urban farmers, to create a weekly organic farmers' market. As a result, Biokultura now has its own organic certifying institute.

Many cities in the USA and Canada also provide space for farmers' markets for organized local farmers. Examples include the city of Vancouver (Canada) and the work of the Rainbow Coalition in Milwaukee and Chicago, which organizes the cooperative sale of organic farm produce through farmers' markets and food box schemes (Vancouver Food Policy Task Force, 2003).

The municipality of Governador Valadares (Brazil) has prioritized the marketing of urban agricultural products in different ways: 1) By providing incentives for the formation of co-operatives for the production and commercialization of products; 2) By creating sales and distribution centres as well as farmers' markets in the city; and 3) By buying agricultural products from urban farmers' groups to supply to schools, community kitchens, hospitals and other service organizations.

The creation of networks connecting local farmers to buyers for restaurants and institutional food programmes including, for example, airports and government-, health- and educational-institutions, could play a role in maintaining the viability of small urban and peri-urban farms.

Supporting micro-enterprise development. Various municipalities are promoting the development of small-scale enterprises: suppliers of (often ecological) farm inputs (such as compost, earthworms, open pollinated seeds and plant materials and bio-pesticides) and processing enterprises (such as food preservation, packaging, street vending and transport) by:

- providing start up licences and subsidies or tax reductions to micro- and small entrepreneurs;
- providing technical and management assistance to micro- and small enterprises;
- providing subsidies and technical assistance for local infrastructure and equipment for small-scale food preservation and storage facilities.

In Ghana, the Tema Municipality has cooperated with the Ministry of Food and Agriculture to establish a milk collection system to encourage dairying in the peri-urban areas of Tema. In Brasilia FD (Brazil), the PROVE programme supports the development of small agro-processing and/or packaging units managed by urban farmers' groups and assists them in setting up quality labels and other marketing strategies. The PROVE products began to be sold in supermarkets as a result of an agreement between the local government, super-markets and producers. Based on this example, agro-industries were also established in Rosario (Argentina), the products of which are sold at weekly urban markets and in municipal offices, for example.

The small-scale of production and rapid turnover of capital of small urban producers also often impedes them from buying even small amounts of good-quality inputs at affordable prices. Therefore, some municipal programmes develop mechanisms for collective purchasing and sales in small units to urban farmers. In Havana (Cuba), farmers' stores (*Tiendas del Agricultor*) have been installed in various neighbourhoods. In these stores, urban farmers can buy equipment, seeds, natural fertilizers, and bio-formulas in small quantities and at low prices. In addition, these stores offer technical assistance.

Measures to promote social inclusion and gender equity

Urban agriculture projects may be designed that specifically involve disadvantaged groups such as youth, disabled people, women heading a household with young children, recent immigrants without jobs, or elderly people without a pension, and with the aim to integrate these groups into socio-economic city-life. Many of these groups are especially at risk of food insecurity, given their often lesser access to rural and urban land, as well as to technical assistance and credit resources.

Gender affirmative actions. The percentage of poor female-led households is generally increasing and in many cities, women constitute the majority of the urban producers. However, they often experience limited access to education, land ownership and access to financial resources. In Fortaleza (Brazil), Banco Palmas created the *Incubadora Femenina*, a food security project seeking to involve women at risk (Melo Neto Segundo, 2002). The project provides information, facilitates visits to farmers' markets and manages an 'urban agriculture laboratory' where women learn farming activities. Women are thus assisted to start their own family farming operations and to cultivate fresh vegetables and medicinal herbs. The municipality of Oña (Ecuador) promoted the use of municipal and private land for farming as part of the municipal Economic Development Plan, prioritizing women and senior citizens. The micro-credit PROQUITO programme, in the municipality of Metropolitan Quito (Ecuador), offers preferential access to credit for urban agriculture to women who are heads of households and to people under 30 years of age, two groups that have the highest unemployment rates in the city (IPES/UMP-LAC, 2002).

School and children's gardens. Amongst many other cities, the cities of Antananarivo (Madagascar), Rosario (Argentina), Bulawayo (Zimbabwe) and Gampaha (Sri Lanka) are promoting school garden programmes. Extensive evidence exists that school-based garden programmes have significant health effects on young people. In these non-traditional learning labs, children become familiar with fresh and nutritious food, especially the fruits and vegetables critical to reducing obesity and chronic diseases. It is precisely these foods that are missing from poor urban children's usual diets. School garden programmes teach a skill and a lifetime hobby that provides exercise, mental stimulation and social interactions. Children receive a practical introduction to biological and environmental sciences, mathematics, geography and social studies.

Supporting youth entrepreneurs through urban agriculture. For a growing number of urban youth, males and females, in the face of shrinking formal employment, market-oriented urban agriculture and related enterprises provide a relatively accessible entry into the urban job market. Young people can earn an income, save on food, learn another trade and perhaps set up a small business. In Portland (USA), a youth employment programme, Food Works, engages 14–21 year olds in all aspects

of planning and running an entrepreneurial farm business (Janus Youth Programs, 2009, www.diggablecity.org). Working side by side with gardens' staff, community residents, local farmers, business owners and non-profit leaders, Food Works' Crew Members learn business, leadership, organic agriculture and other work skills. Similar youth-oriented programmes are currently being set up in Freetown (Sierra Leone) and Porto Novo (Benin).

Urban agriculture projects may be designed to involve specific groups, such as youth

Credit: René van Veenhuizen

HIV/AIDS mitigation through urban agriculture. Families affected by HIV/AIDS tend to have higher expenses due to costs related to treatment of the infections and special diet requirements of the infected persons. Meanwhile, family income tends to decrease due to loss of strength and status of HIV/AIDS-affected family members leading to further socio-economic deterioration. Urban agriculture projects can make important contributions to mitigate the impacts of HIV and AIDS at the individual, family and community level. Its benefits include improved nutrition of HIV/AIDS-affected families, savings on food expenditures, added income from the sale of surpluses, and community mobilization to respond to HIV and AIDS. In Bulawayo (Zimbabwe) 12 allotment gardens were recently established by the city council in selected areas in the high-density and low-income areas of the city. The beneficiaries of the garden allotments are HIV-affected households, the elderly, widows and the destitute. In order to avoid the stigmatization associated with HIV, each garden draws from a mixed group of beneficiaries. The garden allotments, which largely produce vegetables, have contributed to food security and local community development. The HIV-affected households also feel less discriminated against now as they work with other community members in their gardens (Mubvami and Manyati, 2007).

Supporting migrants. In Cologne (Germany) intercultural gardens are promoted to allow immigrants to rent plots of land and start gardening (Stiftung Interkultur, 2009). Migrants (from Turkey, Iran, Congo, Cambodia, Japan and Poland) work alongside German-born residents, pursuing their gardening hobby, carving out a niche for themselves in a foreign country and improving their language skills. Many of the migrant gardeners cultivate crops and herbs from their home countries, which they otherwise cannot obtain in Germany. In Beijing (China) half a million peri-urban migrants are producing a large share of the city's fruits and vegetables consumption, without any acknowledgement or support until recently. The Beijing Agricultural Bureau is now supporting these migrants to form cooperatives and provides technical assistance in ecological production techniques and marketing (Liu et al., 2003).

Measures to reduce the health and environmental risks associated with urban agriculture

Rather than restricting urban agriculture, out of an often unspecified fear of health and environmental risks associated with urban agriculture, cities can instead better design a series of accompanying measures to reduce these risks. The following measures are regularly recommended to reduce risks that can be associated with urban agriculture.

Improved coordination between health, agriculture and environmental departments. The first measure to be taken is to create mechanisms of cooperation between agriculture, health and environment/waste management departments to assess actual health and environmental risks associated with urban agriculture and to design effective preventive/mitigating strategies for which the participation of all these sectors is required. In Kampala (Uganda), health, agricultural and town planning specialists have closely cooperated in the development of the new ordinances on urban agriculture livestock and fisheries (Yeudall et al., 2007). In Phnom Penh (Cambodia) steps are being taken to improve the coordination between municipal departments, universities and private organizations for controlling and monitoring the microbiological and chemical quality of wastewater-fed fish and plants in order to reduce a number of health problems (especially skin infections) related to wastewater-fed aquaculture (Bunting et al., 2006). In Kumasi (Ghana) small kits have been made available to various local organizations to periodically test the quality of the irrigation water. The Accra Metropolitan Assembly has drafted revised bylaws on the use of wastewater and has supported an awareness campaign on health risk minimization strategies in production and marketing (Farm to Fork) of urban vegetables (Obuobie et al., 2006). The Ministry of Housing, Construction and Sanitation of Peru (MVCS) is formulating policy guidelines for the promotion of the productive use of treated wastewater in intra- and peri-urban agriculture and the recreational use of wastewater (including the irrigation of parks and other public green areas).

Health considerations when setting aside zones for urban agriculture. Many cities identify zones where certain types of urban agriculture are allowed (often defining required management practices) and other types are excluded (due to expected negative effects in the given local circumstances) in order to reduce health and environmental risks. When preparing such a zoning and related regulations, factors such as population density, the ecological sensitivity of the area concerned, closeness to polluting industry and closeness to sources of drinking water should be taken into account. Furthermore, the available means to enforce zoning and related regulations should be taken into account.

A city may want to avoid free roaming cattle and major concentrations of stall-fed dairy

Credit: Philip Amoah / IWMI Ghana

Health risks can be reduced if farmers are made fully aware of associated risks

cattle or piggeries in central districts (to avoid traffic congestion, bad smells, flies and waste management problems). Further, intensive horticulture and poultry keeping in areas that are sources of drinking water (risk of water contamination) or mono-cropping in river stream beds (erosion problems/siltation of dams) might need to be avoided. Proper location of crop fields in relation to sources of contamination is also important in order to reduce the effects of air pollution. Within 50–75 m of a main road, leafy vegetables can better be avoided; and production of food crops close to industries that emit certain toxic elements should also be discouraged.

Farmer education on the management of health and environmental risks. Health risks associated with urban farming can be reduced substantially if farmers are made well aware of these risks and know how to prevent them. Examples of preventive measures that can be implemented by farmers themselves are the following:

- Apply ecological farming methods to reduce risks related to intensive use of agrochemicals.
- Adopt adequate animal waste management, regular cleaning and disinfection of stables and proper handling of animal feed in order to prevent health risks related to raising animals in the proximity of homes.
- Use of adequate irrigation practices and proper crop choice can reduce health risks related to the use of wastewater. Untreated wastewater should preferably not be used for food crops (especially not fresh leafy vegetables), but may be used for growing trees or shrubs, crops for industrial use and other non-edible plants (such as ornamentals and flowers). In Xochimilco (Mexico) urban producers have shifted from vegetable growing to a lucrative floriculture when untreated canal waters have become unfit for food growing (Canabal, 1997). In Hyderabad, India, farmers have shifted from the production of paddy to fodder

grass production when river water that is used for irrigation gradually became more polluted (Buechler and Devi, 2006).

- Food fish farmers in Bangkok (Thailand) facing increasing pollution and food safety problems have been encouraged to switch to ornamental fish production. Vegetable producers
in Ho Chi Minh City (Vietnam) have begun cultivating ornamental plants for the urban
middle class to reduce the risks of growing vegetables with wastewater. Municipalities in
Ghana, Jordan and Senegal are field testing the various methods and procedures proposed
by the WHO to reduce the risk of use of wastewater in urban agriculture in situations
where comprehensive wastewater treatment is too expensive and not feasible in the near
term – as is common in many cities in developing countries – (WHO, 2006; Drechsel
et al., 2009).

Education of food vendors and consumers. During production, processing and marketing crops
can become contaminated. Access to clean water and sanitation facilities should therefore be
provided in markets and food-hygiene training should be provided to small food processors and
vendors. Consumers need to be educated regarding the washing or scraping of crops, heating
of milk and meat products and securing hygienic conditions during food handling. Consumers
also need education regarding the importance of fresh nutritious foods and medicinal herbs
and their preparation. A United Nations Food and Agriculture Organization (FAO) project on
making street foods safer in Dakar (Senegal) is training food vendors, food inspectors and
consumers in food hygiene issues. In Accra (Ghana) a multi-partner project resulted in the
training of more than 3,000 street food vendors on improved hygiene practices as well as
increased consumer awareness.

Prevention of industrial pollution of soils and water by industry. Contamination of soils, rivers
and streams by industry is a growing obstacle to safe urban food production. Separation of city
waste (residential and office areas) and industrial waste streams and treatment of industrial
wastes at the source should be promoted. In areas where contamination might occur (such as
downstream of industrial areas) periodic testing of soils and water quality in agricultural plots
might be needed. Increasing pollution and contamination of the city's domestic wastewater
with industrial wastewater effluents is a major constraint to the continued viability of irrigated
urban agriculture as well as to aquaculture. In many South-east Asian cities, the continuity
of the existing potential for growing aquatic vegetables and fish using urban wastewater
will depend on the city planners' ability to coordinate and develop strategies for effective
separation of toxic industrial waste from domestic sewage. There are already encouraging
examples in Hanoi (Mubarik et al., 2005) and Ho Chi Minh City (Vietnam) of relocation and
zoning of urban industries to industrial parks which allow for more effective treatment and
monitoring of effluents. In the medium term, enforcing existing pollution control legislation
to control contaminants at their source and monitoring and regulating industrial wastewater
discharge in public water sources can be effective in reducing health risks.

Inclusion of urban agriculture in local climate change adaptation and disaster risk reduction strategies

The World Meteorological Organization (WMO, 2007) has recommended an increase in urban and indoor farming as a response to climate change and as a means to build more resilient cities. Various cities are already including urban agriculture as part of their strategies to reduce their ecological food/t-print, knowing that urban agriculture has lower energy use (less transport, less cooling, more fresh products sold directly to consumers) and enables cyclical processes and effective use of waste (such as use of urban organic wastes as compost or as raw materials for production of animal feed; and use of excess heat of industry in greenhouses). Urban and peri-urban agriculture also contributes to keeping flood plains and wetlands free from construction and storing and infiltration of excess storm water.

In order to strengthen climate change adaptation in urban areas, the city government may take measures such as:

• preferential food procurement from family and community-based farms located within the city region (for government canteens and school feeding programmes, for example) and facilitating direct marketing of fresh and ecologically produced food from regional sources (less packaging, transport and cooling);
• protecting and stimulating sustainable urban and peri-urban agriculture in flood zones and wetlands and on steep slopes in order to prevent construction in such areas, to slow down water runoff and facilitate infiltration;
• promoting/maintaining multifunctional parks and greenbelts and promoting agro-forestry, involving urban poor and farmers in the maintenance of such green zones (multi-functional land use) in order to reduce the urban heat islands effects, reduce runoff and enhance biodiversity;
• facilitating (safe) reuse of urban wastewater and organic wastes in order to reduce the disposal of wastes into open water systems, reduce fresh water use, promote recycling of nutrients and reduce emissions of methane from waste dumps. In that context, a shift to decentralized and low-cost treatment of wastewater allowing the reuse of wastewater and nutrients close to the source needs to be supported (for example, through stabilization ponds, a cluster approach and constructed wetlands) as well as the decentralized collection and (co-)composting of organic wastes and excreta systems. The health risks associated with the productive reuse of untreated waste water (and polluted streams) have to be reduced through complementary health risk reduction measures as outlined in the new WHO guidelines for safe use of excreta and wastewater (WHO, 2006).

Interesting experiences with the planning and implementation of such urban agriculture related adaptation measures to climate change are being gained by the Climate change programme for Asian cities of the Rockefeller Foundation (Rumbaitis del Rio, 2009). Investing in climate adaptation must involve low-income groups (who often live in the areas most vulnerable to climate impacts) and fully involve them in plans to reduce flooding and other risks (Reid and Sattertwhaite, 2007). In order, for example, to create and maintain a buffer between the city and the river, especially in view of possible changes in the river's water table, the cities of Zwolle (The Netherlands) and Rosario (Argentina) have decided to protect the flood zone from urbanization and maintain it as an attractive multifunctional area for agriculture, nature and recreation. Climate change adaptation through urban agriculture links enhancing urban resilience with better living environments, increased food security and income and, most importantly, enhances the adaptive management capacity of the urban poor.

The IASC Task Force on Meeting Humanitarian Challenges on Urban Areas (IASC, 2009) recommended that in the aftermath of humanitarian crises, support programmes should focus on the revival and diversification of livelihoods for the most vulnerable groups, rather than seeing food distribution as their main intervention. This should be done especially through enabling various forms of urban agriculture and related community-based agro-enterprises (such as compost making, food processing, transport, marketing and home-based manufacturing of tools) by providing tools, seeds, access to land and essential services (including training, organizational support, and training for entrepreneurs).

Integration of urban agriculture into national policies

The overview provided above indicates the wide range of policy measures and actions that municipalities may apply to stimulate and regulate the development of urban and peri-urban agriculture depending on local conditions, needs and policy priorities.

But the local stakeholders will also need the support from national policy makers. Local initiatives on urban and peri-urban agriculture are often constrained by restrictions in mandates and in national legislation. This makes local authorities sometimes hesitant to develop more pro-active policies and programmes on urban agriculture as long as no adequate policy, financial and technical support is provided from the national level.

Urban and peri-urban agriculture needs to be integrated in national policies, such as the agricultural policy, the national food security and poverty reduction strategies, national SCP (sustainable consumption and production) and Agenda 21 plans etc. Several developing countries have already taken such initiatives: Cuba some time ago developed a comprehensive policy to support highly productive – and mainly ecological – urban and peri-urban agriculture. This started off as a crisis measure (oil crisis) but has become a crucial component of its national agriculture and food security policies. Brazil developed an urban agriculture programme as part of its 'Zero Hunger' policy. Sierra Leone included urban agriculture in its 'Operation Feed the Nation', Ghana in the national food and agriculture sector development policy (FASDEP II) and Sri Lanka in its National Campaign to Motivate Domestic Food Production 2007–2010 while China included it as a central component in its 'New Countryside' policy (RUAF Foundation, 2009b).

In countries where such initiatives have not been taken yet, it is recommended to undertake a *scoping exercise* to review past research, ongoing and new initiatives, needs and opportunities, potential actors at all levels as a basis for selecting priority areas, setting targets and defining policy measures and actions required. An important step will be the creation of an institutional home for urban agriculture. Conventionally, sector policies have been defined under the assumption that agriculture refers to the rural sphere. As a consequence, urban and peri-urban agriculture often does not receive proper attention and support either from the agricultural institutions or from the urban authorities. The Ministry of Agriculture seems in most countries the best equipped to take a coordinating role regarding urban and peri-urban agriculture, but experiences to date reveal that close cooperation with other Ministries is also required (Health, Social Development, Economic Development) and that these Ministries have to play an active role in the design and realization of urban agriculture programmes (either as part of their own sector policy or as inputs to the agricultural policy or programme).

Pro-active policies are needed to stimulate local initiatives

Final remarks

Conventionally, city governments looked upon agriculture as a relic that had survived from rural–urban migration and was incompatible with urban development. The expectation was that agriculture in the city would dwindle as cities and urban economies would grow. Urban agriculture was not given any policy attention, other than restricting it as much as possible or permitting it only temporarily at certain sites.

The many examples given in this book demonstrate that local authorities in many countries have recognized that urban and peri-urban agriculture form an integral part of the urban socio-economic and ecological system, link to several critical urban challenges, and deserve proper policy attention and support.

Such recognition has led to policy changes in many cities and the design of action programmes on urban agriculture, involving various stakeholders from governmental and private sectors.

The urbanization of poverty and food insecurity have become serious concerns and national governments and international agencies are increasing their support for the development of safe and sustainable urban agriculture systems and the integration of these within the urban planning system.

With this book we have sought to share the experiences gained and lessons learned in the RUAF 'Cities Farming for the Future' programme (2004–2008) in two partner cities and by so doing to provide some building blocks for stakeholders in developing countries to participate in policy formulation and action planning on urban agriculture.

After an introduction to urban agriculture and a discussion of potentials for responding to key challenges with which cities in developing countries are confronted (Chapter 1), we have presented the Multi-stakeholder Policy formulation and Action Planning approach as applied by RUAF CFF in 20 cities in close cooperation with municipal authorities, urban farmer groups, universities, NGOs, governmental organizations and other stakeholders in urban agriculture (Chapters 2 and 3).

In this chapter (Chapter 4), we have shifted focus from the participatory process of policy and programme development through to the question of what kind of policy measures and actions best promote the development of sustainable and safe urban agriculture.

We hope and expect that the readers of this publication will have been stimulated to engage in participatory planning on urban agriculture in their own cities, combining the lessons learned from participatory multi-stakeholder processes with the lessons learned regarding effective policies and courses of action for the development of sustainable urban agriculture.

References

Azuba, S.M. and McCans, S. (2006) 'Effecting policy change and implementation in urban agriculture, Kampala, Uganda', *Urban Agriculture Magazine* 16: 60–61.

Boudjenouia, A., Fleury, A. and Tacherift, A. (2006) 'Multi-functionality of peri-urban open spaces in Setif, Alegria', *Urban Agriculture Magazine* 15: 28–29.

Buechler, S. and Devi, G. (2006) 'Adaptations of wastewater-irrigated farming systems: A case study of Hyderabad, India', in R. van Veenhuizen (ed.), *Cities Farming for the Future: Urban Agriculture for Green and Productive Cities*, pp. 267–70, RUAF Foundation, IDRC and IIRR, Philippines.

Bunting, S., Little, D. and Leschen, W. (2006) 'Urban aquatic production', in R. van Veenhuizen (ed.), *Cities Farming for the Future: Urban Agriculture for Green and Productive Cities*, pp. 267–70, RUAF Foundation, IDRC and IIRR, Philippines.

Canabal, B. (1997) *Xochimilco una identidad creada*, Universidad Autónoma Metropolitana-Xochimilco.

City of Cape Town (2006) *Urban Agriculture Policy for the City of Cape Town*. Available from: http://www.capetown.gov.za/en/ehd/Documents/EHD_-_Urban_Agricultural_Policy_2007_8102007113120_.pdf [last accessed 25 March 2010].

Cooley, R. (2006) 'Municipal and civil society food systems policy development', *Urban Agriculture Magazine* 16: 54.

Dongus, S. (2001) *Urban Vegetable Production in Dar es Salaam (Tanzania) – GIS-supported Analysis of Spatial Changes from 1992 to 1999*, APT-Reports 12, pp.100–44, Freiburg, Germany.

Drechsel, P., Scott, C.A. and Rashid-Sally, L. (eds) (2009) *Wastewater Irrigation and Health: Assessing and Mitigating Risk in Low-income Countries*, Earthscan, UK.

Dubbeling, M. (2004) *Optimising use of vacant space for urban agriculture through participatory planning processes*. Paper presented at workshop on IDRC supported initiatives on urban agriculture and food security, Ryerson University, Toronto, August–September 2004.

Fang, J., Hong, Y., Shenghe, L. and Jianming, C. (2005) 'Multifunctional agro-tourism in Beijing', *Urban Agriculture Magazine* 15: 14–15.

Foeken, D. (2006) *To Subsidise My Income: Urban farming in an East African Town*, Brill, Leiden.

Governador Valadares (2003) *Proposals for the inclusion of UA in the City's Master Plan based on the City Statute*, Governador Valadares, Brazil (original text in Portuguese, (translation by M. Dubbeling and R. Huber), IPES-UMPLAC/UN Habitat.

Governador Valadares (2004) *Proposals for the use of progressive and regressive taxing policies to encourage the productive use of private spaces*, Governador Valadares, Brazil (original text in Portuguese, translation by M. Dubbeling and R. Huber), IPES-UMPLAC/UN Habitat.

Holmer, R., Clavejo, M.T., Dongus, S., Drescher, A. (2003) 'Allotment gardens for Philippine cities', *Urban Agriculture Magazine* 11: 29–31.

Homem de Carvalho, J.L. (2005) *ASPROVE, Association of the PROVE producers*. Case study for the IDRC/IPES/ETC project on 'Social organizations of urban and peri-urban producers: Management models and innovative alliances for policy influencing', (unpublished). Available from: http://www.ipes.org/au/osaup/english_version/organizaciones/asprove/Pdf/Estudio%20-%20ASPROVE%20-%20%20ingles.pdf [last accessed 25 March 2010].

Hovorka, A., and Keboneilwe, D. (2004) 'Launching a policy initiative in Botswana', *Urban Agriculture Magazine* 13: 46.

IASC (2009) *Meeting Humanitarian Challenges in Urban Areas: Assessment and Strategy*, Draft annotated outline, Task Force on Meeting Humanitarian Challenges in Urban Areas, Inter-Agency Standing Committee, Geneva.

International Potato Center (IPC) (2007) *Impacts of urban agriculture: Highlights of Urban Harvest research and development 2003–2006,* Urban Harvest, Lima.

IPES/ UMP-LAC (2002) *Policy Briefs on Urban Agriculture*, IDRC, IPES, UMP-LAC. Available from: http://www.ruaf.org/node/419 [last accessed 25 March 2010].

Jacobi, P., Amend, J. and Kiango, S. (2000) 'Urban agriculture in Dar es Salaam: providing for an indispensable part of the diet', in N. Bakker, M. Dubbeling, S. Guendel, U. Sabel-Koschella and H. de Zeeuw (eds), *Growing Cities, Growing Food: Urban Agriculture on the Policy Agenda*, pp. 257–83, DSE, Feldafing.

Janus Youth Programs (2009) *Urban Agriculture Services*. Available from: http://www.janusyouth.org/what-we-do/urban-agriculture-services.php [last accessed 25 March 2010].

Keboneilwe, D. (2006) *Urban and Peri-urban Agriculture*, Working Paper (approved by the Policy Advisory Committee on 21 March 2006).

Laeremans, L. and Sourani, A. (2006) 'Urban agriculture in the Gaza Strip, Palestine' *Urban Agriculture Magazine* 15: 26–7.

Liu, S., Cai, J. and Yang, Z. (2003) 'Migrants' access to land in peri-urban Beijing', *Urban Agriculture Magazine* 11: 6–8.

Mbaye, A. and Moustier, P. (2000) 'Market-oriented urban agricultural production in Dakar', in N. Bakker, M. Dubbeling, S. Guendel, U. Sabel-Koschella and H. de Zeeuw (eds), *Growing Cities, Growing Food: Urban Agriculture on the Policy Agenda,* pp. 235–56, German Foundation for International Development, Feldafing, Germany.

MDP (2002) *The Nyanga Declaration on Urban and Peri-Urban Agriculture in Zimbabwe*. Available from: http://www.ruaf.org/node/2132 [last accessed 25 March 2010].

Melo Neto Segundo, J.J. de (2002) 'Urban agriculture project in the Conjunto Palmeira slum, Fortaleza-Ceará, Brazil', *Urban Agriculture Magazine* 7: 10–11.

Mendes, W, (2006) 'Creating and implementing food policies in Vancouver, Canada', *Urban Agriculture Magazine* 16: 51–4.

Merzthal, G. and Soto, N. (2006) 'Integration of urban agriculture in municipal agendas: Experiences from Lima, Peru', *Urban Agriculture Magazine* 16: 27–31.

Mougeot, L.J.A. (ed.) (2005) *AGROPOLIS: The Social, Political and Environmental Dimensions of Urban Agriculture*, Earthscan, London.

Mubarik, A., De Bon, H. and Moustier, P. (2005) 'Promoting the multifunctionality of urban and per-iurban agriculture in Hanoi', *Urban Agriculture Magazine* 15: 11–13.

Mubvami, T. (2006) 'The policy framework and practice of urban agriculture in Bulawayo', *Urban Agriculture Magazine* 16: 38–40.

Mubvami, T. and Manyati, M. (2007) 'HIV/Aids, urban agriculture and community mobilisation: cases from Zimbabwe', *Urban Agriculture Magazine* 18: 7–10.

Municipality of Rosario (2002) *Ordinance 7341* (original text in Spanish, translation by M. Dubbeling and R. Huber), IPES-UMPLAC/UN Habitat.

Municipality of Rosario (2003) *Ordinance related to the establishment and management of a Municipal Land Bank for UA* (original text in Spanish, translation by M. Dubbeling and R. Huber), IPES-UMPLAC/UN Habitat.

Ministerio de la Agricultura y Grupo Nacional de Agricultura Urbana de Cuba (2004) *Lineamientos para los sub-programas de la agricultura urbana para el 2005 al 2007 y sistema evaluativo*, National Group for Urban Agriculture of the Ministry of Agriculture, Havana, Cuba.

Mutonodzo, C. (2009) 'The social and economic implications of urban agriculture on food security in Harare, Zimbabwe', in M. Redwood (ed.), *Agriculture in Urban Planning, Generating Livelihoods and Food Security*, pp. 73–90, Earthscan, London.

Obuobie, E., Keraita, B., Danso, G., Amoah, P., Cofie, O.O., Raschid-Sally, L. and P. Drechsel. (2006) 'Irrigated urban vegetable production in Ghana: Characteristics, benefits and risks'. IWMI-RUAF-IDRC-CPWF, Accra, Ghana: IWMI, 150 pp.

Pothukuchi, K. (2006) Contribution to the Comfood Listserv April 10, 2006. Available from: http://www.foodsecurity.org/list.html [last accessed 29 March 2010].

Potutan, G.E., Schnitzler, W.H., Arnado, J.M., Janubas, L.G. and Holmer, R.J. (2000) 'Urban agriculture in Cagayan de Oro: a favourable response of city government and NGOs', in N. Bakker, M. Dubbeling, S. Guendel, U. Sabel-Koschella and H. de Zeeuw (eds), *Growing Cities, Growing Food, Urban Agriculture on the Policy Agenda*, pp. 413–28, DSE, Feldafing, Germany.

Purnomohadi, N. (2000) 'Jakarta: Urban agriculture as an alternative strategy to face the economic crisis', in N. Bakker, M. Dubbeling, S. Guendel, U. Sabel-Koschella and H. de Zeeuw (eds), *Growing Cities, Growing Food, Urban Agriculture on the Policy Agenda*, pp. 453–66, DSE, Feldafing, Germany.

Reid, H. and Sattertwhaite, D. (2007) Climate *change and cities: Why urban agendas are central to adaptation and mitigation*, Sustainable Development Opinion, IIED, UK.

RUAF Foundation (2009a) *Report on the Networking Event 'Urban and Peri-urban Agriculture for Green, Productive and Socially Inclusive Cities'* at World Urban Forum IV, November 2008, Nanjing, China, RUAF Foundation, Leusden. Available from: http://www.ruaf.org/node/2022 [last accessed 25 March 2010].

RUAF Foundation (2009b) *Cities Farming for the Future Programme Final Progress Report (Activities realised in 2008 and Results obtained 2005–2008)*, RUAF Foundation, Leusden. Available from: http://www.ruaf.org/node/448 [last accessed 25 March 2010].

Rumbaitis del Rio, C. (2009), *Cities, Climate Change Resilience and Urban Agriculture*, Powerpoint presentation at Strategic Partnership meeting on Urban Agriculture, IDRC, Marseille, July 2, 2009.

Silva-Ochoa, P. and Scott, C.A. (2002) 'The impact of a treatment plant on wastewater irrigation in Mexico', *Urban Agriculture Magazine* 8: 33–4.

Socorro, A. (2003) 'From empty lots to productive spaces in Cienfuegos', *Urban Agriculture Magazine* 11: 26–7.

Stiftung Interkultur (2009) *Sponsoring partner of processes of integration in a multicultural society.* Available from: http://www.stiftung-interkultur.de [last accessed 29 March 2010].

Terrile, R. and Lattuca, A. (2006) 'An enabling policy framework for urban agriculture in Rosario', *Urban Agriculture Magazine* 16: 62.

Toronto Food Policy Council (2009) *Food Policy.* Available from: http://www.toronto.ca/health/tfpc_index.htm [last accessed 25 March 2010].

UMP LAC (2000) *Quito Declaration: Urban Agriculture in 21st Century Cities.* Available from: http://www.ruaf.org/node/2132 [last accessed 25 March 2010].

Vancouver Food Policy Task Force (2003) *Policy report on Action Plan for Creating a Just and Sustainable Food System for the City of Vancouver*, prepared for presentation to the Vancouver City Council on 20 November 2003. Available from: http://www.vancouver.ca/ctyclerk/cclerk/20031209/rr1.htm [last accessed 25 March 2010].

Van Veenhuizen, R. (ed.) (2006) *Cities Farming for the Future: Urban Agriculture for Green and Productive Cities*, RUAF Foundation, IDRC and IIRR, Philippines.

Visser, S. (2006) 'Concrete actions: Cape Town's urban agriculture assistance programme', *Urban Agriculture Magazine* 16: 48–50.

Wilbers, J. (2005) *Bond van Volkstuinders, BVV (Association of Gardeners)*, Case study for the IDRC/IPES/ETC project on 'Social organisations of urban and peri-urban producers: Management models and innovative alliances for policy influencing', (unpublished). Available from: http://www.ipes.org/au/osaup/english_version/organizaciones/bvv/Pdf/Estudio%20-%20BVV%20Amsterdam%20-%20ingles.pdf [last accessed 25 March 2010].

Wilbers, J. and De Zeeuw, H. (2006) 'A critical review of recent policy documents on urban agriculture', *Urban Agriculture Magazine* 16: 3–9.

World Health Organization (WHO) (2006) *WHO Guidelines for the Safe Use of Wastewater, Excreta and Greywater*, WHO, Geneva.

World Meteorological Organization (WMO) (2007) *UN Agency calls for urban agriculture*, WMO press release 7 December 2007

Yeudall, F., Sebastian, R., Cole, D.C., Ibrahim, S., Lubowa, A., and Kikafunda, J. (2007) 'Food and nutritional security of children of urban farmers in Kampala, Uganda', *Food and Nutrition Bulletin* 28 (2 Suppl.): 237–46.

RESOURCES

Key readings on urban agriculture

Bakker, N., Dubbeling, M., Guendel, S., Sabel-Koschella, U. and De Zeeuw, H. (eds) (2000) *Growing cities, growing food: Urban agriculture on the policy agenda*, DSE, Feldafing, Germany.
This reader contributes to the debate on the value of urban agriculture for sustainable urban development in a thematic way. Definitions and presence of urban agriculture are explored. From there, potential contributions of urban agriculture to food security, household economics and city ecology are examined. Policy and institutional options and implications are also discussed. The second part of the reader contains case studies from selected cities in Asia, Africa, Latin America and Europe which pursue a system-oriented approach to understanding urban agriculture and its ecological, economic and food security impacts in different political, economic, demographic and ecological conditions. The authors include urban planners, researchers, project coordinators and NGO staff from both developing and northern countries. http://www.ruaf.org/node/54

Barker, C., Prain, G., Warnaars, M., Warnaars, X., Wing, L. and Wolf, F. (2007) *Impacts of Urban Agriculture, Highlights of Urban Harvest research and development 2003–2006*, **International Potato Center, Lima.**
Organized within a research framework that encompasses the themes of Ecosystem Health, Livelihoods and Markets and Stakeholder and Policy Analysis and Dialogue, Urban Harvest presents the impacts of innovative work undertaken in Africa, Asia and Latin America to enhance the food, nutrition and income security of the urban poor through agriculture. http://www.database.ruaf.org/ruaf_bieb/upload/2887.pdf

Cole, D., Lee-Smith, D. and Nasinyama G. (eds) (2008) *Healthy City Harvests – Generating evidence to guide policy on urban agriculture*, **CIP/Urban Harvest and Makerere University Press.**
This book presents research results on potential health risks of crop and livestock production in the city, as well as nutritional and food security benefits of urban farming, embedded in the policy context of Kampala, but with relevance to other cities in Africa. It addresses the role of urban agriculture in a time of global urban food crises and rapid, unplanned city growth, and how these were re-integrated in a public policy debate. http://www.uharvest.org/

De Zeeuw, H. (2005) Gardens of Hope; *Urban agriculture as a complementary strategy for the mitigation of the HIV-Aids pandemic.* **Report on the workshop and study visit to Johannesburg and Cape Town, 5–11 August 2005, ETC/RUAF, CTA and Abalimi Bezekhaya, Leusden.**

This report gives an introduction to the background and aim of the study visit and workshop and an introduction to the key issues on urban micro-farming and HIV/AIDS. It includes 20 cases presented during the study visit and gives a summary of the main conclusions and recommendations to local and national policy makers and donor agencies as well as an overview of the follow up actions planned by the participants themselves.
http://www.ruaf.org/node/1329

De Zeeuw, H. and Dubbeling, M. (2009) *Cities, food and agriculture: Challenges and the way forward.* **Discussion paper for the RUAF-FAO Technical consultation on 'Food, Agriculture and Cities', 24–25 September 2009, Rome, RUAF Foundation.**
The discussion paper discusses a number of key challenges encountered by cities today (including increasing urban poverty and food insecurity; growing scarcity of fresh water; waste disposal problems; flooding and rising urban temperatures) and provides research data on the contributions urban and peri-urban agriculture can make to respond to these challenges. Finally a number of policy recommendations are formulated at local, national and international level to strengthen the resilience of urban food systems. http://www.ruaf.org/node/2135

Drechsel, P. and Kunze, D. (2001) *Waste composting for urban and peri-urban agriculture: Closing the rural-urban nutrient cycle in sub-Saharan Africa*, **CABI Publishing, Wallingford, International Water Management Institute, Colombo, and FAO, Rome.**
This book addresses the subject of waste management and environmental protection in a rapidly urbanizing environment. The book is mainly based on papers presented at a workshop on 'Closing the nutrient cycle for urban food security and environmental protection' held in Ghana by the International Board for Soil Research and Management (now part of the International Water Management Institute) and FAO. Special reference is given to sub-Saharan Africa, with acknowledgement to experiences from other parts of the world.
http://www.amazon.co.uk/Waste-Composting-Urban-Peri-urban-Agriculture/dp/0851995489

FAO (2007) *The urban producer's resource book: A practical guide for working with low income urban and peri-urban producers organizations*, **FAO, Rome.**
This manual focuses on issues of central concern to urban producers worldwide: access to resources for production; financial constraints; policy and regulatory environment; local government and institutional support; environmental and food quality; and safety standards and group organization. It explains how urban producers can be assisted in forming themselves into organizations or how they can strengthen their existing organizations.
http://www.fao.org/docrep/010/a1177e/a1177e00.htm

Hovorka, A., De Zeeuw, H. and Njenga, M. (eds) (2009) *Women Feeding Cities – Mainstreaming gender in urban agriculture and food security*, **Practical Action Publishing, Rugby.**
The book analyses the roles of women and men in urban food production, processing and marketing in case studies from three development regions and includes field-tested guidelines and tools for gender mainstreaming. It is essential reading for researchers, policy makers and

development practitioners. The publication is based on experiences gained in the context of Urban Harvest, the CGIAR System-wide Initiative on Urban and Peri-urban Agriculture and The Cities Farming for the Future programme of the RUAF Foundation.
http://www.database.ruaf.org/gender/index.htm

Knuth, L. (2006) *Greening cities for improving urban livelihoods: Legal, policy and institu-tional aspects of urban and peri-urban forestry in West and Central Asia* **(with a case study of Armenia), FAO Livelihood Support Programme (LSP), Working Paper 37, FAO, Rome.**
This paper is one of a series which addresses the linkages of poverty and forests in West and Central Asia within the context of sustainable livelihood approaches. It presents a livelihoods analysis of the contribution of forests and trees to urban poor livelihoods.
http://www.mountainpartnership.org/common/files/pdf/5_Greening.pdf

Koc, M., MacRae, R., Mougeot, L.J.A. and Welsh, J. (eds) (1999) *For Hunger-proof Cities – Sustainable Urban Food Systems*, **IDRC, Ottawa.**
This is the first book to fully examine food security from an urban perspective. It examines existing local food systems and ways to improve the availability and accessibility of food for city dwellers. It looks at methods to improve community-supported agriculture and coopera-tion between urban and rural populations. It explores what existing marketing and distribution structures can do to improve accessibility and what the emerging forms of food-distribution systems are, and how they can contribute to alleviating hunger in the cities. The book discusses the underlying structures that create poverty and inequality and examines the role of emergency food systems, such as food banks. It includes contributions from farmers and professors, young activists and experienced business leaders, students and policy makers, and community organizers and practitioners. http://www.idrc.ca/en/ev-9394-201-1-DO_TOPIC.html

Mougeot, L.J.A. (2005) *AGROPOLIS – The Social, Political and Environmental Dimensions of Urban Agriculture*, **IDRC, Ottawa.**
This book presents the first harvest of graduate research on urban agriculture supported by the AGROPOLIS small grant facility of Canada's International Development Research Centre (IDRC). All studies are preoccupied with higher-order (institutional) constraints or enabling conditions and their effect on the performance and benefits accruing to small (peri-)urban producers. The various authors creatively combined methods developed by different disciplines into batteries which they applied to researching urban agriculture issues.
http://www.idrc.ca/en/ev-84289-201-1-DO_TOPIC.html

Mougeot, L.J.A. (2006) *Growing Better Cities: Urban Agriculture for Sustainable Development*, **IDRC, Ottawa.**
This book reviews the research experience of IDRC and its partners, including local govern-ments, into the issues surrounding urban agriculture, with a particular emphasis on the influ-ence that research has had on government policies. It describes the growth of city networks in Africa and Latin America that focus on accommodating urban agriculture and improving

the lot of urban food producers. And it offers specific recommendations aimed at helping policymakers at all levels of government to maximize the potential of urban agriculture. The book concludes with a vision of how such policies might transform cities in the near future. http://www.idrc.ca/en/ev-95297-201-1-DO_TOPIC.html

Obuobie, E., Keraita, B., Danso, G., Amoah, P., Cofie, O.O., Raschid-Sally, L. and Drechsel, P. (2006) Irrigated Urban Vegetable Production in Ghana: Characteristics, Benefits and Risks, IWMI-RUAF-CPWF, Accra, Ghana.
This book gives a comprehensive overview of urban and peri-urban vegetable farming in Ghana's major cities with a special focus on wastewater use. It gives recommendations on how the health risks for consumers could be effectively reduced in a low-income country like Ghana, while simultaneously supporting the important contribution of open-space urban and peri-urban agriculture. The book highlights further research needs and will serve as an important resource for students, academics and decision makers. http://www.ruaf.org/node/1046

Redwood, M. (ed.) (2008) *Agriculture in Urban Planning: Generating Livelihoods and Ffood Security*, IDRC and Earthscan, London.
This volume written by researchers working in urban agriculture examines concrete strategies to integrate city farming into the urban landscape. Drawing on original field work in cities across the rapidly urbanizing global South, the book examines the contribution of urban agriculture and city farming to livelihoods and food security.
http://www.idrc.ca/en/ev-133761-201-1-DO_TOPIC.html

Schiere, J.B. (2000) *Peri-Urban Livestock Systems: Problems, Approaches and Opportunities*, Ventana Agricultural Systems A&D, FAO/IAC, Rome/Wageningen.
This report reviews information from case studies on peri-urban livestock systems across the world – from Ho-Chi-Minh City, via Karachi to Dar-Es-Salaam and Quito and Mexico City. It also includes additional references and interviews with consultants.

Schiere, J.B. and Van Der Hoek, R. (2001) *Livestock keeping in urban areas: A review of traditional technologies*, Animal Production and Health Papers 151, FAO, Rome.
This publication uses a not so widely publicized FAO report with cases on urban livestock around the world as a background document. The emphasis of this publication is, however, on practical aspects of animal production in urban conditions, such as feeding, breeding and animal species, husbandry techniques, product processing and waste management.
http://www.fao.org/DOCREP/004/Y0500E/Y0500E00.htm

Shackleton, C.M., Pasquini, M. and Drescher, A.W. (2009) *African Indigenous Vegetables in Urban Agriculture*, Earthscan, London.
This book provides a comprehensive synthesis of current knowledge of the potential and challenges associated with the multiple roles, use, management and livelihood contributions of indigenous vegetables in urban agriculture in sub-Saharan Africa.
http://www.earthscan.co.uk/?TabId=56958&v=451875

Van Veenhuizen, R. (ed.) (2006) *Cities Farming for the Future: Urban Agriculture for Green and Productive Cities*, **IIRR, Philippines.**
This publication presents the current state of affairs in the development of sustainable urban agriculture and as such indicates what progress has been made since the first major works on urban agriculture were published (the UNDP book 'Urban Agriculture' by Smit et al. published in 1996 and the DSE book 'Growing Cities, Growing Food: Urban Agriculture on the Policy Agenda' by Bakker et al. published in 2000). http://www.ruaf.org/node/961

Van Veenhuizen, R. and Danso, G. (2007) *Profitability and sustainability of urban and peri-urban agriculture*, **Agricultural Management, Marketing and Finance FAO Occasional paper 19, FAO, Rome.**
This paper integrates the results of three earlier studies on the profitability and sustainability of farming in UPA sites, mainly in Africa and Asia, putting them in a wider context by using additional published and unpublished information available at the International Network of Resource Centres on Urban Agriculture and Food Security (RUAF), and also to appraise aspects on policy. Coordination and improvement of further research on the multiple functions of UA and monitoring of its impacts are recommended to provide municipalities and other city stakeholders with proper information and tools to include UA into sustainable city development. http://www.ruaf.org/sites/default/files/2838.pdf

Urban Agriculture Magazine
UA Magazine no. 1   – Maiden issue
UA Magazine no. 2   – Livestock in and around cities
UA Magazine no. 3   – Health aspects of urban agriculture
UA Magazine no. 4   – Integration of UPA in urban planning
UA Magazine no. 5   – Methodologies for UA research, policy development, planning and implementation
UA Magazine no. 6   – Transition to Ecological Urban Agriculture: A Challenge
UA Magazine no. 7   – Economic Aspects of Urban Agriculture
UA Magazine no. 8   – Wastewater Reuse in Urban Agriculture
UA Magazine no. 9   – Financing Urban Agriculture
UA Magazine no. 10 – Appropriate (Micro) Technologies for Urban Agriculture
UA Magazine no. 11 – Availability, Access and Usability of Land for Urban Agriculture
UA Magazine no. 12 – Gender and Urban Agriculture
UA Magazine no. 13 – Trees and Cities – Growing Together
UA Magazine no. 14 – Urban Aquatic Production
UA Magazine no. 15 – Multiple Functions of Urban Agriculture
UA Magazine no. 16 – Formulating Effective Policies on Urban Agriculture
UA Magazine no. 17 – Strengthening Urban Producers' Organizations
UA Magazine no. 18 – Building Communities through Urban Agriculture
UA Magazine no. 19 – Stimulating Innovation in Urban Agriculture

UA Magazine no. 20 – Water for Urban Agriculture
UA Magazine no. 21 – Linking Relief, Rehabilitation and Development – A role for urban agriculture?
UA Magazine no. 22 – Building Resilient Cities
Available at: http://www.ruaf.org/node/101

Multi-stakeholder policy formulation on urban agriculture

Critchley, W., Verburg, M. and Van Veldhuizen L. (eds) (2006) *Facilitating multi-stakeholder partnerships: Lessons from PROLINNOVA*, **International Institute of Rural Reconstruction (IIRR), Philippines.**
This concise booklet looks at ways to foster participatory innovation development (PID) at a regional, national and global level, drawing on lessons from Prolinnova projects in Africa and Asia. Development professionals interested in the mechanics of agricultural innovation and management will find this a useful, readable resource.
http://www.prolinnova.net/fmsp-booklet.php

De Zeeuw, H., Dubbeling, M., Van Veenhuizen, R. (2008) *Courses of action for municipal policies and programmes on urban agriculture*, **RUAF working paper 2, RUAF Foundation, Leusden.**
This working paper outlines how urban agriculture can contribute to various policy goals (social, economic and ecological) and shortly describes four types of policy instruments that can be used for urban agriculture. The main body of the paper presents a series of key issues to be considered in formulating policies and intervention strategies related to urban agriculture and possible courses of action for each of these issues.
http://www.ruaf.org/sites/default/files/WP_02.pdf

Drechsel, P., Cofie, O., Van Veenhuizen, R. and Larbi, T.O. (2008) Linking research, capacity building, and policy dialogue in support of informal irrigation in urban West Africa', *Irrigation and Drainage* **57: 268–78.**
This paper describes the capacity development and multi-stakeholder processes initiated in Anglophone West Africa, their lessons and successes with special reference to Ghana, where research had already produced a favourable knowledge base on urban and peri-urban agriculture in general and irrigated urban farming in particular.
http://www.database.ruaf.org/ruaf_bieb/upload/2918.pdf

Dubbeling, M. (2006) *Policy Briefs on Urban Aquaculture.*
The PAPUSSA Programme has made available an increasing amount of information on peri-urban aquatic production systems in South-east Asian cities. An overall description of the importance, the need and recommendations for development and policy making on (peri-)urban aquaculture is given in a first and introductory Policy Brief. Each of these

recommendations has further been addressed in greater depth in four additional Policy Briefs. All guidelines are based on PAPUSSA research and output, and aim to assist in the process of decision-making rather than to provide definitive answers. http://www.papussa.org/publications.html#article9

Dubbeling, M. (2008) *Multi-stakeholder policy development and action planning on urban* *agriculture*, **RUAF working paper 1, RUAF Foundation, Leusden.**
This first working paper gives an overview of lessons learned under the Cities Farming for the Future programme with Multi-stakeholder Policy formulation and Action Planning (MPAP). It discusses the importance of interactive and participatory processes of policy formulation and action planning, presents the MPAP process and the different steps to be taken, and highlights lessons learned thus far by RUAF partners and several other organizations. http://www.ruaf.org/sites/default/files/WP_01.pdf

Faysse, N. (2006) 'Troubles on the way: An analysis of the challenges faced by multi- **stakeholder platforms',** *Natural Resources Forum* **30 (3): 219–29.**
The article analyses the challenges Multi-stakeholder Platforms (MSPs) face in an unfavour-able context, and identifies five main issues: Power relationships; Platform composition; Stakeholder representation and capacity to participate meaningfully in the debates; Decision-making power and mechanisms; and finally the Cost of setting up an MSP. The analysis is mainly based on two case studies: the first on water user associations in South Africa, and the second on a negotiation platform set up to resolve conflicts over a water and sanitation project in Bolivia. http://publications.cirad.fr/une_notice.php?dk=538626

Hemmati, M. (with contributions from F. Dodds, J. Enayati and J. McHarry (2002) *Multi-* *Stakeholder Processes for Governance and Sustainability: Beyond Deadlock and Conflict*, **Earthscan, London, UK.**
This practical guide explains how multi-stakeholder processes (MSPs) can be organized and implemented. It includes detailed examples of MSPs in practice and provides functional checklists, explaining how to bypass adversarial politics and achieve positive results. This important contribution to the understanding of participatory approaches to decision-making will be invaluable to policy makers, NGOs, business unions, local authorities and activists. http://www.earthscan.co.uk/?tabid=705

Hooton, N., Lee-Smith, D., Nasinyama, G. and Romney, D., in collaboration with Atukunda, **G., Azuba, M., Kaweesa, M., Lubowa, A., Muwanga, J., Njenga, M. and Young, J. (2007)** *Championing urban farmers in Kampala: Influences on local policy change in Uganda*, **ILRI** **Research Report No. 2, in collaboration with ODI, Urban Harvest and KUFSALCC, International** **Livestock Research Institute, Nairobi, Kenya.**
This working paper presents an analysis of actors, events and influences affecting a policy change on urban agriculture in Kampala. It is an output of the International Livestock Research Institute's (ILRI's) and Overseas Development Institute's (ODI's) 'Process and Partnership

for Pro-poor Policy Change' project, which, through case studies with national and international partners, seeks to identify and institutionalize innovative research and development mechanisms and approaches that lead to pro-poor policy.
http://www.database.ruaf.org/wuf/pdf/urban_kampala_uh.pdf

Lundy, M., Gottret, M.V., Ashby, J. (2005) *Learning Alliances: An approach for building multi-stakeholder innovation systems*, **CGIAR, ILAC brief 8.**
This brief describes how the Rural Agroenterprise Development Project of the International Center for Tropical Agriculture is addressing the problem of a lack of exchange between researchers, policy makers and other stakeholders. Through building learning alliances that engage multiple stakeholders in processes of innovation, the initiative is enhancing learning and improving effectiveness in rural enterprise development.
http://www.database.ruaf.org/ruaf_bieb/upload/2186.pdf

Rabi, A., Laban, P., Rifai, S., Sarsour, S. and Tabakhna, O. (2005) *Improving Local Water Governance through Stakeholder Dialogue*, **EMPOWERS Regional Symposium: End-Users Ownership and Involvement in IWRM 13–17 November 2005, Cairo, Egypt.**
The paper highlights some of the practical experience developed under the EC funded EMPOWERS Partnership to facilitate stakeholder dialogue and ensure end user participation in local water management in three countries (Palestine, Jordan and Egypt). Moreover, it will show how such dialogue could improve good local water governance in that area. The paper will further elaborate on the possibilities for institutionalization of the facilitation process.
http://www.project.empowers.info/page/1981

Urban Management Programme (UMP) and IPES (2003) *Policy briefs on urban agriculture*, **IDRC, UMP, IPES.**
Series of guidelines based on scientific and technological research, reflecting innovative practices on nine urban agriculture themes. This work was coordinated and financed by IDRC, the Urban Management Program for Latin America and the Caribbean in Ecuador and IPES, Peru. http://www.ruaf.org/node/419

UN Habitat/UNEP (1999) *Sustainable Cities Programme Source Book Series.*
Experiences with the environmental planning and management approach of the Sustainable Cities Programme (UN Habitat/UNEP) have been captured and translated into effective tools – in the form of manuals – that can be used to inform, support and guide the environmental planning process in cities.

Source Book Series manuals provide guidance on the step-by-step process.
http://www.unchs.org/programmes/sustainablecities/SCPProcess.asp

United Nations Centre for Human Settlements (UNCHS) (2001) *Tools to Support Participatory Urban Decision Making*. **Urban Governance Toolkit Series, United Nations Centre for Human Settlements (UNCHS Habitat), Nairobi.**

This toolkit aims to support participatory urban decision-making. It has been prepared as one of the products of the 'Global Campaign on Urban Governance', led by UN Habitat in collaboration with a range of partners. It provides tools and short case studies on aspects such as mobilizing stakeholders, building collaboration and forging consensus, identifying key issues and formulating priority strategies, negotiating and implementing action plans, monitoring and evaluation and institutionalization.
http://www.unhabitat.org/pmss/getPage.asp?page=bookView&book=1122

Vermeulen, S., Woodhill, J., Proctor, F., Delnoye, R. (2008) *Chain-wide learning for inclusive agrifood market development: A guide to multi-stakeholder processes for linking small-scale producers to modern markets*, **Bunnik, The Netherlands.**
This guide provides concepts and tools for working with actors along the entire value chain so that modern markets can be more inclusive of small-scale producers and entrepreneurs.
http://www.database.ruaf.org/ruaf_bieb/upload/2907.pdf

Warner, J. (ed.) (2007) *Multi-stakeholder Platforms for Integrated Water Management*, **Ashgate, Surrey, UK.**
Taking a positive but critical look at experiences with multi-stakeholder platforms in both the developed as well as developing worlds, the book argues that care should be taken not to promise too much or expect that political barriers will automatically be broken down and equal participation will be achieved. Suggestions for improving success and sustainability are made. http://www.irc.nl/page/37623

Websites

http://www.ruaf.org
Visiting this site allows you to learn about the RUAF Foundation and its work (the Cities Farming for the Future and the From Seed to Table programmes), and download most of its publications, including all the Urban Agriculture Magazine issues. One can also find thematic references and a searchable bibliographic database on urban agriculture.
RUAF website in Spanish language: http://www.ipes.org/au
In Portuguese: http://ipes.org/index.php?option=com_content&view=article&id=268:videos-em-portugues&catid=7:agricultura-urbana&Itemid=100
In French: http://www.iagu.org/RUAF/index.html
In Chinese: http://www.cnruaf.com.cn/
In Arabic: http://www.urbanagriculture-mena.org/webar/main.php

http://www.communitygarden.org/
The American Community Gardening Association is a bi-national non-profit membership organization of professionals, volunteers and supporters of community greening in urban and rural communities. The website displays, among other information, resources for starting a garden and contact details for existing gardens.

http://www.fao.org/fcit/en/
Food for the Cities is the interdepartmental programme on urban agriculture at the FAO, and offers fact sheets, working papers and thematic publications in three languages.

http://km.fao.org/fsn
The Global Forum on Food Security and Nutrition Policies and Strategies (FSN) is an online community whose members share experiences, identify resources, provide peer coaching and support and find collective solutions to food security and nutrition issues, focusing on policies. It is supported by the FAO.

www.farmingsolutions.org
Farming Solutions, the Future of Agriculture, is a site supported by ILEIA, OXFAM and Greenpeace that seeks to share examples of successful, environmentally responsible farming systems from all over the world that illustrate how farmers can protect the environment while at the same time increasing the food supply where it is most needed.

http://www.foodsecurity.org/index.html
The Community Food Security Coalition is a non-profit, North American organization dedicated to building strong, sustainable, local and regional food systems that ensure access to affordable, nutritious and culturally appropriate food for all people at all times.

http://www.globalhort.org/
The Global Horticulture Initiative is a worldwide programme intended to foster more efficient and effective partnerships and collective action among the stakeholders. This GlobalHort Information Portal offers information on the activities of the partners related to horticulture.

www.iclei.org
The Local Agenda 21 Campaign promotes a participatory, long-term, strategic planning process that helps municipalities identify local sustainability priorities and implement long-term action plans. It supports good local governance and mobilizes local governments and their citizens to undertake such a multi-stakeholder process. The ICLEI website offers a variety of resources on Local Agenda 21 and urban governance, which include case studies, publications and toolkits.

http://www.idrc.ca/upe/
The Urban Poverty & Environment Program (UPE) funds research and activities in developing countries that apply integrated and participatory approaches to reducing environmental burdens on the urban poor and enhancing the use of natural resources for food, water and income security.

http://www.idrc.ca/en/ev-92997-201-1-DO_TOPIC.html
The IDRC website features under the 'in-focus' programme a variety of resources on urban agriculture, including slide presentations, short stories, case studies, research reports and books. These are only part of the reported results of IDRC-supported research.

www.iwmi.cgiar.org/health/wastew/index.htm
Here you can learn more about IWMI's Water, Health and Environment research including objectives, projects, outputs and impacts on the issue of wastewater reuse for agriculture.

http://knownetgrin.honeybee.org/
Honeybee Network is a global initiative to give voice to creative and innovative people at the grassroots level. The Honeybee Network is run by SRISTI (Society for Research and Initiatives for Sustainable Technologies and Institutions) in India. The Network has an online database of innovations, primarily from India but also from other countries. Honeybee tries to connect innovators with each other through communication and networking in local languages. Innovations can be submitted via the innovation registry form on the website and, after verification, will be added to the innovation database.

www.leisa.info
The Centre for Information on Low-External-Input and Sustainable Agriculture (ILEIA) is an independent organization that seeks to contribute to alleviating poverty by promoting agro-ecological approaches. Documentation, analysis and publication of successful experiences in low-external input and sustainable agriculture (LEISA) are the major activities. The website provides access to large, searchable databases on LEISA and PTD.

http://www.livablecities.org
The International Making Cities Livable Council is an interdisciplinary, international network of individuals and cities dedicated to making our cities and communities more liveable.

http://www.megacitiesproject.org
The Mega-Cities Project is a transnational non-profit network of community, academic, government, business and media leaders dedicated to sharing innovative solutions to urban problems. Its aim is to make cities more socially just, ecologically sustainable, politically participatory and economically vital.

www.prolinnova.net
PROLINNOVA is an international NGO-led initiative to build a global learning and advocacy network on promoting local innovation in ecologically-oriented agriculture and Natural Resource Management. The focus is on the dynamics of indigenous knowledge, and on how research, extension and other actors in development can strengthen the capacities of farmers to adjust to changing conditions: to develop and adapt their own site-appropriate systems and institutions of resource management.

www.purple-eu.org

Peri-urban regions in Europe are facing extreme pressure on their rural areas. The balance between sustainable open space, sustainable agriculture and urban spatial and economic dynamics needs to be re-established. This demands a combination of European, national and regional policy strategies and objectives. Therefore it is essential to recognize the specific peri-urban agenda in the new European regulations on rural development and structural funds.

http://puvep.xu.edu.ph/index.php

The Peri-urban Vegetable Project (PUVeP) is a research and outreach unit of Xavier University College of Agriculture (XUCA), Cagayan de Oro City in the Philippines and provides research, training and education related to urban natural resources management and food production in the city.

www.sarnissa.org

Sustainable Aquaculture Research Networks In Sub Saharan Africa (SARNISSA) is an EU (FP7) programme on Aquaculture Research Networks and Policy dialogue in sub-Saharan Africa. RUAF collaborates with Stirling University, CIRAD, World Fish Center, CABI-UK, IRAD (Cameroon) and Bunda College (Malawi) in this project, which includes aquaculture in urban settings, on a critical review of national aquaculture policies in 10 African countries.

www.susana.org

The SuSanA is not a new organization, but rather a loose network of organizations working along the same lines, and open to others who want to join and be active in the promotion of sustainable sanitation systems.

http://sustainablecities.net/

The International Centre for Sustainable Cities (ICSC) was created to bring the idea of urban sustainability into practical action. ICSC is a 'do tank', rather than a think tank, and serves as a broker, bringing together the business community, civil society organizations and various levels of government to tackle urban issues.

www.sustainablefoodcenter.org

The Sustainable Food Center (SFC) supports and is active in local food system development in the USA. SFC teaches sustainable food gardening practices to children and adults, organizes markets for locally grown produce in urban areas accessible to low-income residents, donates produce to area food pantries, and develops training courses for individuals and institutions on how to prepare healthy and affordable meals.

www.switchurbanwater.eu

SWITCH aims to bring about a change in urban water management. The website contains information on the work in the cities, learning alliances, the SWITCH partners and published research reports.

http://www.uharvest.org/

This website offers information on the achievements and publications of Urban Harvest, the CGIAR system-wide initiative on urban and peri-urban agriculture.

http://portals.wi.wur.nl/msp/

This website provides practical information on how to facilitate participatory learning processes with various stakeholders. It gives theoretical foundations, concrete case studies, methods and tools to create learning processes, facilitation tips, examples, literature and links. The aim of providing this information is to build capacity for multi-stakeholder processes and social learning. Tools include those that can be applied for collecting information, stakeholder analysis, planning and decision-making.

Partners of the International Network of Resource Centres on Urban Agriculture and Food Security (RUAF)

International coordination

ETC-Urban Agriculture
Global coordinator RUAF: Ms Marielle Dubbeling

PO Box 64, 3830 AB Leusden
The Netherlands

P +31-33-4326039
F +31-33 4940791
E ruaf@etcnl.nl
www.etc-urbanagriculture.org & www.ruaf.org

Eastern and Southern Africa

MDP (Municipal Development Partnership)
Regional coordinator RUAF: Mr Takawira Mubvami

7th Floor, Hurudza House
14–16 Nelson Mandela Avenue
Harare, Zimbabwe

P 263-4-774385
F 263-4-774387
E tmubvami@mdpafrica.org.zw
www.mdpafrica.org.zw/ua_cffp

Latin America and the Caribbean

IPES (Promoción del Desarrollo Sostenible)
Regional coordinator RUAF: Mr Gunther Merzthal

Calle Audiencia 194, San Isidro
Lima 27, Peru

P +51-1-440-6099, 421-9722, 421-6684 Ext.110
F +51-1-440-6099, 421-9722, 421-6684
E gunther@ipes.org.pe
www.ipes.org/au

South and South East Asia

IWMI-India (International Water Management Institute Regional Office India)
Regional coordinator RUAF: Ms Priyanie Amerasinghe

c/o ICRISAT Patancheru AP 502 324
Hyderabad, India

P +91-40-3296161
F +91-40-3241239
E p.amerasinghe@cgiar.org
http://ruaf-asia.iwmi.org/

West-Africa (Francophone)
IAGU (Institut Africain de Gestion Urbaine)
Regional coordinator RUAF: Mr. Moussa Sy

BP 7263, Dakar
Senegal

P (221) 33 869 87 00
F (221) 33 827 28 13
E moussa@iagu.org
www.iagu.org/RUAF/index.html

China
IGSNRR (Institute of Geographical Sciences and Natural Resource Research, Chinese Academy of Sciences)
Regional coordinator RUAF: Mr Jianming Cai

11A Datun Road, Anwai, 100101
Beijing, China

P +86-10- 64889279
F +86-10-64851844
E caijm@igsnrr.ac.cn
www.cnruaf.com.cn/

West-Africa (Anglophone)
IWMI-Ghana (International Water Management Institute Sub-regional office West Africa)
Regional coordinator RUAF: Ms Olufunke Cofie

PMB CT 112, Accra
Ghana

P +233-21-784753
F +233-21-784752
E o.cofie@cgiar.org
http://ruaf.iwmi.org/

North Africa & Middle East
AUB-ESDU (Environment and Sustainable Development Unit, American University of Beirut)
Regional coordinator RUAF: Mr Ziad Moussa

PO Box 11-0236/ AUB, Riad El Solh, Beirut
1107 2020, Lebanon

P + 961-1- 374 374 or 350 000
E zm13@aub.edu.lb / ziadmoussa@yahoo.com
www.urbanagriculture-mena.org/